Risks
Reading Corporate Signals

Risks
Reading Corporate Signals

HAIG J. BOYADJIAN
and
JAMES F. WARREN

JOHN WILEY & SONS
Chichester · New York · Brisbane · Toronto · Singapore

Library of Congress Cataloging-in-Publication Data:

Boyadjian, Haig J.
  Risks: Reading Corporate Signals.

  Includes index.
  1. Business enterprises—Finance. 2. Company
reports. 3. Financial statements. 4. Investments.
5. Risk management. I. Warren, James F. II. Title.
HG4026.B66 1987   658   86-15661

ISBN 0 471 91207 7

British Library Cataloguing in Publication Data:

Boyadjian, Haig J.
  Risks.
  1. Business enterprises—Finance
  I. Title II. Warren, James F.
  658.1′51   HG4026

ISBN 0 471 91207 7 (ppc)
     0 471 93177 2 (Standard Chartered)
     0 471 93178 0 (pbk)

Typeset by Acorn Bookwork, Salisbury, Wiltshire
Printed and bound in Great Britain by Dotesios Ltd., Trowbridge, Wilts.

To

Contents

Foreword

I discovered this book, quite by accident, in a bookshop in the City of London, and was instantly impressed by the articulate style in which it is written. The focus is placed clearly and succinctly on the understanding of the cash generation and its unique ability to link it to the asset conversion cycle of a business, together with the risks involved. Too frequently these pivotal aspects of credit analysis are obscured.

This book is refreshing in the sheer practicality of its professionalism but remains both literate and enjoyable to read. The reception to this text from my colleagues in Standard Chartered Bank, from bright young MBA graduates to old but well seasoned campaigners, has been unfailingly enthusiastic.

Young bankers find it enlightening, older ones feel vindicated by its sound common sense and simplicity of purpose.

If we as bankers carry out our assessment of customers using *Risks* as our guideline we should reduce our own risks and ensure long and profitable relationships.

For this reason Standard Chartered Bank has selected *Risks* as the standard text for our comprehensive range of credit training programmes.

Profit from Credit

D. B. Northrop
Standard Chartered Bank
London, May, 1991.

Introduction

Banking is the surest, safest, easiest business I have ever known. If you are not actually stupid or dishonest it is hard not to make money from banking.
George Moore, *The Banker's Life*

In *Risks*, we have set out to write a readable piece in understandable language, designed primarily for those who do not have specialized backgrounds in accounting or financial analysis but who want to be able to use company reports in an intelligent and sensible way to make important decisions. Anyone who has ever received the Annual Report of a company will know that the value of that document to a reader wanting to invest wisely, or to lend prudently, can be remarkably limited. The information that is critical and essential for responsible decision making is mostly missing or expressed in esoteric language. Explanation is often inadequate or downright misleading. Self-aggrandisement by the management is the order of the day.

Learned dissertations from business schools and financial theorists hardly ever bother to tell you this. Most such literature is packaged for elitist audiences and is replete with mathematical equations better suited to astrophysics than the fundamental task of enlightening an audience with a legitimate need to understand and interpret the accounts of a business operation.

The study of business is a serious matter but it is not an end in itself for most of us. People labour at this vast, multifaceted subject usually for intensely practical reasons. So it is with this book. Lenders want to be reasonably sure that, upon the maturity of an obligation, they will be repaid in cash. That assurance must rest on some acceptable level of knowledge about a company's future liquidity and solvency. Equally, the investor is anxious that his investment remain whole and will either bring in an adequate return or appreciate in capital value.

Academic literature and the press have not really helped such people; they have convinced almost everyone over the past 50 years that the repayment of loans and the generation of an adequate return on an investment are secured almost exclusively by good profitability in a company. While this is not entirely wrong, the lengths to which this idea has been taken are becoming ridiculous and dangerous.

Modern business is complex and risky. To understand it one has to unravel the complexity and focus upon the risks. It is no good reducing analysis to statistics and probabilities. Analysis calls for insight and judgement, and above all the ability to decipher the mysteries of accountancy. Most business textbooks, once done with their metaphysical speculations, quickly turn to simplistic illustrations involving single product companies with surprisingly uninvolved accounting procedures. The majority of the biggest loans and the largest investments simply do not involve these types of business organizations at all.

Loans and investments running into billions of dollars, pounds, yen, deutschmarks and other currencies are made every day. The recipients are huge multinational concerns that not only produce a multitude of products but even operate in diverse, often unrelated industries. Typically, such firms use extremely sophisticated accounting which, it is unkind but fair to say, is little understood by most lenders and investors. And all too often lenders have virtually no worthwhile information about their borrowers apart from the company's own published statements and press comments.

In the US business schools, a veritable industry has

grown up churning out ever more intricate models to explain the workings of corporations. Each model is hailed by its inventive author as a radical improvement on all of its predecessors. Considerable ingenuity goes into these creations, but the sad truth is that, in the main, they neither inform on the subject nor do they influence the way companies are actually assessed. Largely, this is because they are stronger on statistics than they are on accountancy; and the issue of risk usually receives a very low priority.

However, no serious attempt to offer insights on modern business can ignore the vast and kaleidoscopic experience of the United States. The boldness and success of American business are distinguishing hallmarks of the twentieth century and the consummate skill of American business in the use of debt as an instrument of wealth is awesome. We cite in our examples and cases principally US corporations, but we have not neglected the international aspect and have included also, for diversity and variety, a number of British companies. We have not felt the need to be parochial in our choice of terminology, though generally American business vocabulary has been preferred.

London and New York are, of course, different in countless ways, but just as there are underlying universal patterns in human behaviour, regardless of cultural differences, so there are many similarities in business practices around the world. Insight depends, in our view, not so much on specialist knowledge as on the strength of the analyst's methodology!

Behind this book lies the work that we ourselves have done in establishing, teaching and marketing a unique seminar in financial analysis at one of the largest banks in the world. In our teaching, as in our writing, we have had to consider always the practical implication of our ideas in an action oriented environment where analysis, often done under pressure, has to justify the placement of substantial funds at risk. There are many others who have a similar

need for reaching informed risk decisions quickly, effectively and imaginatively, not being misled by the many
false pointers along the road. It is for them that this book
has been written. The views expressed in this book are
entirely our own and do not necessarily reflect or represent
the views of any institutions with which we have been
associated.

HJB
JFW

Postscript

On May 19th, 1987, Citibank made a $3 billion provision against loans
which has been interpreted by the marketplace as primarily directed at
their Latin American portfolio. This bold and decisive action caused a
major stir, not least among other banks who have had to engage in
similar painful provisions. These provisions are almost at $15 billion at
this writing.

1

The Annual Report— A celebrated fiction?

'I can tell you', said Tigg in his ear, 'how many of 'em will buy annuities, effect insurances, bring us their money in a hundred shapes and ways, force it upon us as if we were the Mint; yet know no more about us than you do of that crossing-sweeper at the corner. Not so much. Ha, ha!'
Charles Dickens, *Martin Chuzzlewit*, Chapter 27

If you have ever been a shareholder in a company or corporation, from time to time you will have received from it a very interesting document. This document, known in the United States as the Annual Report and variously described in other parts of the world, purports to outline, in words and figures, the recent performance and consequent financial position of the company in question and stands in the form of an extended letter from the directors, those charged with running the company's affairs, to the shareholders, those who actually own the business.

Why is this an 'interesting document'? Naturally, it cannot fail to be of great concern to the individual shareholder whose money is at stake in the enterprise. He or she is bound to want to know on a regular basis how the company is faring, whether his or her investment is growing or shrinking, what developments have taken place, both financially and in broader economic terms. The individual investor cannot fail to take a lively interest in the Annual

Report of his company, since most other sources of information, of which there are potentially a great many, will give only a partial or biased and therefore a generally unsatisfactory picture. Annual Reports will also be eagerly awaited by a whole host of others who have an interest in a company's performance. These might include bankers, analysts, investment advisers, government officials, trade union leaders, industry competitors and so on.

So runs the accepted wisdom, and to some extent it is the truth. Annual Reports are sent regularly to shareholders and they are interesting to them and to others. Yet there is something seriously amiss with the cosy situation implied just now. The world of business is a world of risk, opportunity and the struggle for power. At times it is a cruel place and there is many a mixed motive. These aspects are missing.

The conventional view of business and the relationship between a company, its shareholders and other concerned parties can be read in innumerable books. The rules of accountancy which control the preparation and presentation of financial information are easily available in countless learned and not so learned volumes. In this book we shall do something different. It is not a textbook on business or accountancy and very little of its content could be considered academic or technical. We shall ask some simple but searching questions and come across some simple and perhaps embarrassing answers. For the truth about financial reporting, accountancy and the nature of business is not at all the same as it is usually represented. There are some surprises in store.

Our investigations should logically start one stage back from the Annual Report by asking the question, 'What is a company?' A limited liability company is a curious invention often taken for granted because of its very familiarity. There are several million of them in the United States and hundreds of thousands in most European countries. It is the predominant vehicle of modern business. It has not always been so.

A viable company is, in reality, a repository of economic wealth, a legal entity which owns in its own name certain property or assets and which incurs, in the course of trading, financial and other obligations. Companies have existed for thousands of years, as long as men have been buying and selling. Their primary initial purpose was the raising of capital. One trader might not have sufficient cash to undertake a major enterprise on his own. What would be more natural than to find some other like-minded entrepreneurs so that they could all pool their resources? The rewards and the risks would be shared among the participants in proportion to the amount each had contributed.

Today, we would probably call this type of organization not a company but a partnership. Partnerships still exist as trading organizations, particularly in some European banking centres, but the partnership has been almost totally superseded by the company in modern industry and trade.

The difference between a partnership and a company, and the principal reason for the emergence of the latter can be contained in one phrase, *limited liability*. In a partnership, all partners are individually liable for the obligations of the partnership. That is to say, if the partnership borrowed a large sum of money, invested it in a worthless venture of some kind and was incapable of repaying when the money fell due, the duty of repayment would fall squarely on the shoulders of the partners.

Such an arrangement was hardly a great injustice, since it was pretty clear where the responsibility lay from a moral point of view. On the other hand, as societies developed, and particularly with the coming of the industrial revolution in Europe, it became increasingly difficult to find entrepreneurs prepared to invest if the arduous responsibility of personal liability was attached to the deal. Rich men wanted to invest, but they wanted too to set a limit on the maximum they might lose if all did not go according to plan. The solution was to limit the liability of the entrepreneur in a venture by allowing a company to have a legal existence separate from that of the owners and to do business without making them responsible for all the consequences. In order to warn the world that one needed to be careful in dealing with an organization not backed by the full resources of personal wealth, it was decreed that limited liability companies must advertise their status in their name. English companies have the word 'limited' or the acronym 'plc' (for 'public limited company') as part of their name for precisely this reason and similar expressions are to be found in almost all other countries.

This simple fact is now almost forgotten and if anything one is often chary of doing business with unincorporated bodies, believing, usually quite rightly, that limited liability status is the mark of an established and reliable trading organization. Trading partnerships, sole traders and unincorporated organizations tend to be very small and have little financial strength even if the owners' homes and chattels are thrown in.

The creation of the limited liability company brought with it one other great advantage for businessmen. If the company could trade without totally involving the owners it could also employ managers and staff bound not to the owners directly but merely to the company. This meant that another onerous duty—management—which had previously been attached to entrepreneurship and which must have deterred potential investors could be delegated easily and without too many complicated problems to others with the time, talents and possibly youth to undertake the necessary duties. Thus was born the professional manager.

Today's company, therefore, need not involve its shareholders, as the owners are grandly called, to any great extent. What the company really needs in order to function is their money or investment. It calls on them neither for management expertise nor to meet losses in excess of the amount actually committed. The managers manage the business and the shareholders sit back and reap the rewards, if any.

It will be obvious from what has been said that the legal 'shape' of a company was engineered in the interests of the shareholders. One has only to glance at the situation in a modern multinational, however, to see how it all works in practice. Those entrusted with overall responsibility for the running of the corporation are the directors who are appointed by the shareholders at the Annual General Meeting. The directors in turn hire the senior management, who attend to the implementation of the policies decided upon by the directors and head up the management hierarchy, which supervises and organizes the work of the entire workforce.

When the company is successful and its achievements are perceived to be meeting expectations, the system functions more than adequately. Everyone appreciates his particular role and no awkward questions arise about blame and responsibility; the chain of command is secure. What happens, though, when the company starts accumulating losses? Perhaps it has invested in a new product which could not ultimately be developed because of technical problems or, for some reason, once it was on the market no one wanted to buy it. Who suffers what consequences?

Consider the different parties involved. First, the shareholders are the ones who suffer the financial loss as it was their money which was put at risk and which was imprudently spent. Their liability is limited to the extent of their investment in the shares they originally purchased, but that money will be deemed forfeit by custom and law before any creditors of the company are asked to accept any reduction in their investment.

Quite understandably, the shareholders will probably be none too pleased at their hard-earned wealth being dissi-

pated in this way, and as they did not make the management decision which led to the loss, they are likely to look
around to see who can be made to accept the blame. They
will not have to look very far. The directors, appointed to
run the company, will have to do some explaining if they
wish to retain their often prestigious and well remunerated
jobs.

Here we come to the point where theory and practice
diverge. In theory, the shareholders have an absolute right
to hire and fire the directors by the simple expedient of
calling a meeting and passing a resolution appointing
certain people to the board and dismissing others. The legal
power of the shareholders to take this action is unques-
tioned. Actually, it almost never happens. Directors do not
like the prospect of removal from office and will usually
take vigorous defensive action. Particularly powerfully
entrenched are those directors who are also executive
officers of the company, so running its affairs from day to
day. Such 'chief executives', 'presidents' and 'executive
vice-chairmen' have at their disposal the whole awesome
power apparatus of the corporation, which they can and do
use to fend off the shareholders. Dissident shareholders
have no such advantages; they will find that contacting
other shareholders is a problem as companies will not
normally open the share register to casual inspection and it
costs time and money to make the necessary arrangements.

Even when a director of a substantial company is forced
out by the shareholders, he can usually count on compensation at a level to make ordinary mortals blanch.

Dismissal of directors inevitably engenders a good deal
of acrimony and consequent publicity. These may not be
crucial factors in a small, privately held company and
occasionally directors are replaced by dissatisfied shareholders. Such action is virtually never taken by the shareholders in large public concerns, however, for one other
basic reason, the existence of stock exchanges. It is vastly

easier to pick up one's phone, call one's stockbroker and instruct him to sell the shares of a company which has failed to meet expectations. Most investors feel that life is too short to waste it seeking retribution from incompetent directors. How much better to cut one's losses and hope for better luck next time.

Management does not like to see people selling the company's shares and will often adopt a highly hostile attitude to analysts or journalists who make such a recommendation, denying them interviews and invitations to briefings. The sale of shares depresses the price, which is often, at least in the United States, a measure of management performance and the basis of certain executive bonuses. A low price also increases the cost of raising new equity and possibly even the cost of new debt as the market perceives a heightened degree of risk. Lurking corporate predators are also a threat. Even if their jobs are not in jeopardy, the directors have a big stake in maintaining or raising the share price on the stock exchange.

The option to sell is not always available to the shareholder in a private company because the company's own rules may specifically limit the market by restricting eligible shareholders, possibly to members of a family. It may also be difficult for an investor with very large sums invested in a sizeable proportion of the equity of a public corporation to sell out owing to the shallowness of the market.

The bulk of commercial equities quoted on the New York and London stock exchanges belong to pension funds, insurance companies, mutual funds and the like. Although there has been some improvement lately, some are notorious for their lack of involvement in the management of the companies they virtually own, to the real detriment of the small, individual minority shareholder. Institutional investors do start to apply a certain amount of pressure if things get really bad, but they too are mostly interested in preserving the value of their holdings and will sit back or sell rather than risk an adverse market and the publicity and unpleasantness associated with sacking for incompetence a director who may be a well-known public figure.

It is an amazing fact that it is extremely uncommon for a shareholder to stand up at an Annual General Meeting of a major company and ask a pertinent, well-informed question of the directors about the way the company is run. Evasion, prevarication and ridicule are, in any event, the most likely outcome. Questions asked are almost always about involvement in South Africa, environmental concerns, employment practices and the like—important but peripheral matters.

The directors, inclusive of top management, thus are comparatively safe from paying the price for any inefficiency or incompetence. Does that relative immunity apply too to the rest of the management and to the workforce? By no means! Anyone who can be held responsible for a major and costly error in a corporation is in danger of losing his job or at least being demoted. The extent to which this goes on in business depends largely on the cultural environment. In Europe, employment protection laws backed up by long custom ensure that outright sackings are difficult to effect and comparatively rare. Even in the United States where a tougher, results oriented philosophy prevails, summary punishments are not nearly so common as outsiders usually imagine. An incompetent manager in the United States is likely to be fired eventually, but not until he has had several opportunities to demonstrate his incompetence. In Europe, particularly in Britain, he is more likely to be shunted into a job of lesser responsibility and left to work out his career in an obscure corner of the organization with pay and pension rights intact!

Just to complete the picture, we should note that even though, in all probability, totally innocent of incompetence or malfeasance, the workforce may well lose their jobs on a wide scale if, as a consequence of losses, plants have to close and the company embarks on what is euphemistically called 'rationalizing' or 'restructuring'. Strikes and other union organized non-cooperation or inactivity ('industrial action' as the British often call it!) may have played a part in the company's problems but it is the responsibility of management to manage the workforce and that means, among other things, educating them and treating them in such a way that they do not embark on precipitous behaviour in furtherance of their ambitions but which leads only to the disappearance of their own jobs.

From this discussion, it appears that when losses are made everyone to some extent pays the price—shareholders, directors, management and workers. It is also the case that those who might be deemed most responsible, the directors, are generally those who pay the least. This perverse outcome of our industrial democracy is not often remarked upon and needs to be borne in mind by the reader throughout this book. The relationship that exists between the shareholders and the directors is thoroughly unbalanced and this imbalance colours the material that a company publishes about itself in subtle and not necessarily innocent ways.

Let us turn now to the Annual Report, the 'interesting document' with which our chapter began. Why should the company go to the considerable expense of producing this extravagant, finely printed document and sending it to all the shareholders? The reason usually given is that the law requires any limited company to produce its figures, for these to be deposited at some central registry (Companies House in London or the Securities and Exchange Commission in Washington DC, for example) and for copies to be sent to the shareholders so that they can have a direct report on what is happening.

The law in all developed industrial countries also lays down certain minimum requirements as to what information must be given. In the United States, the power and influence of the investing community have brought about heavy disclosure requirements; at the other extreme, Third World and developing countries require very little public disclosure. Most European countries have requirements falling somewhere in between.

In order that the directors, the nominal authors of the Annual Report, may not get away with any falsification of the facts, the financial statements have, almost invariably, to be subject to external audit. Contained in the Annual Report is a short letter from a firm of accountants stating that the figures have been scrutinized and subjected to established auditing procedures, and that the belief of the auditors is that a basically true picture has been painted. In Britain, the expression is 'a true and fair view'.

Many people, relying on the legal requirements and the auditors' certificate, hasten to the conclusion that an Annual Report is 'the truth, the whole truth and nothing but the truth'. Look at the Annual Report of a large public company and see what it actually contains.

The exact format varies from country to country. Just inside the front cover there is usually a page of 'highlights' showing a few key numbers from the financial data presented by the management as a thumb-nail sketch of what the rest of the Annual Report supposedly reveals. 'Your Company at a Glance' or some such snappy expression will be printed at the top. After this will come an account in words of the company's recent performance and present condition, frequently backed up by several pages of slick pictures illustrating the company's different activities and possibly some of their cuter personnel. It is no exaggeration to say that the pictures usually highlight the company's employment of women, ethnic minorities and handicapped people. In a company which is successful or which is trying to appear so, these pictures and accompanying text occupy around half the report.

It can be stated that although the auditors would be

unlikely to tolerate outright falsehood, the bulk of this material is pure propaganda for the company. Being generally the work of public relations 'consultants' it is written in a friendly, uncomplicated style and paints the rosiest picture possible of the company's culture, ethics and activities. The whole purpose of this section is to encourage the shareholders to the view that the company is a good, wholesome investment and that the individual shareholder can feel proud and confident in his shareholding.

No legal requirements anywhere in the world specify the use of the chairman's and chief executive's portrait in an Annual Report and the cost of publishing such material falls inevitably and directly on the shareholders it is designed to impress.

The directors are, in effect, using the shareholders' own resources to convince them that they should perpetuate them in office, which they would probably do anyway, and more importantly to keep their money in the company. It is possible that in the future more investment will be needed from the shareholders and, so the argument runs, they need to be kept informed and, if possible, well disposed.

It is far from being the purpose of this book to attack the capitalist system which has substantially created the economic and industrial wealth of the world, or to suggest that directors and senior management are engaged in some sort of wholesale fraud against their investors. The pictures and the accompanying commentary in an Annual Report are genuinely of interest to investors and there is usually no conscious dishonesty or deception. However, it is contended that the relationship which exists between directors and shareholders is one where the directors have very much the upper hand. They have a strong vested interest in maintaining that relationship and the concern for the shareholder exhibited by the directors in the Annual Report is not intrinsically different from that of the salesman for the customer. First and foremost, the salesman needs to sell. His desire to see the customer a happy man, prominent in the sales pitch, is totally secondary.

Next we turn to the financial data. At this point the mood changes. Few investors really understand accounting and the financial parts of an Annual Report are often printed on a different, darker coloured paper as if to warn off the uninitiated from the arcane mysteries on which they are about to stumble. Here there are no pictures, except possibly a few graphs, and the language becomes at once technical, abstruse and forbidding. The print is usually smaller, too. What is the poor investor to do when confronted by these awesome pages of unfathomable complexity? In theory, he does some analysis. He examines and digests every one of the numbers, reads all the notes and the exegesis thereon and appraises the company accordingly.

In fact, the typical investor does nothing of the sort. He turns back to the highlights page, looks at the trends in sales and profits and makes his decision on the basis of that plus his own intuition and knowledge of the industry and the world. Very few non-professional investors do any more than that. They do not, as a group, read the financial data.

It may well be wondered why the company goes to the expense of producing all this complicated material if the principal market ignores it. Something psychological seems to be at play here. Many investors are quite happy with a basic summary because they believe that the disclosure requirements ensure that there are no skeletons in the cupboard and there are, after all, 'experts', highly paid analysts, who will study the figures and reveal their findings in the press and elsewhere. The auditors' certificate too gives comforting reassurances that all is correct and above board.

The terrible truth is that the emperor has no clothes! Neither of the two assumptions just given is really true beyond a certain point and the limitation of the safeguards could usefully be much better understood by the general public.

In general, analysts do not digest and absorb all the information given. There is simply too much of it and to a great extent it is presented in ways which make analysis of it almost impossible. The analyst cannot cope with pages of six or seven digit numbers. All he can do is employ certain established techniques to try to catch the most significant items in the elegantly arranged morass of information.

His first task will be to *spread* the basic statements. All banks and investment houses have computer programs to do this although until recently it was done manually. Spreading consists of rearranging the numbers in a standard format, putting them into a computer and then having the machine calculate a number of simple ratios, one key number divided by another, before printing out the whole package. The ratios, which vary slightly between analysts according to personal preference, illustrate general trends in the figures and, broadly speaking, show which direction the company is moving in. Particular emphasis is given to the income statement (or profit and loss account in Britain) since to most people's minds profitability and success are two sides of a coin.

It is the dozen or so ratios in common use plus a few specific totals which form the basis of most analysis. Analysts usually look through the notes, particularly in countries like Britain where important details tend to be buried there, but on the whole the analysis will be based on a much simpler computer-based summary. Given the nature and quality of the information produced, this is, so far as it goes, a perfectly reasonable means of operation. It should not, though, be thought by the inexperienced that every number has some vital analytical significance. The bulk of the numbers published cannot be made to tell anything of importance to investors or bankers.

The audit report is often misunderstood too. Published statements are prepared not by the auditors but by the company's own management. Annual Reports are not the work of auditors, they are the products of companies themselves. The auditors' duty is to cast an independent eye over the process and in particular to give an opinion on whether or not the financial statements are presented fairly. In essence, they check that the job is done properly, that no deception is being practised, and only when they are satisfied will they sign a clean audit report.

Auditors are under a duty to exercise independent judgment but they are not independent in every sense since they are paid by the company and if they and the company regularly disagree on important matters they can resign or can be dismissed. By law, the auditors are appointed by the shareholders each year at the Annual General Meeting and could if dismissed by the management appeal to the shareholders. Such action is, needless to say, virtually unheard of. The auditors, in fact, engage in a process of discussion with the management as to what will be tolerated in the final publication.

Generally, auditors are respected people who give useful advice but head-on clashes do occur from time to time. There is no doubt that auditors are often faced with dilemmas as no accounting firm wishes to run the risk of losing a major corporate account but standards of integrity and independence must prevail. There are many reasons for a change of auditors and sometimes an unexpected change can indicate a fundamental difference of opinion between the company's management and its auditors as to the interpretation of financial information. A qualification in an audit report to the effect that the accounts contain serious distortions could damage a multinational company irreparably. Confronted by a choice between tolerating such a situation and damaging the company resignation can be the only course to take.

Although an auditor's role is that of a watchdog rather than that of a bloodhound there is an increasing tendency to try to make auditors accountable for business failures. Many business failures in the last few years have led to lawsuits against auditors alleging failure to alert the business community. Most lawsuits are defended and are settled out out of court but the London and American insurance markets are becoming wary of providing negligence insurance for accountants because of the incidence of claims being made against accountants and the colossal sums being sought.

A word here about fraud. Fraud is an ugly word but it is a good deal more common in business than is usually realised. Most recently in the news have been some of the most prestigious top drawer corporations, investment houses and banks who have stood accused of and been found guilty of dishonest practices. At the smaller end, every large employer suffers a degree of petty embezzlement from its employees, much of which is dealt with under internal disciplinary procedures. It is comparatively rare for a company to be engaged in wholesale fraud but cases do occur and in Britain even the august portals of Lloyds, the insurance broking market, have recently been sullied. Officially, the reason why there are so few successful prosecutions for fraud in the City is not that it does not occur, but that juries have difficulty understanding the documents in complex cases.

Fraud is by its nature hard to detect and it will almost never be apparent from published figures. That does not mean that it does not exist, merely that one should not rely on the auditors to point it out and in that sense an auditors' report is in reality worth less than might at first appear.

The rules of accountancy, 'generally accepted accounting principles', are not the product of a disinterested council of the great and good deciding issues along the lines of natural justice. They emerge from negotiation, companies generally lobbying for techniques which tend to understate their risks and increase their profits, bankers and investors arguing for more conservative methods. These are not technical and esoteric matters, of importance only to the experts. In the next chapter we will show how different accounting methods can make enormous differences to the picture revealed in the accounts; and investors and bankers ignore developments in accounting at their peril. Auditors do not help here. They simply affirm that the statements have been properly prepared in accordance with the prevailing standards. No more, no less.

Before we proceed to consider the techniques that analysts use to assess the condition of a company, it will serve us to point out a few other facts about Annual Reports, the significance of which is often not appreciated. One such matter is the question of consolidation.

The financial statements published in the Annual Report are not those of the company whose name appears on the cover. Rather, they are the consolidated figures of that company *and* all its subsidiary companies, that is, the other quite separate companies which it owns in whole or in major part and which are often listed at the back of the Annual Report. Typically, in a major industrial group the principal company, the one which bears the familiar name, will be a holding company. That means that the actual operating assets of the organization belong not to the principal company directly but to some subsidiary company whose shares are held by the holding company.

It is quite common for very complex structures to exist with many layers of holding companies. Thus, the actual financial statements of XYZ Inc. will show that the only assets of XYZ Inc. are its investments, the shares in all the subsidiary companies that it owns. Although the holding company balance sheet is often published it is not of much use to anyone and receives very little analytical attention.

Presentation instead focuses on the *consolidated* figures which are founded on the reasonable but totally untrue assumption that the group may be considered as a single entity. By aggregating the assets and liabilities and the incomes and expenditures of all the subsidiaries, and by netting out intercompany transactions, management produces a combined statement, something akin to an alloy of lead and gold. The consolidating figures, which would show the working underlying the consolidation, are virtually never made available to even the largest lenders.

Now, there are many perfectly legitimate reasons why an industrial group should consist of a hundred or more separate companies. Each subsidiary will have its own specific purpose within the whole. Some will almost certainly be located abroad. Some will be operating subsidiaries, some financing vehicles, some holding companies. All this is quite ordinary and normal. The point, however, is that the financial data are founded on a premise in direct contradiction to the legal arrangements. Why is this anomaly permitted?

Until the 1930s, companies regularly produced financial statements showing that on one side of their balance sheet there was the owners' equity, on the other a portfolio of investments. For a large group, this type of accounting was obviously inadequate since if the principal operating subsidiary had assumed a large level of indebtedness to a bank or other lender, this fact was not presented to the readers. In order to prevent this sort of abuse it became the custom, later enshrined in law, that the companies had to produce consolidated accounts where all the assets and, more importantly, the liabilities of all group companies were included.

Analysts are much concerned with a company's level of debt, and from this point of view the introduction of consolidated statements was a step forward. From the asset point of view, it must be considered a step backwards. While we see, supposedly, the total indebtedness of the group on one side of the balance sheet, we see on the other the amalgamated assets of the holding company and all the subsidiary companies. That would be acceptable if we could, to some extent, see which assets were supported or financed by which liabilities. But such detail is totally absent from an Annual Report. Many US companies will indicate broadly the percentage of assets in the United States and in other countries where the group companies trade, but there is absolutely no way to identify which subsidiaries own which assets and have which liabilities. Lenders and investors blithely carry on in blissful ignorance of this crucial information.

The consequence is that anyone dealing with an individual member of a group on the basis of the group consolidated figures has to assume that the group is in reality one economic unit, and that if one company gets into trouble the others will provide funds to support it. Indeed, this may well be the case. However, unless formal guarantees are given by other group companies there is no certainty that support will necessarily be forthcoming. As with all limited liability companies, the strict liability of the 'group' for the debts of one of its members, is only the paid up capital of the company in question.

There is in business considerable reluctance to give guarantees to banks or other lenders to subsidiary companies since such guarantees are recorded in the Annual Report as contingent liabilities and a sharp rise in this number might disconcert trading partners and members of the analytical fraternity. To get around the problem, the habit of issuing letters of comfort—also known as 'monkey letters'—has grown up in the last few years. Strictly speaking, these have no legal enforceability and are merely statements from a parent company that they would not abandon a subsidiary if it were to become distressed. Bankers are never very happy to rely on such documents, totally lacking as they are in substance, but this type of letter, issued by a reputable name, is certainly better that nothing at all and is, in practice, rarely dishonoured.

Consolidated accounts are not just a problem for lenders. Anyone looking at the consolidated balance sheet should be aware that of the list of assets a sizeable proportion may be situated in foreign countries and in no way available for immediate repatriation. Assets must be considered from two aspects: value and liquidity. It will be explained later why balance sheet numbers are in any case a poor guide to value. Liquidity means the ease and speed with which an asset can be converted into cash, and cash that is free to meet maturing financial obligations. Assets tied up in, say, South Africa or India (where there are exchange controls) and owned by a remote subsidiary do not have the same value or liquidity as similar assets back at home and under direct head office supervision. In consolidated accounts, however, they look identical!

Finally, it is worth remarking that not all the assets shown in consolidated figures belong to the group and not all liabilities are recorded. Overstatement of group assets arises from the practice of consolidating all subsidiaries which are more than 50 per cent owned as opposed to showing them as investments. Where this occurs there will be a compensating entry on the liabilities side for minority interests. Again, note that no indication is given as to which assets are fully owned by the group and which are owned by subsidiary companies partly held by outsiders.

As to the understatement of liabilities, this is a major shortcoming of published financial data and will be addressed later. Suffice it to say here that where the group holding in a company is less than 50 per cent it will usually not be consolidated and any debt that it has will not appear.

In many cases, this will not matter since it is not normally expected that a group will make good on debts incurred by companies in which there is only a minority shareholding, unless specific guarantees have been given. It is of relevance in the case of groups involved in capital projects undertaken through joint ventures. These operations often borrow heavily and the entrepreneurs are usually liable to some extent in the event of failure. Joint venture indebtedness does appear sometimes in Annual Reports but only in the notes, where, of course, it tends not to get noticed amid the welter of other detail.

Even more serious understatement of liabilities occurs when significant financial subsidiaries are excluded. Accounting rules permit the non-consolidation of captive finance companies, banks and insurance companies and also of subsidiaries engaged in businesses so different from those of the rest of the group that the result would be confusing and indeed meaningless. Wholly owned subsidiaries engaged in totally alien industries are particularly common in the United States because the antitrust laws discourage the acquisition of companies in the same line of business. To expand, as it were, one has to go for something completely different.

Captive finance companies are a particular problem. In a nutshell, a company sells its accounts receivable (debtors) to a subsidiary specially set up for that purpose. The sale is for cash, the subsidiary providing this cash by borrowing against the receivable. Bankers are tolerably keen to lend to captive finance companies, considering them more liquid than parent corporations. Their assets are, in their view, closer to being turned into cash, which is true provided the underlying inventory has actually been sold to the end consumer and not merely dumped on a wholesaler. The parent company also has the satisfaction of seeing its own liquidity position greatly improved as debtors are replaced with cash and the subsidiary borrowing does not have to be reported. Details are normally provided in the notes to the financial statements but usually given little more than a cursory glance by investors. This is a mistake, for the captive finance company reflects the general health of the parent.

Even at this stage of our survey of the nature of business reporting, it should be obvious that simple ratio calculations applied to consolidated figures are going to provide a picture at best only approximating to the truth. Analysts tend to assume that changes in the numbers from one year to the next reflect mainly trading developments. They usually ignore, mainly because they are told virtually nothing about such matters, the fact that changes in the numbers could equally well reflect the acquisition or disposal of subsidiaries, the changeover from accounting for a partially owned subsidiary as an investment to full consolidation or vice versa, possibly but not necessarily accompanied by some increase or decrease in the actual ownership, that a captive finance company may have been recently established, that gains in one subsidiary may have been offset by losses elsewhere and that other structural changes may have occurred which make comparing this year's figures with those of last a clear case of apples and banana peels. While it is true that there is usually some reference to such developments, there is invariably insufficient detail to enable an analyst to calculate the total effect on the statements. He can only guess. More often, he will not bother.

So, despite all the apparent detail contained in the financial section, the amount of real, useful knowledge to be derived from that source is severely limited. Figures are there in abundance, schedules, tables and impressive technical sounding language, but there are also fundamental underlying assumptions so broad and pervasive and really so inaccurate that the value of the whole is much diminished. Imagine an old steam engine. The question is how fast can it go up a certain hill. You are told that the engine was made in 1923, is painted red and gold, the driver's name is Fred and for 40 years the train ran every day between Leeds and Sheffield. It is 18 feet from the rail to the top of the funnel and its boiler was the largest ever made at a certain factory in Wales. Well, how fast can it climb the hill? There is, of course, absolutely no way to tell from what we have. The facts that we need to do the calculation—the gradient of the hill, the engine capacity, the weight of the engine and so forth—we have to guess.

But, what is interesting is that, as presented, the question is meaningless. We have not specified whether we are talking about the maximum speed of the train on its own, or pulling a string of carriages or using what grade of fuel. Analysing a company from its Annual Report is rather similar. We are given bundles of extraneous information which give us only the vaguest hints of what we are really after, how that company will perform next year and the year after. We need to know what weight the train has to pull (say, what interest rates will be), what the weather conditions will do (how the company's market, competitors and economy will behave), as well as a lot more about the technical dimensions of the train's working parts (the subsidiary companies) before we can begin to form an intelligent opinion.

Let us return briefly to the 'highlights' page at the beginning of the Annual Report. If much of the crucial data are missing from the detailed financial section, we may be sure that the 'highlights' page, an extract from the figures of a few 'key' numbers, is unlikely to provide any sensible answers. Annual Reports are written with a view to impressing the reader and it is worth a look to see what numbers the directors most wish to have their shareholders concentrate on.

While the actual layout and content varies between companies and some are more detailed than others, three numbers are almost always prominent: sales, profits and assets. We shall see later how none of these is quite as uncomplicated as it might appear. For now, let us say that the sales and assets figures give an idea of the size and the rate of growth of the group. Other things being equal, rising sales tends to indicate, to most people, prosperity and increasing total assets, strangely, suggests the same.

Actually, both sharply rising sales and burgeoning assets may be danger signs, particularly where the growth is of such a nature as to increase significantly the risk attaching to the company's operations. Also, the ratio between sales and assets may be regarded as a measure of efficiency. Asset turnover ratio, sales/assets, is supposed to give the number of times that assets are 'turned over' during the year. Assets do not, of course, 'turn over' in this way, but as assets have to be financed (and the holding of assets is expensive) there is certainly an advantage to many companies in attempting to increase their sales without incurring an equivalent percentage growth in the asset total. Each company in each industry has its optimum velocity of sales/assets.

The real focus of the shareholder's attention is profits, what Americans like to call 'the bottom line'. This figure may be quoted before tax, as often in the UK, or net as is customary in the United States.'Net Income' or 'Earnings Attributable to Ordinary Shareholder' will usually be supplemented by a figure for earnings per share — EPS for short—and just underneath (and less prominent) dividend per share.

Of all the numbers contained in an Annual Report, the single most influential is that of earnings per share. In American public corporations, this figure is announced quarterly and can have an immediate and profound effect on the share price. By contrast, the effect on the share price of the publication of the quarterly or Annual Report is minimal unless very serious news is disclosed there for the first time. Provided dividend per share is not cut, an event which shareholders invariably find distressing, it is earnings per share which hogs the limelight.

What is this magic number? To answer that we need to go back to a more basic question: *What does it mean to say that a business made a profit?* Let us clear away some misconceptions. *It does not mean that the company has amassed that amount of cash in the bank* and is looking for ways of investing or spending it. It does not mean that the business has 'grown' by that amount. It does not mean that the business is that much further away from bankruptcy or liquidation. It means, simply that according to the company's accountants (and with the tacit blessing of the auditors) the amount deemed to have been received from trading and other activities exceeded the amount deemed to have been incurred in expenses by the stated figure for profit.

The word 'deemed' is important. The revenues, in most types of company the result of sales, are *not* what was received in cash during the period; the figure represents, in common parlance, the amount the company reckoned it had sold, probably the amount shipped from its factories. It may or may not include sales tax, discounts, returned merchandise, freight and other adjustments. Other income may include dividends declared (not necessarily received), interest income (again accrued), a share in the profits of non-consolidated associate companies (almost certainly not received in cash) and any other inflows which it is considered will not have to be repaid.

Accountants have written long tracts on the problem of 'revenue recognition' explaining the very complex rules which define what is or is not income. There are many grey areas. Thus, for example, how does one treat a government grant? Is it income in the year that it is received? Should that £1m windfall go straight to this year's profits— tempting if this has not otherwise been a good year—or should we spread it over 5, 10 or even 20 years. There are rules to control the treatment of such items, and, by and large, where alternatives are possible the company must say (in the notes) what it has done. But, as we know, few people read the notes. They do read the profit figures and for the most part they are unaware what a difference alternative accounting policies can create! The answer is, of course, as much as £950 000 as in this case.

Sales and other income figures contain assumptions. These numbers are not factual; they are, if you like, estimates. Also, and momentously critical, they are not cash numbers.

In the same way, expenses give rise to difficult problems of allocation. A cost is included in the profit and loss account if it is attributable to a particular period or if it is related to an item of income which has been attributed to that same period. Just consider the kind of costs that a large corporation incurs and imagine how difficult and, more to the point, how arbitrary such allocation must inevitably be. It is comparatively easy to attribute the cost of property taxes, rent, electricity and salaries to individual periods. But what about the cost of raw materials whose price fluctuates daily and which are held in store for some time before they are used? What about the costs incurred when a new factory is built and equipped? Should not those be spread over the time that the company will be benefiting from its new asset? Indeed they should, but it is anyone's guess how long that will be especially when the asset is new. The factory may be designed to last 20 years; its output may become obsolete after 2 and it may have then to be retooled, rebuilt, scrapped or even abandoned! All at further cost.

Allocation of costs is based on educated guesswork. And if the numbers put forward for revenues and expenses have a goodly level of assumption, guesswork and rule of thumb artifice among the ingredients, the profit figure, revenues less expenses, will be no better than the two numbers from which it is derived. The stated profit for a period is an estimate. If a company made a profit, it is telling its shareholders that given the generally accepted parameters and the conventions which govern the production of accounts, income attributed to the period in question exceeded expenses attributed to the same period by that amount. It is not that the figure is fraudulent, inaccurate or invalid. It is merely artificial and misleading because it is founded upon assumptions which may or may not be reasonable and accurate, and which are only partially disclosed.

Within the accrual concept, it is the allocation of costs which carries the greatest uncertainty. Costs are incurred by large companies which are amortized over many years. Companies need to plan far into the future but even the most perspicacious treasurer would be hard pressed to predict with any confidence what will be happening in his industry at the end of next year. We live in an uncertain world. It is an easy step from this recognition to the statement that quarterly profit figures are, at least potentially, enormously inaccurate. Any attempt to define into exactly which quarter the cost of a long-term investment will fall can only be a guess. It follows too that the preoccupation of American investors with quarterly earnings per share must be misplaced, at least in so far as the number is deemed to be an accurate reflection of the company's performance. Little detail is published in quarterly reports and, as already noted, it is the number not the commentary which moves the market.

The trouble is that quarterly results have to be observed by investors because they do affect share prices, not necessarily from what is revealed about the company, but because of investor behaviour. The prophecy is self-fulfilling. In fact, it is an ill-kept secret that most companies which report quarterly try to manage their earnings to avoid violent fluctuations. There are innumerable ways in which this can be done, the most effective being the deferral of expenses until such time as the company has sufficient other profit to absorb them. If, for example, a company realizes that its investment in a new factory, which it was intending to write off (or 'depreciate') to expenses over 20 years, is found to be worthless after 3 years, the remaining cost should be put through the profit and loss account immediately. Any delay is a fraud against the shareholders since income is being overstated. In practice, even some large and reputable companies hold meetings with their accountants and auditors to decide when and where the company can afford to 'take a hit' to its earnings. There is usually no intention to deceive. It is merely that everyone is locked into this weird short-term quarterly earnings rigmarole and it is just too painful and costly to attempt to defy it.

The final quarter of 1985 saw a spate of such write-offs by American companies, which aroused the suspicion of many analysts that these companies were taking advantage of the stock market boom to take a 'big bath' at a time when the share price would be least affected. As it happened, the shares of some of them actually rose on the news as investors interpreted the action as 'house cleaning' and looked forward optimistically to better results in 1986. Some companies were even accused of charging excessive write-offs so that they could report higher quarterly earnings in subsequent periods!

Ironically, most investors and analysts know that quarterly figures should be treated with caution, the stated reason being that they are not audited. Actually the audit is irrelevant. The way the figures are prepared should alone undermine any credibility they might have.

To some extent the same provisos apply to annual statements. Even though these are audited, the underlying assumptions are the same; it is just that problems of revenue recognition and cost allocation assume less prominence if longer periods are taken, as the errors and grey areas are proportionately smaller. Ideally, perhaps, company profits should be stated over periods longer than a year, especially for companies which have long productive cycles. Although quite sophisticated techniques exist for handling long-term contracts, how can it possibly make sense to report annual profits for a company engaged solely in a 10-year construction enterprise to build a dam in a highly inflationary foreign country? The question how much profit has been made is devoid of meaning until the work is at least nearing completion. After 1 year, let alone 3 months, it is absurd to pretend that some profit has been made. Correspondingly, the argument has less force for companies such as supermarket chains which deal predominantly for cash settlement and can allocate revenues and costs in a reasonably convincing manner.

Investors are impatient people, hungry for details of performance and even more avid for profit. Their enthusiasm and demands for quarterly information are not misplaced—after all, the investors are entitled to know how their company is performing—but they display extraordinary optimism if they imagine that a quarterly earnings report is worth much more than the paper it is written on.

The last line of note on the 'highlights' page is that for dividends per share. Unless a company is doing badly and still wishes to maintain its dividend, this number will usually be a fraction of the number for profits per share. The way the numbers are presented gives a reader the distinct impression that dividends are a proportion of profits and that the undistributed portion is 'reinvested' in the business for the shareholders' benefit. Such an impression is confirmed by the use of the expression 'paying dividends out of reserves' to describe the situation just mentioned and the existence of laws in most countries forbidding distributions which are not 'earned'. Buried deep down seems to be the feeling that profits are a crock of gold in the bank which shareholders can have a share in before the wealth is ploughed back into the operation to yield yet more money next year.

Quite how this extraordinary notion gained acceptance is a mystery. The ability of a company to pay dividends to its shareholders does not depend, physically, upon profits. It depends upon having the cash to make the dividend payment when it is due. We have seen that profit and cash, while related, are quite different and it is easy to see that in some circumstances a highly profitable but illiquid company could be forced into liquidation by attempting to pay away cash that it does not have while a cash-rich, perhaps declining, company could easily pay a dividend even when loss making. Businesses do not build up profits and then think about distributing them. Rather, they buy and sell, attempting to bring in enough cash from selling and investing to meet their obligations as they come due and to keep the (profitable) gap between revenues and costs to a maximum.

Profit is an abstract concept. It does not physically exist. By contrast cash is real! It does tend to exist nowadays in intangible form, say in bank accounts, but its basic reality is undisputed and it is certainly very hard to make a payment without it.

Say one buys a house for £30 000 and after 5 years sells it for £60 000 and buys another more or less identical. Is there a profit over the 5 years? Certainly—a profit of £30 000. Could one pay a dividend? Certainly not, unless one had other resources or could raise *cash* on the house. Alternatively, suppose that the house was sold after 5 years for £10 000, a clear loss of £20 000, and the proceeds not reinvested. Paying a dividend is physically no problem because the cash is still on hand waiting to be spent.

To conclude, it may be well to draw together some of these strands and to summarize the problem of analysing a company's Annual Report. We have seen that the relationship between a company and its shareholders is bedevilled by certain tensions which are not conducive to full and impartial disclosure and we have discussed at length the elementary principles and assumptions which lurk largely undeclared beneath the figures as presented.

A suggested list of the questions an investor, a lender or a financial analyst researching a company should think of asking might run as follows.

(1) What are the assets of the company actually worth? Are the book amounts a true reflection of value?
(2) What assets and liabilities exist which are not included in the figures, perhaps because they have no cash flow associated with them, or simply because accounting practice does not require their inclusion?
(3) To what extent does the income statement mirror flows of cash and to what extent are these concealed by adusting bookkeeping entries and the accrual system generally?
(4) What clues exist as to how the company will perform in the future? Will past trends continue or be reversed?

This list might, of course, be multiplied many times over as the analysis becomes more detailed and as we proceed further.

To ignore such questions, or to suppose that they do not matter, leads inexorably to analysis that lacks penetration and effectiveness. The conventional responses to these questions are without exception wrong.

(1) It is almost invariably assumed that the balance sheet is a valuation statement. It is not!
(2) Assets and liabilities not included are virtually ignored by virtue of their non-appearance!
(3) It is assumed that there is a close link between the income statement and the cash flow and that profit is the source of dividends. Simply not so!

(4) Past performance is deemed to be the best guide available to future developments, in the absence of more detailed information about next year's business conditions. Next year the business could be dead!

In this chapter, we have defined at least with a broad brush the extent of the misunderstandings. From now on the approach will be more constructive. Not all the obstacles *can* be surmounted; some will always be impenetrable. On the other hand, much remains to be discovered and in the unilluminated areas; we shall, like Socrates, be wise in knowing that we know nothing. And that is a celebrated truth, not a celebrated fiction.

2
Accounting matters—Magic by the numbers

The beauty of reporting quarterly should be that companies can smooth the flow of information to the market and avoid shocks—which was precisely what Plessey failed to do with its 1984–85 results yesterday.
Lex column, *Financial Times*, 24 May 1985

Double entry bookkeeping, the simple process of entering debits and credits into a daybook or ledger in such a way that the sum of the debits is always equal to the sum of the credits, has been a feature of business for so long that we take it for granted. Rarely, if ever, do we stop and wonder whether it is really quite such a powerful tool as it is usually assumed to be. One possible reason is that the system has such elegance and cunning simplicity, though most people find it very hard when they first encounter it, that few have the heart to challenge its awesome claim to have the power to define each and every business transaction by the passing of balancing debit and credit entries. It is as though the majesty of the algebra blinds the young bookkeeper and accountant to the prosaic limitations of the method.

A second cause of the well-nigh unqualified and universal acceptance of double entry lies in the unsophisticated nature of the examples which are usually presented in support of it. Double entry was invented in the late fifteenth century by an Italian monk, and business in those days was a good deal less complex than it is today. Imagine the differences: there were no limited companies, no complicated leasing transactions or pensions to worry about, foreign exchange rates did not fluctuate from hour to hour and above all inflation was extremely low, where it existed at all. In these blissful conditions double entry worked like a charm and doubtless some thought that Paccioli, its inventor, was in league with the devil!

Double entry continues to work best today in similarly unthreatening circumstances, such as are found in very small businesses or on the pages of accountancy textbooks. It was not, though, designed for modern multinational companies and considerable skill and determination have been necessary to create the accountancy systems found around the world, all of which are based on double entry even though this is not too obvious from a first glance at an Annual Report. To be sure, the balance sheet balances but the words 'debit' and 'credit' are nowhere in evidence (except in Italian accounts) and it is not an easy task, as we shall see, to work back to even a summary of the accounting entries which were passed during the year.

Until the early twentieth century the principal statement to be produced by any company was a balance sheet. A balance sheet, according to the textbooks, is a list of the assets and liabilities of the company, and it is often compared to a 'snapshot' of the business taken at a particular moment, the close of business at the end of the accounting period. Obviously, there is some merit in these definitions and they are not wholly misleading. However, technically a balance sheet is something quite different. It is a list of the open balances outstanding in the ledger at the time that the balance sheet is struck.

Why is the difference important? The popular view of a balance sheet implies that the numbers shown represent value, that the assets and liabilities are 'worth' the amount at which they are entered. The technical view takes no cognizance of value, holding that a balance sheet is simply a product of the double entry system. What the assets and liabilities shown are actually 'worth' is irrelevant.

A major difficulty is beginning to emerge here. A balance sheet that is just a list of meaningless numbers is not much use to anyone. What the owner of the business wants to know is what the business has, how much of that is owed to external parties and how much belongs to him. He wants to be able to use the balance sheet to encourage others to do business with his company. He needs a statement of values.

The numbers thrown up on the asset or debit side in a very crude double entry system are historical costs. To take the simplest case of so-called 'fixed assets', the number ascribed in a balance sheet to the factory purchased by the company will be the price paid for it, less the amount written off through the process of depreciation. Accountants produce all manner of justifications for the 'historical cost principle', suggesting, for example, that it provides an objective valuation while other valuation methods are tainted by subjectivity and hence inaccuracy. The truth is that double entry strongly implies historical cost: the factory cost us £1000 so we debit the fixed assets account £1000 and reduce or credit the cash account with the same figure. The historical cost goes automatically onto the balance sheet and will stay there until the asset is sold. We may depreciate the asset by transferring a portion of the cost to the income statement but the basic 'valuation' will not be changed unless we specifically choose to revalue, and there is nothing intrinsic in the double entry system that compels or encourages that revaluation.

It tends to be forgotten now that until comparatively recent times, the balance sheet was considered a company's principal financial statement. The American term, still sometimes used, 'statement of financial position' testifies to the traditional dominance of the balance sheet, as does the comparative dearth of detail contained in the profit and loss account of a British company, particularly prior to the Companies Act, 1981. It is still the custom in some European countries for the smaller private companies to publish only a balance sheet, the profit and loss account being regarded as 'not relevant', a euphemism for 'private'. The practice is, though, becoming rare since few lenders or investors or even trading partners, especially those of a more international disposition, are likely to have much faith in a balance sheet alone, and companies have to concede the issue of privacy in the interests of doing business.

Balance sheets are not produced for their aesthetic qualities. Their primary purpose until the 1920s was to justify applications for short-term credit from banks. We have to imagine ourselves back before the days of medium-term bank lending, when any sort of semi-permanent debt finance would have been very hard to procure for all but the largest and best-known companies. Companies were basically 'equity funded', that is, run on the proprietor's own money, and might enjoy trade credit through delaying the payment of expenses. Bank support would have been strictly short-term and largely restricted to the discounting of trade bills with recourse to the borrower if the drawee of the bill failed to honour his obligation.

Bankers, being by nature a prudent and cautious bunch, were interested in seeing what assets the company had available to meet obligations. They knew from experience that a proportion of discounts and short-term loans were dishonoured and in those cases the chance of ultimate repayment was enhanced if there were, belonging to the company, assets which could be readily converted into cash, known in the trade as 'liquid assets'. If the underlying transaction were specifically secured, perhaps on the goods the loan was intended to finance, there was little need to look at a balance sheet. There certainly was such a need if the loan were unsecured, or secured on the assets of the company generally, as with the British floating charge. In these cases, a banker looked to see what liquid assets were shown on the balance sheet as a way of assuring himself that the loan would not turn bad.

The earliest known examples of bank lending—and its history can be traced back to Mesopotamia in the third millennium BC—are of agricultural lending. A farmer would borrow to buy seed and would repay the loan with interest out of the proceeds of the harvest. Consequently, while the seed was growing he would be quite heavily borrowed, after the harvest was over and the debts paid off he would not be borrowing until the next seed time.

In a situation of this type, it is easy to see that repayment of the loan really did come from liquidation of the current assets. The need for money is a seasonal one and the short-term loan is obviously the correct medium for financing it. Farming is a more intricate and involved process these days but the same pattern of borrowing is familiar to all rural bank managers. Different crops and products have, of course, different seasons but virtually all have an annual cycle. Bankers lending to finance this cycle would naturally see a year as the touchstone or definition of liquidity; they lent money for an absolute maximum of a year, usually much less, and they were interested in seeing assets of a similar maturity. They quite correctly reckoned that it was the current or liquid assets which essentially repaid the current liabilities including their own lending.

The balance sheet was a tool ideally suited to this type of analysis. First, the value of the cash and debts owing to the company, 'debtors' for short, was correctly given by historical cost. Cash is its own measure of value and 'debtors' was easily quantifiable in cash terms on the not too outrageous assumption that most of the debtors would pay up. Stock-in-trade or, as we shall follow the Americans in calling it,

inventory is somewhat more difficult since the whole purpose of being in business is to convert that inventory into a
larger sum of cash than was paid for it, but a degree of
conservatism was acceptable given the undoubted risk that
it might not be sold at all. Agricultural inventories turn
over pretty quickly and there was little time for the other
bugbear of modern inventory accounting, fluctuating
prices, to affect the valuation. On the liability side, it was
quite easy for the short-term external liabilities to be listed.
By watching the balance sheet as it changed over the year a
banker could keep well in control.

Notice that the banker does not need to worry about
whether the farmer makes a profit. In the long term, losses
will drive anyone out of business, but in the short term it is
essential only that sufficient cash be raised from the inventory to repay the loan. The banker's interest is in cash, not
profit.

As the banker is largely unconcerned about profit, he is
not much interested in seeing an income statement. In any
case, last year's income statement will not tell him anything
about this year's trade. This is particularly true of farming
where so much depends upon the weather! In short, historical cost balance sheets were perfectly adequate for controlling short-term seasonal lending.

After the industrial revolution, agriculture came to
occupy a much smaller part of a banker's business. Manufacturing companies abounded and sought finance from
their bankers, not for seasonal needs to fund the growing
of crops, but for keeping them in business while they produced the goods and waited for their customers to pay.
These trade debts, evidenced by accepted bills of exchange,
could be sold to the bank at a discount in advance of their
maturity.

Even now, there was no need for a banker to concern
himself with profit. Whether his customer made a profit on

the goods the banker was financing was largely irrelevant. Crucial, on the other hand, was his customer's liquidity. Provided that the company had assets that could be readily turned into cash, the banker reckoned correctly that he was unlikely to lose money.

The balance sheets that we see today in published accounts reflect the preoccupation of earlier generations of bankers with liquidity. Under the American system the assets appear on the left in descending order of liquidity, the liabilities and equity accounts on the right with the most current items standing at the top. Current assets and current liabilities are separately subtotalled. It is evident from the layout and the accompanying discussion in an Annual Report that liquidity and the existence of 'working capital' (defined as the difference between current assets and current liabilities) are supposed to be important elements in any analysis.

In the UK, a vertical rather than a horizontal format is preferred for balance sheets and the concept of working capital receives even greater prominence since the current liabilities, instead of being listed with the other liabilities and equity, are regularly shown as a deduction from current assets, the resultant figure being described as 'net current assets'.

It is worth noting what a strange convention this actually is. The strong implication is that the current liabilities are actually matched in some way against the current assets. It is as if the company is saying, 'There are our current assets and here are the current liabilities which have to be paid out of them.' Now, we have seen that this is not an unreasonable way to look at a seasonal, agricultural operation. It is also not unreasonable for a short-term lender or trading partner to want to see a fairly liquid position. It is, however, for most modern businesses, particularly large international ones, a wholly unrealistic approach.

Traditional analysis claims that current assets are those which will be converted into cash within a year, current liabilities those that have to be paid within a year. Accounting conventions throughout the world support these definitions. The trouble is that there is no direct link between the liquidation of the current assets and the payment of the current liabilities. Take a non-seasonal, stable business like the wholesaling of electrical components. As the debtors pay for their consignments and as the inventory is sold, cash flows into the company's bank account. During the year the company will pay its operating expenses, interest, dividends and all other outflows out of the same bank account. Because it is in a stable industry and the company's balance sheet will not change much over the year, there will always be debtors and inventory, and always liabilities to be settled. Although current assets are turned into cash and current liabilities do have to be settled, there is no direct correlation between the two processes.

Consider it another way. In the course of the year not only will the company liquidate the current assets on its books at the end of the previous year, it will also generate much more cash from trading. The vast bulk of its debtors and inventory will never appear on a year-end balance sheet, a document that reveals only the totals outstanding at the year end. Similarly, the company will during the year have to pay many other items beyond those shown on its last balance sheet as current liabilities. Salaries, overheads and maturing debts of all types have to be paid continually. If the year end is 31 December, salaries due on 31 January will not appear. A dividend, though, deemed to be an allocation of profit earned during the previous calendar year and payable on 31 January, will be shown on the year-end balance sheet as a current liability. Accountants say that this is because the dividend 'belongs' with the previous year's transactions and needs to be accrued, that is, deducted from equity and shown as a liability. The same is not true of the salaries because, as at 31 December, they had not been earned and were not a liability.

Come 31 January, though, both payments have to be made and in cash. Whatever logic the accountants' argument may contain, it is quite absurd to suggest that the dividend has to be paid out of the year-end current assets while the salaries do not. On 31 January, cheques must be drawn on the bank and there must be cash available to cover those cheques. Artificial distinctions about what should appear on a balance sheet have no impact one way or the other on whether or not the cash will be there when required.

There is really nothing profound in these observations. Historically, what has happened is that a tool and a type of analysis which worked very well for simple business situations has been stretched beyond its capacity. When business began to develop beyond its origins in agriculture and primitive trading, lenders and analysts did not move quickly to develop new tools but relied on the old ones they knew and trusted. Only very recently has the liquidity approach to balance sheet analysis started to fall into disuse in tacit acknowledgement that it does not work very well for modern businesses.

Anyone who worked for an English clearing bank prior to, say, 1980 would have become quite an expert in applying a highly developed version of this tool. It used to work like this. Let us suppose Mr Brown, main shareholder in Brown Manufacturing Ltd, came to see his bank manager for a loan. We need not concern ourselves too much with what Brown Manufacturing Ltd actually manufactured or what type of loan he was seeking since the underlying method was always the same. Let us suppose that Brown Manufacturing Ltd's last balance sheet, rearranged for convenience in the American style, looked as follows:

Brown Manufacturing Ltd
Balance Sheet as at 31.12.19XX

	£		£
Cash	1 000	Short-term loan	3 000
Debtors	2 500	Creditors	3 500
Inventory	4 000	Current liabilities	6 500
Current assets	7 500	Medium-term loan	5 000
Fixed assets	10 000		
(net of			
depreciation)		Equity	7 500
Goodwill	1 500		
	£19 000		£19 000

The medium-term loan, we may assume, was secured on the fixed assets which had been purchased with the bank's assistance some time previously. How would the manager assess the safety of his short-term loan? He would do it by evaluating the assets on a liquidation basis, estimating how much he would receive in the unhappy event that Brown Manufacturing Ltd were to go into liquidation that afternoon. 'No company, in my experience, has ever had any cash on hand when it went into liquidation, so we can forget about that,' the manager would say (to himself, of course, not to Mr Brown!). Let us assume that 80 per cent of the debtors would be collected and that the inventory could be sold for about 50 per cent of its book value in a distress sale. The fixed assets, let us say, 75 per cent, and the goodwill obviously nothing. The liquidation value of Brown Manufacturing Ltd is 80% × £2500 + 50% × £4000 + 75% × 10 000 minus the creditors, £3500. That comes to £8000. Just sufficient to pay out the bank! Not a case for any more lending though.

What would Mr Brown say in response, in the unlikely event that he was privy to this analysis?

First of all, he would say that his business was not going into liquidation. On the contrary, it was flourishing. For the bank to start on the assumption that Brown Manufacturing Ltd was a basket case was absurd; like taking one's wife to the doctor only to be told that the best way to diagnose her ailment was to kill her and do a *post mortem*! Next, he would question the coefficients or percentages the bank had applied to his company's assets. How did the 80 per cent, 50 per cent, 75 per cent arise? Was it a guess? Or founded on some esoteric statistical analysis? Being truthful, the manager would have replied that these numbers were estimates based on experience and would vary according to the nature of the business under examination. It is unlikely that Mr Brown would have been very impressed! How about the goodwill? This had arisen because the company had recently taken over another operation at a price in excess of the book value of the assets. Far from being worthless, the goodwill was extremely valuable; the acquisition had been the best thing that the company had done for years and the new operation was performing splendidly. Why did the manager want to count it as worthless?

In a real situation the manager would, of course, have taken these factors into account. Break-up analysis was not his only tool for making credit decisions. But this approach was very widely used and has not disappeared today entirely. We have noted some of the shortcomings. What advantages did it have for the bank?

The principal virtue of break-up analysis was its undoubted conservatism. The bank assumed the worst, and limited its lending to what the company could repay from assets in a catastrophic situation. As there were no rosy, optimistic assumptions built into the calculation, the bank was unlikely to be disappointed if the worst actually did happen. Some companies obviously do go into liquidation owing the bank money and the use of break-up did much over the years to control the banks' losses. It was also an easy approach which could be handled by clerical staff with a minimum of training. It does not take highly skilled analysts to do break-ups.

The disadvantages of this approach lie in its two major assumptions, that the company will fail and that the balance sheet can be used to obtain the value of assets. The first of these is wholly unrealistic as an analytical starting point. Most established businesses do not fold up; the bank's money is used to develop the business and is repaid from the cash flow generated by the business. With break-up analysis no attention is paid to performance, past, present or future, it being assumed that the venture will not pay off.

Inevitably, break-up analysis will discourage the bank from taking on much good lending. If the bank can be sure that a business will survive (and that is admittedly a big 'if') it can make loans even to companies lacking the asset backing necessary to pass the break-up test. There are plenty of creditworthy corporate customers in the world that do not have readily saleable assets on their balance sheets but whose pattern of trading ensures that they can meet their obligations as they mature.

Secondly, the use of coefficients and balance sheet values to assess the worth in liquidation of a company's assets, is hopelessly naïve. It works, as we have seen, tolerably well for the simple agricultural company where the current assets are expected to be liquidated at something like their book value to repay seasonal lending. It does not work with fixed assets and to a large extent it does not work with the inventory of a manufacturing company.

Consider for a moment Brown Manufacturing Ltd's £10 000 in fixed assets and let us assume that this represents a factory which cost £15 000 some 5 years ago and which is being depreciated on the straight line method over 15 years. The double entry system produces the value £10 000 by saying that the cost price was £15 000 and 5/15 of the value has been consumed or expensed, that is, charged to income, and therefore £10 000 is the remaining, unexpensed, outstanding value.

That is fine so far as it goes, but it does not go very far. That factory's value might be assessed in various ways. For the purpose of break-up analysis, the bank wishes to know what it would sell for at auction if it were put up for sale. To find this out the bank should be asking an industrial valuer for an opinion. It might be that the factory is on a prime industrial site and that its value has risen many times in the last 5 years. Inflation may also have raised the selling price. If the factory is equipped with standard fittings it may be very easy for another manufacturer to set up there without extensive and expensive refitting. Perhaps the true value of the factory is £100 000. Conversely, it may be that, as recently in the UK with the recession closing many factories, it is very difficult to give a factory away. Perhaps it has been poorly maintained, the local seaport has closed or there is a shortage of suitable workers. Perhaps the area is simply no longer fashionable for new factories, or the government has taken away incentives to new businesses opening in the area. It may be that Brown Manufacturing Ltd had the factory fitted with highly specialized equipment and fixtures which make it virtually impossible for another company to manufacture a different product in it. In this case the liquidation value of the factory might well be nil.

The figure of £10 000 thrown out by the bookkeeping is meaningless. It will not do to say that by multiplying this meaningless sum by an arbitrary coefficient we shall come up with a meaningful value for the factory. Value is determined by what something can be sold for. Historic cost is a very poor guide to value when that cost was incurred some years before, especially in inflationary circumstances. In the long term, inflation makes a nonsense of historical cost as a method of valuation.

Partly in recognition of this, it is permissible in the UK

and some other countries, but not the USA, to revalue assets periodically to their market value. The problem is, though, that there is no obligation to effect this revaluation on any periodic basis. A company may just revalue its assets when it needs particularly to strengthen its balance sheet, perhaps in advance of a rights issue. After the revaluation, the assets will continue to be depreciated, on the new book value, and before very long the stated book value will again have become unrealistic.

If the difficulties inherent in valuing fixed assets seem complex, they pale into insignificance before those attaching to the valuation of inventory. Accounting practice in the UK and virtually everywhere else dictates that inventory shall be shown at the lower of cost or net realizable value. *Cost* means the price at which the company purchased the inventory plus the amount expended in processing that inventory at the balance sheet date.

Net realizable value means the amount for which the inventory could be sold net of the costs involved in finishing the production process and selling it. In practice, inventory is normally valued at cost unless the auditors insist that net realizable value is lower, a decision which tends to necessitate major and expensive write-downs in the inventory valuation.

In a small business it is sometimes possible to follow each item of inventory and say what its cost price was; by keeping careful record of each and every item of inventory and the costs expended on it, some companies may reflect the true historic cost of the inventory physically in their possession. Typically, these would be companies handling a small number of large-ticket items. For most companies, however, the valuation of the inventory at the year end is very much more difficult. Just imagine the picture. Over the year the company has, perhaps, bought thousands of different components, some of which are lying unopened, some are half-processed, some are finished and waiting to be shipped. The prices at which the same components were bought over the year has fluctuated, as have the labour costs.

There are, of course, sophisticated control techniques for keeping track of the bookkeeping and it is not the function of this book to describe these in detail. It is certainly possible to devise methods which will produce, at the year end, a number representing the cost of the inventory still on hand. The crucial point is that the number produced will depend entirely upon the method. In an Annual Report there is usually some indication of the valuation method used. It will be a method agreed with the company's auditors and with the tax authorities. It will be in accordance with good accounting practice. It will not, in any meaningful sense, tell you what the inventory is worth. The resultant number is not even an estimate of the value of the inventory. It is the cost of the inventory as determined in accordance with the company's method of inventory valuation.

One reason why the inventory figure needs to be viewed with circumspection lies in the fact that much inventory in process of manufacture has no particular value apart from that process. Raw materials may have a price in the commodity markets. Finished goods have a value related to their selling price. But half-finished goods are, on their own and to anyone except the company which owns them, virtually worthless. No one is likely to buy half-made cars or stereos. Their value depends upon the certainty of their ultimate completion. As accountants say, the inventory has to be valued on a 'going concern' basis.

Another factor which readers of Annual Reports should bear in mind is the extreme difficulty of attaching specific costs to specific pieces of inventory, particularly when large numbers of identical units are processed each year. Where inventory items have been purchased at different prices over the year, perhaps because of inflationary price rises, one quite realistic view is to say that the items on hand at the end of the year are basically those purchased last. To give a very simple example, suppose the company purchased five shipments of inventory over the year at the following prices: £1.0m, £1.2m, £1.3m, £1.4m, £1.6m. At the end of the year it has the equivalent of one and a half shipments on hand. What is the cost price to go into the balance sheet? Under this sytem, known as FIFO (first in, first out), the answer would be $1 \times £1.6m + \frac{1}{2} \times £1.4m = £2.3m$.

You would not imagine that anyone would quarrel with that, but you would be wrong. If £2.3m is the stock valuation, and let us assume for the sake of simplicity that at the beginning of the year inventory consisted of one and half shipments valued at £1.3m, and also ignore production costs, the charge to income or cost of goods is $£1.3m + £1.0m + £1.2m + £1.3m + \frac{1}{2} \times £1.4m = £5.5m$. There is a direct, pound for pound relationship between the inventory valuation and the cost of sales. If our company sold the year's product for £7.0m, it should report a profit of £1.5m on which, ignoring other deductions, we assume it pays tax.

Will the company's owners be happy with this situation? Almost certainly they will be very unhappy indeed. They will point out to the tax authorities that the profit being shown is largely fictitious. To stay in business, just at the same level, inventory must be replaced as it is processed and sold. The taxation system is not taking into account the additional cost of replacing inventory and the company, not having increased its physical inventory at all, has in effect incurred an unexpected cost of £1.0m which it cannot set off against its profits. It is having to pay tax in cash on paper or inflationary profits.

There is considerable merit in the argument, although the tax authorities will not willingly concede the point as they will not wish to forgo the revenue. If they were, say, to allow the company to use àn average cost system, total costs of £7.8m divided by six and half shipments would yield a cost of sales of $5/6.5 \times £7.8 = £6.0$m and an inventory valuation figure of $1.5/6.5 \times £7.8 = £1.8$m. Clearly, less tax would be payable.

Best of all for the company in a period of rising prices would be a LIFO (last in, first out) system whereby it is assumed that it is the latest items purchased which have been consumed, and the oldest which remains in the balance sheet. In our example, cost of sales would be £6.5m giving a taxable profit of £0.5m and inventory would be valued at £1.3m, inflation having had no effect on the balance sheet figure.

The lower the inventory valuation, the lower the profit and, provided that the tax system recognizes the same valuation for tax purposes, the less tax that is paid. Unfortunately, the lower the inventory valuation, the lower the profit, and we can see at once that valuation of inventory is not simply a matter of giving as impartial and 'accurate' a number as possible. The number given against inventory in an Annual Report is not the value of the inventory. It is the sum of expenses incurred for raw materials and direct labour which have not been passed through the income statement.

As a broad guide it can be said that FIFO comes closest in times of inflation to showing current value in the balance sheet; average costing systems will tend to underestimate inventory value, and LIFO will, especially if a company has been using it for some time, give a value substantially below the current cost. This is because, provided physical, year-end inventory levels do not fall, they will be represented in the balance sheet by costs associated with the purchase of that quantity of inventory at the time that company first acquired an equivalent level and showed it on its balance sheet at year end. In our example, if the company maintains inventory levels at year end of one and a half shipments every year for the next 20 years, it will always show inventory of £1.3m. After 20 years, unless inflation is extremely low, £1.3m will be a ridiculous underestimate.

The method of inventory valuation in any company will depend upon a number of factors, not least the type of business and the nature and cost structure of the inventory. LIFO is rarely seen outside of the USA because the tax authorities either forbid it, as in the UK, or allow it only when the inventory can be shown to behave in accordance with LIFO principles, as in some European countries. (An example might be coal poured into a cellar and removed for consumption from the top. The oldest coal is never actually consumed and stays for ever at the bottom!)

In the USA, most major companies are on LIFO with the aim of reducing taxes. Many were slow to adopt LIFO, partly, as they claimed, because the bookkeeping is more complicated and therefore expensive, partly because the Internal Revenue Service and the Securities and Exchange Commission together decided that a company on LIFO must use the same method for its Annual Report and consequently show shareholders reduced profits. American shareholders tend to take a dim view of reduced profits and some managements preferred to pay extra tax rather than try to explain LIFO to their shareholders. Some idea of the true value of the inventory may be deduced from the notes to the accounts where the size of the LIFO reserve is revealed. Add that to the stated inventory valuation—and this will often more than double the number—to see the FIFO value of the same inventory.

The British and others addressed the problem of paper inventory profits in a different way by creating a system of 'stock appreciation allowances', essentially to permit companies not to pay tax on the fictitious profits created by inflation. Now that inflation has been reduced these allowances have largely been abolished.

Our discussion of inventory valuation has so far only hinted at one little-known aspect of corporate analysis. What appears on a balance sheet to a large extent is a function of what does and does not go through the profit and loss account. The valuation of inventory makes a difference to the shape of the balance sheet, but it also makes a direct, pound for pound difference to the profit and loss account. It is obvious, in double entry terms, that purchases of inventory and expenses involve ultimately cash outflows, credits to the cash account. For every credit there must be a matching debit. Either the debit goes to the balance sheet where it becomes an asset, or it goes to the profit and loss as an expense. There are no other options! Assets are, in a sense, unexpired expenses, or alternatively, but mathematically much the same thing, revenues which have not yet been received. A balance sheet is not, at the most basic level, a list of assets and liabilities. It is a list of open ledger balances.

It is possible to adjust a balance sheet so that the values it gives are realistic. As the balance sheet by definition balances, there must ultimately be balancing adjustments over the owners' equity accounts. Adjustments to equity are in common parlance called profits or losses and the obvious way to make these adjustments is by debiting or crediting the income statement, itself little more than a summary of the trading entries over the equity accounts. Since adjustments to equity which do not pass through the income statement are in general discouraged except in very specific circumstances (e.g. the issue of new capital), it becomes extremely difficult to adjust either the balance sheet or the income statement without some effect, possibly undesirable, on the other.

This brings us to what is probably the biggest problem faced by an analyst in evaluating a balance sheet. Since the Wall Street crash in 1929 and the Great Depression which followed it, the public, particularly in the USA but also elsewhere, has kept a much closer watch on corporate performances. It is investor pressure for more information which has led to the now ubiquitous income statement assuming its modern degree of prominence.

The public and the markets perceived that traditional liquidity was not a satisfactory measure of the risk attaching to dealings with a company, particularly over the long term, and shareholders and long-term lenders, bond holders and institutional lenders turned instead to looking at profitability. Economic business theory was developed to show that profitable companies survived where loss-making ones did not and here was born the notion that the market price of shares was related to historical profitability. Inevitably, by the process described above, the balance sheet faded in significance against the income statement. An unholy alliance of accountants, company managements, shareholders and to some extent accounting standards bodies all came to the conclusion that if the double entry bookkeeping system was inadequate for describing faithfully the business of large successful modern companies, then the consequences should be suffered by the balance sheet and not by the income statement.

A glance at a modern Annual Report will show how this process has proceeded. LIFO accounting makes sense on the income statement, not on the balance sheet. By the same token, there is resistance to the regular revaluation of fixed assets, a move that is on one level attractive because it makes a company look bigger and stronger, as it necessarily involves charging depreciation at a higher level in subsequent years as the revalued assets are expensed. The revaluation, by convention, does not go through the income statement as a profit, but the depreciation does, as an expense. Accordingly, revaluations are rare except when there is a sudden desire on the part of a company to show itself in its rosiest colours, principally in advance of an equity issue.

The multitude of deferred items on both sides of a balance sheet arises because the debits or credits that created them are an embarrassment. Often they will be expenses, perhaps for research and development, starting the company, buying another company for a value in excess of book value, or just prepayments of some sort, that are to be spread over the income statements of several periods. They are not assets as the word is usually understood. They are unexpensed expenses. Alternatively, deferred items may arise from entries it is deemed appropriate to pass through the income statement, like taxes, which may or may not be matched by cash flow at some unspecified future date; in the interim a matching entry goes on the balance sheet. Again, these entries do not really represent the creation of liabilities or assets; they are simply the largely unwanted by-products of the double entry bookkeeping system operating under strain.

In extreme cases, the treatment of some items may become a hotly contested issue. One good example concerns the treatment of foreign exchange translation gains and losses. A company with operations abroad has assets and liabilities expressed in foreign currency—generally more assets than liabilities. At the year end these must be included in the final figures for the Annual Report and the balances translated into the home currency. The strength of the US dollar in the years preceding 1985 meant that, in dollars, the overseas assets of multinational companies were apparently worth less each year as the exchange rate rose. If the assets were worth less, there was a loss to be accommodated somewhere in the accounts.

American business, which had not been dissatisfied when the dollar was weak, and foreign exchange translation profits were being 'earned', started objecting strongly to the old practice of putting the gain or loss through the income statement. It was not fair, they argued, to have their domestic earnings wiped out by translations. They did not trust the public and the markets to understand. Instead, they argued that the effect should be shown on the balance sheet where it did not attract attention (although they did not put it quite like that!)

The usual place for a capitalized loss is on the asset side under intangibles. This alternative was not too attractive since American business is also sensitive to return on assets which would be depressed by this treatment. Furthermore, if the number became large there might become pressure to set up an amortization schedule, as for fixed assets, with deleterious effects on the income statement. Finally, it was settled that accumulated translation gains and losses should be included as an equity account. In the USA this is shown separately; in the UK the number is rolled into the general reserves. It remains to be seen what will happen now that the dollar has weakened and it is translation gains that are being hidden in this way. There will undoubtedly be many voices clamouring to have the gain put back into the income statement!

It follows from all this that the number the company publishes as its total assets needs to be treated with some caution. We need not doubt, as a general rule, that a company with total assets of £50m really is smaller than another company with assets of £100m. To deny that would be to push the argument too far. But we should recognize that total assets is at best an approximation. It is not an estimate. It is the sum of the asset figures produced by the accounting rules as applied in one particular case.

Now, if total assets is a suspect figure, it follows that total liabilities plus equity is similarly suspect, since it is the same number. If we can be sure that the liabilities are correctly stated, we must have our doubts about the equity value.

It will come as no surprise to hear that balance sheet equity values bear little resemblance, except in order of magnitude, to market values as defined by the stock exchange prices. Successful companies usually trade at a substantial premium to their book value, weak or unsuccessful ones not infrequently at a discount. The stock market does not value companies primarily by reference to the book value of their shares.

Does this matter? It does, not so much because there is a divergence in the two valuations as because that divergence should alert us to some more of the pitfalls to be avoided in balance sheet analysis. The question of liquidity has already been addressed. There remains the other great test that bankers and investors apply to company balance sheets, that of gearing or leverage, to which the value of equity is of crucial importance.

The basic notion is very simple. To set up a business requires money. Some of this money will come from the entrepreneurs who take the primary risk in the venture. To them belong the rewards and the losses. Other money comes from outsiders and is borrowed. It may come from banks or others who charge interest, it may come in the form of trade credit, the temporary forgoing of payment in the normal course of doing business. Money that is borrowed has eventually to be repaid with interest as appropriate. Failure to pay renders the company liable to liquidation. Borrowed money brings risk. By contrast, the owners' money and the accrued profits of the business do not have to be repaid. Dividends are at the company's discretion and there is no risk. Owners' money is in short supply and expensive, partly because it is scarce, more importantly because dividend payments are not tax deductible to a company, whereas interest payments are. Accordingly, the more use that is made of borrowed money, the more profitable the business tends to be, when it is successful. However, borrowed money also brings risk and the more there is the greater the risk. Poor trading performance will quickly lead to the collapse of a company heavily dependent upon borrowed money.

In order to attempt a quantification of the risk, company watchers like to compare the relative amounts of borrowed money and equity. Various related techniques are used by different analysts, but two of the most widely employed are the gearing ratio, that of interest-bearing borrowings divided by equity, and the leverage ratio, that of total liabilities excluding equity divided by equity. The higher the ratio the riskier the company is perceived to be. Naturally, the figures in the Annual Report are used as the raw data.

The underlying argument is beyond reproach. Companies with little equity in proportion to their size are at risk and many of them fail in difficult times. What one needs to beware of is the belief that the numbers produced by these ratios are always accurate and valid.

We may begin by considering a couple of notions that have enjoyed long popularity in the UK and which are in truth at least highly questionable if not totally invalid. The first is that it is a refinement to the technique to deduct intangible and deferred assets from equity to produce a difference known as 'net capital resources'. This practice is reminiscent of the bankers' break-up approach and appears to suggest that as intangible assets have no liquidation value they should be counted as worthless. It is simply incorrect to say that all intangibles are worthless. We know that the equity figure is in itself suspect, and simply to deduct the intangibles, while making no adjustment in respect of the often highly curious values ascribed to other assets, is unhelpful. One artificial number deducted from another is not going to yield any special insight.

The second bugbear is more a matter of banking practice. Banking textbooks often state that the bank should not put more money into a business than the entrepreneurs. It is they, so the argument runs, who should be bearing the risk. In effect, this is saying that gearing should not exceed unity. As a rule of thumb, this idea has served the banks well over the years. For most British companies unity would be a very high, not to say dangerous, level. But it is not true to say that if gearing goes above this level the bank is suddenly taking all the risk, as bankers tend to imply. The bank is still entitled to its principal and interest and it will have priority over the shareholders in a liquidation. The shareholders will still lose all their money invested before the bank loses its loan. In other words, the risk of dealing with a company is not directly correlated to the amount lent. Account must be taken of the terms.

The most serious problem with the use of these ratios lies in the vexed and recurring question of the asset and liability values. If the value of total assets is a weird number, equity must inevitably be a weird number too. We have not yet addressed the difficulties associated with the value of the liabilities, but this adds yet another crucial level of uncertainty.

Current liabilities are not really an issue. As they are short-term and payable in cash, it is not difficult to measure them accurately. Nor is it difficult to account for long-term borrowings. Readers of Annual Reports do not always appreciate that there exist other long-term liabilities which are not mentioned at all! What are these strange items? Principal culprits are leases, unfunded pension liabilities, contingencies, deferred taxes, and debt subject to defeasance arrangements.

Strange to relate, these are all, except the last, areas where obligations arise without there being concomitant cash flows. If a company borrows to purchase a fixed asset, the accounting treatment is obvious and uncontentious. If, on the other hand, the company can rent or lease the asset it will not create necessarily an asset or a liability on the balance sheet; the rental may merely be charged to income as an expense. Corporate treasurers much prefer the latter treatment since it keeps both debt and total asset figures down. Actually, the difference between the two is largely cosmetic and leases are often only thinly disguised purchase and borrowing arrangements, sometimes with tax advantages.

In the USA, rules are specified by the accounting bodies to the effect that leases which are tantamount to purchases should be capitalized, that is, the effective value of the asset and the payout obligation should be shown on the balance sheet. The imposition of such rules spawned an industry in the USA among tax advisers and accountants in the writing of leases which did not have to be so capitalized.

Companies are genuinely interested in keeping leases off their balance sheets. In theory, analysts will never be fooled because details have to be disclosed in the notes to the accounts. In practice, most companies know that most analysts would not or could not make the necessary adjustments. They guess, correctly, that it is the numbers on the main statements which count. The UK is in the process of adopting stricter accounting for leases, and capitalized leases may now be seen on some companies' accounts. Elsewhere in the world the capitalization of leases is almost unknown.

Unfunded pension liabilities arise when a company chooses to charge pension costs to income as they are paid (later) rather than when the beneficiaries accrue the vested interest (earlier). In the interests of keeping profits up, the matter of pensions can easily be overlooked. The acquisition of vested pension rights by workers is a gradual process not involving cash flow and so it does not give risk to immediate bookkeeping entries, a convenient circumstance which works in the company's favour in the short term. Some major US companies now have actuarially computed pension liabilities rather in excess of their net worth. These companies, needless to say, are in the forefront of opposition to suggestions that the liability should be disclosed on the face of the balance sheet—by debit to owners' equity, naturally!

Contingencies are obligations like guarantees, potential liabilities or bills discounted, liabilities which may or may not one day have to be paid. Again, these arise without cash flow and so tend to be ignored. In almost every country it is required to disclose contingencies by way of footnote, although details are invariably absent. A proportion of contingent liabilities will inevitably have to be met, and an estimate could reasonably be included on the face of the balance sheet. Contingencies contain risks and are certainly not a factor to ignore in assessing the adequacy of capital. If a bank issues a performance bond in support of an overseas construction project and the project fails, the bank is just as likely to lose money as if it had made a straight loan.

Deferred taxes are one of life's engaging mysteries except to the initiated. The rest of the world, dutifully paying its income tax, wonders uncomfortably how a company manages to defer its tax! Deferred taxes are simply taxes charged to income but not deemed payable in the short term. Principally, they arise because certain deductions are allowed for tax purposes, often as part of government strategy to encourage capital investment, which are not allowable immediately in the accounting statements. An example might be the use in the UK of capital allowances. Effectively, capital allowances reduce the tax payable in the early years of an asset's life as a large proportion of the cost is deducted from taxable income in the first year. For accounting purposes, the deduction of the cost from income takes place under the process known as depreciation, over the useful life of the asset. If the standard tax rate is applied in the accounts to the reported profits, tax will be overstated in the early years. The overstatement is deferred tax. The timing difference will unwind over the life of the asset and the total tax paid will be the same, provided the rate remains constant, since the cost of the asset can only be deducted a total of once. Debits to the profit and loss account for tax which is not immediately paid are balanced by credits which are passed to the balance sheet account entitled 'deferred tax'.

In the USA it is mandatory to make full provision for deferred tax, that is, for the income statement to take no cognizance of the possibility of tax deferred. British practice is to insist on provision for deferred tax only so far as the tax is likely to be paid in the foreseeable future. Obviously, if a company is continuously buying assets, it is continually taking capital allowances and in the end deferring some of its tax for ever. In the UK this may be reflected by reducing the tax charge shown on the profit and loss account. That done, it is not necessary to pass such large credits to the deferred tax accounts. In many parts of the world, the concept of deferred tax does not exist and the tax shown in the profit and loss account is what is actually paid. This is particularly a feature of West German and Japanese accounting. Balance sheets which do not reasonably reflect the deferred tax liability are understating the liabilities. Unless the reader understands the treatment, and only with US and UK accounts will he get the slightest help, he is likely to be misled.

Finally, debt defeasance is a bold new American way of making debt vanish. By creating a trust to assume liquid assets and the debt to be 'defeased' it is permissible in some circumstances to remove both asset and liability from the balance sheet. The process is actually wasteful of resources and costly to the shareholder. Shareholders will, however, be mollified as the matter will not be mentioned in the Annual Report except possibly as an item of extraordinary income on the supposed redemption of the debt. This profit is wholly fictitious.

The above is by no means a definitive list of what is wrong with a corporate balance sheet. It is just an indication of the kinds of problems which exist. One cannot attribute too much to the numbers. Not only do they arise from a system in many ways ill adapted to the modern world, but considerable ingenuity may well have been exercised in making the numbers as seductive as possible.

Since the company's shareholders are paying for this self-deception the only beneficiaries are likely to be the management. The point is not that the numbers are wholly unrealistic, although in many cases they are; it is rather that they are numerical approximations, often attempting to define the undefinable down to several decimal places.

Ratios are merely the result of dividing one such number by another. The dynamics they purport to measure do exist. As we have said, more highly leveraged companies are riskier. The mistake lies in assuming that a company with leverage of 3:1 is necessarily more risky than one with leverage of 2:1. It may just be that the accounting standards are different! We should note that consistency is more or less mandatory in the production of accounts over the years and one cannot change the rules every year. So, if we see leverage rising each year that may be a genuine warning signal for the company. Against this a company reveals its position only one day a year. It offers no assurances that the figures were similar the day before or the day after!

The authors know of one US subsidiary of a British company which paid off, for one day, a loan which was otherwise permanent, the money being drawn down again immediately the next day. It was no surprise to receive a letter from the company's auditors a few weeks later asking the bank to confirm the loan balance on the one day that the company had not been borrowing! Such window dressing is extremely common. It may not be illegal or designed to cheat, but it is scarcely consistent with the honourable and trustworthy stewardship of the owners' money.

Before concluding our survey of the weaknesses of published numbers we need briefly to focus on the income statement in particular to examine one of the analyst's favourite tools, the coverage ratio. At its simplest the technique is to divide profit before interest and tax by interest to see how many times the interest was covered by earnings. A similar technique is used by stock analysts to ascertain the coverage of dividends by after-tax profits.

As with the debt equity ratio, the technique is rooted in common sense and does, albeit crudely, measure risk in a numerical sense. The danger lies in reading too much into this technique. Neither dividends nor interest are in reality paid out of profits. They are paid out of the bank account. It is the availability of cash rather than profit which is the acid test. Failure to 'cover' dividends or interest, or indeed other costs, is not necessarily fatal in the short term, though it will be difficult to sustain indefinitely. If the income statement is based on accrual and a generous measure of fairly arbitrary judgement, the coverage ratio is only an indication.

Beware of attempts to make these tools sharper by including other factors. The addition of depreciation to net profit seldom gives a realistic estimate of cash flow, despite the popular legend to that effect, and 'cash flow coverage' ratios are virtually worthless. The inclusion of leasing and other financial costs with interest is not unreasonable but where leasing charges have been deducted above the profit before interest and tax line, they should be added back before doing the division.

In a tolerably stable company the pattern of interest or dividend coverage may be a realistic indication of strength or risk but the calculation should be done with care and interpreted with circumspection. The numbers are not so reliable that fine distinctions can be drawn and precise comparisons made with confidence.

To end, we shall look briefly at an example which illustrates a number of the points made above. We would stress that although the accountancy rules applying in the USA have in this instance been scrupulously observed, the result for the reasons below could be highly misleading for the casual reader, and anyone attempting to analyse developments by the use of simple traditional tools of analysis could come to some totally wrong conclusions.

In 1983 the consumer electronics company, Texas Instruments Inc., decided that their attempt to enter the home computer market had failed. They realized that in competition with IBM, Honeywell and others they would never establish a sufficiently large or lucrative market share and that their home computer operation had simply to be closed down. The investment in home computers made over the previous two or three years had been sizeable and perhaps not unexpectedly the income statement of Texas Instruments made gloomy reading for the shareholders:

	$m
Income (loss) before provision (credit) for income taxes	(323.2)
Provision (credit) for income taxes	(177.8)
Net income (loss)	(145.4)

How much money did Texas Instruments lose? How much tax did they pay or recover? These might seem obvious questions which could be answered merely by reference to the figures quoted.

In fact, the true situation was quite different. First, the loss of $323.2m was not money lost in the period. To a large extent it arose from write-offs. Certain expenditure in previous periods had been debited to the balance sheet as an asset rather than charged to income. This was a realistic treatment at the time since the company expected to recover value for the investment outlay (that is, it invested in inventory which it expected to sell, fixed assets which should have contributed to the ongoing production cycle, etc.). The loss arose from the decision of the company to write off that investment. It decided that it was no longer realistic to consider that past expenditure the purchase of an asset. Now it had to be regarded as an expense. There was no way to alter past statements, so the debit was transferred (by credit to the asset accounts) to the income statement.

The tax position is even more interesting. The accounts suggest that the company received $177.8m in cash, even if the parentheses, the equivalent of the taboo minus sign, ought mathematically to suggest an outflow. Actually,

Texas Instruments paid tax rather than received it in 1983. The notes and the commentary refer to the fact that the tax loss was treated as a tax loss carry forward. That means that Texas Instruments exercised the right to offset this loss for tax purposes against future income, rather than against past income. The latter course would have brought an immediate refund from the Internal Revenue Service (IRS) but, probably because the taxable profits in previous years against which the loss would have been offset were not very heavily taxed, that being the key factor in determining the size of the refund, the company chose to offset its loss against future profits. So, no refund.

Having made this decision it could then choose how to show it on the accounts. One possibility would be to show no tax refund on payment, simply nil tax. This is not very attractive since the crucial net loss figure would have been an unrelieved $323.2m, the accompanying privilege of showing next year's profit similarly free of tax being perhaps too remote. Alternatively, it could show the refund accrued and next year show profits being taxed in the normal way, even though little if any tax would actually be payable. US accounting rules require a company to be reasonably certain that future profits will be made before this approach is permitted.

The rest of the story appears in the note relating to tax appended to the main statement. It reads:

Provision (credit) for Income Taxes

1983	US	Non-US	Elim.	Total
Currently payable	(48)	101	—	53
Net timing differences	(207)	(24)	—	(231)
Total	(255)	77	—	(178)

From this schedule it appears that Texas Instruments paid, or had to pay within the next year, $101m in taxes to foreign governments. It would recover $48m from the IRS and the rest was made up of longer-term deferrals. Texas

Instruments, far from recovering tax in 1983, was in reality paying it out (to the tune of $53m).

It is not, of course, clear from any of this how much tax was paid during 1983 and how much was a short-term liability at year end for settlement in 1984. To find this out we need to look at the balance sheet. At year end $77.2m was shown as short-term tax payable, presumably part of the $101m in foreign taxes though we cannot be sure of the details since the company does not publish a reconciliation of its tax accounts.

But what of the tax refund? If we credit the income statement with a non-cash item, what do we debit? One may well ask. Under the tax note is the following passage:

> Net accumulated tax related timing differences (stated as $231m) including the income tax benefit arising from the US financial statement net operating loss carryforward, which totalled $193m in 1983 are classified in the balance sheet as prepaid taxes and expenses, other assets and deferred charges, and deferred credits and other liabilities, as appropriate.

That means that it is scattered, and all over the balance sheet. The company's balance sheet has been made a victim of the income statement presentation. So long as we realize the $177.8m tax credit is not cash, the income statement presentation is not unrealistic. The balance sheet presentation is. It says that the company has already paid next year's tax in advance. One could make out a mathematical argument to support this presentation but do we really want to see an asset on the balance sheet in respect of next year's (and possibly several subsequent years') tax paid? The treatment of the tax position on the income statement, however, dictates that the balance sheet must include the amount of the 'prepaid' tax, so all that can be done to avoid showing it separately, is to do what Texas Instruments in fact did and roll the debit into sundry other accounts. It is not that the company is trying to conceal anything, merely that a balance sheet showing large amonts of prepaid tax as an asset is not what investors expect to see.

A glance at the balance sheet (see Exhibit 1) shows that not only has the tax credit been liberally dispersed around the balance sheet, but so has the loss. We saw that it was not cash. Partly it was reflected in the lower inventory figure, though by the look of the figures that is not where all of it is. The major part of it seems to lie in accounts payable and accrued expenses, and that is the most probable explanation of the increase in that account of $265m. Analysts usually conclude that disproportionate increases in payables mean that a company is taking longer to pay its suppliers, and here might suppose that Texas Instruments' problems are making it a slow player. Our analysis shows that that is almost certainly not the case here.

This example does not illustrate improper behaviour in the company's managers or its auditors. But somehow it is difficult for the reader to see what has happened unless he does some diligent digging. He is presented with a 'simplified' view on the face of the main statements. He discovers the reality by applying his knowledge of accountancy to the full information available. Even then he can only see through a glass darkly. Few analysts actually take the trouble. Perhaps it will not matter—Texas Instruments is a strong company which will recover.

As business and the world economy becomes ever more complex, the inadequacies of the double entry system loom ever more apparent. But there is great general reluctance to do more than tinker with it, and there is no willingness at all on the part of the accounting profession to address its fundamental limitations. Nowhere is this better illustrated than in the sad story of inflation accounting. The rapid inflation experienced in Western countries during the 1970s brought a flurry of interest in 'inflation accounting', but now that inflation has settled down to more tolerable levels, that interest is waning and we shall soon no longer see in UK Annual Reports the current cost information that supporters of inflation accounting fought so hard for.

Texas Instruments Incorporated and Subsidiaries

	December 31 1983	December 31 1982
Balance Sheet		
Assets		
Current assets		
Cash and short-term investments	$ 184.9	$ 420.0
Accounts receivable, less allowance for losses of $159.2 in 1983 and $72.7 in 1982	664.6	641.7
Inventories (net of progress billings)	335.6	360.0
Prepaid taxes and expenses	266.6	105.2
Total current assets	1,451.7	1,526.9
Property, plant and equipment at cost	2,266.3	2,083.8
Less accumulated depreciation	(1,067.3)	(987.5)
Property, plant and equipment (net)	1,199.0	1,096.3
Other assets and deferred charges	62.6	8.2
Total assets	$2,713.3	$2,631.4
Liabilities and Stockholders' Equity		
Current liabilities		
Loans payable and current portion long-term debt	$ 37.3	$ 49.5
Accounts payable and accrued expenses	1,050.8	784.0
Income taxes payable	77.2	68.8
Accrued retirement contribution	53.2	44.6
Dividends payable	12.0	11.8
Total current liabilities	1,230.5	958.7
Deferred liabilities and credits		
Long-term debt	225.1	214.0
Incentive compensation payable in future years	3.8	6.8
Deferred credits and other liabilities	51.2	91.1
Total deferred liabilities and credits	280.1	311.9
Stockholders' equity (common shares outstanding at year-end: 1983—24,027,538; 1982—23,652,416)	1,202.7	1,360.8
Total liabilities and stockholders' equity	$2,713.3	$2,631.4

Exhibit 1   Reproduced by permission of Texas Instruments, Inc.

Inflation accounting meant in practice little more than historical cost accounting with a few adjustments made for inflation, the effect of which was usually to reduce profits severely. It was natural that producers of accounts had little enthusiasm for such adjustments, though officially their opposition was founded on what they saw as the subjectivity of current cost accounts and the unnecessary expense of preparing them.

But inflation does have an effect. It makes borrowers richer and lenders poorer and in monetary terms it tends to push up the value of fixed assets. Unquestionably some effort should be made to allow for this effect. But no one wants to report lower profits because of inflation, and without some support from the tax authorities, which has not been forthcoming because of the loss of tax revenue that was expected if inflation accounting achieved common acceptance, producers of accounts have had no incentive to press for its adoption.

Historical cost accounting is built on the premise that the value of money is constant and the technical problems thrown up in attempting to reconcile that starting point with a contradictory counter-premise proved intractable. Ultimately, it was inconceivable that the double entry system should be allowed to become obsolescent, and when inflation receded, the issue was permitted to drop, to near universal relief. Few people had ever understood or used the current cost accounts anyway.

It is often not difficult for an analyst to penetrate beneath the surface. All that is needed is a willingness to see the double entry system for what it is, a simple algebraic model, not an inerrant wonder revealing through its workings every aspect of a company's life and peformance. Traditional ratios work well in analysing stable companies in predictable economies, but not so well in hard cases, just those where accurate perception is most necessary if the lender or investor is to hang on to his money. That, after all, is what analysis is all about.

3

How business works— And doesn't!

Again I saw that under the sun the race is not to the swift nor the battle to the strong, nor bread to the wise, nor riches to the intelligent, nor favour to the men of skill; but time and chance happen to them all.
Ecclesiastes, 9:11
(Revised Standard Version)

For all its faults and limitations, there is no getting away from the double entry bookkeeping system and the various financial accounting practices which have evolved from it. Accounting rules vary considerably from one part of the world to another, and different accounting methods can result in widely differing numbers arising, but all financial accounting systems devised for the presentation of the accounts of companies operating in the developed and developing world are fundamentally the same. There is always a balance sheet and an income statement (of some sort) and much the same items inevitably appear on them. Although moves are afoot to create more universal standards, and the rules are constantly changing, it would be fair to say that the criticisms of accountancy outlined so far have not given serious impetus to any radically new approach. Double entry bookkeeping is here to stay and if we wish to understand a chosen company we have no choice but to come to terms with it.

What is within our power is to look at the numbers in original and creative ways, to devise new tests which are more informative about the underlying reality the numbers purport to describe. Before we can do this, though, we need to be quite clear about what it is we are trying to measure. Published accounts do not give a list of debits and credits and leave the reader to judge which numbers are important. The accounts are presented in such a way as almost to tell the reader how those numbers should be interpreted. This is the 'highlights page' approach already described. As analysts we have to regard the whole Annual Report as a large mine of information, an assortment of clues from which we ourselves should take responsibility for extracting the nuggets of truth and insight from the dross of surplus and irrelevant information, of which there is plenty!

In order to decide what it is we should be measuring, we need to consider what a business is and how it works. Businesses are of many types and often highly complex but there are certain fundamental processes common to almost all and only on an understanding of these can a worthwhile methodology be founded.

To start a new business one needs to get busy in several directions. There may be legal formalities to observe, premises to rent or buy, staff to hire, a product to develop or market and a plethora of other matters to be sorted out. But before any of these can be attended to one needs to hold a sum of money, which we may define as cash in the bank. It is impossible to start a business without money.

One of the primary objects of being in business is, of course, to make money, again cash in the bank, yet paradoxically one has to start with some and to spend it in order, as one hopes, to receive it back, more abundantly, from the new venture.

Consider the most straightforward example of a manufacturing company. Our prospective entrepreneur, let us call him Smith, has in the early stages of building his business to pay legal incorporation costs and a down payment to secure an office. He then has to obtain space to manufacture his product and hire workers to convert his raw material into the finished article he proposes to sell. Finally, in this much simplified scenario, he needs to buy a supply of that raw material for his workers to process.

All of this costs money and Smith has a number of ways of obtaining it. He will in all probability be using his own savings and possibly those of others who are prepared to back him on an equity basis, that is, as co-owners of the business; secondly, he may borrow money from a bank that is prepared to lend it. Thirdly, he may take trade credit by delaying payment for the goods and services he is obtaining to set up his business. For a small, new business these are about the only possibilities.

Naturally Smith will not be spending his savings on an office or factory or a lorryload of some industrial material for his personal gratification or because he likes having his money spent in this way. He does it because he expects ultimately to get it back and he hopes that he will get back much more than he put in. The bank likewise will have made it clear that it wishes to receive its money back with interest and will probably have agreed a repayment schedule with Smith. Suppliers of goods and services will all have to be paid in cash before too long. As Smith's business is just setting up and is an unknown quantity, they will be unlikely to be exceptionally patient.

How is Smith to satisfy all these parties, each of them wanting cash? Obviously he sets his workers to the task of turning the raw material he has purchased into something he can sell to potential customers. As the new finished gadgets come off the assembly line, he will either sell them directly to the public or perhaps pass them in bulk to wholesalers. It may be that he can sell for immediate cash settlement but in most markets he will have to sell on credit, that is, he will have to deliver the goods to a retailer who will not pay for them until some agreed period of time has elapsed. Smith, or more precisely Smith's business, will have to wait for the cash. Naturally, the creditors will have to wait too!

As the debtors, those who have bought the output of Smith's business (let us assume it is a limited liability company and call it Smith Ltd), eventually pay, cash becomes available for the purchase of more raw material, to pay the bank interest and to meet the running costs of the office and the factory. The first cycle is now complete, and provided Smith Ltd has sold the articles at a sufficiently high price and has been paid there will be enough cash to keep the business going.

Defining 'sufficiently high' in this context is not easy but, broadly, the cash recovered must be well in excess of that invested initially in the raw material and in the manufacturing and selling process, so that there is a margin to pay the incidental costs of running the cycle—overheads, interest, tax, etc.—and also bring Smith Ltd a profit. Notice though that, in the short term, this cycle will not fail for want of a profit. All that matters is that cash should be available to purchase more raw material and honour the workforce's pay cheques.

As the business grows there will be many such cycles going on simultaneously so that, at any one time, some articles are in the course of production, some will be finished and awaiting sale and some will have been sold with payment expected at some future date.

To talk of a number of separate cycles proceeding simultaneously implies that inventory is purchased and turned into the finished product in discrete amounts and that for each cash outflow at the beginning of the cycle there is a corresponding cash payment to the company at the end of the same cycle. Such an implication is misleading since inventory, like cash, is usually a fungible asset. Individual amounts of any of these lose their separate identity when added to a common pool. Just think of a bank account into which £1000 salary is paid every month and in which the balance is £20 000. If the owner writes out a cheque for £50 worth of groceries, is it possible to say from which month's salary the £50 spent actually came? Industrial inventory tends to behave in the same way.

This type of cycle, which we may call the 'asset conversion' cycle, goes on in some form in virtually all businesses. We have used as our basic example a manufacturing company because in such a company all the stages can be clearly seen. A company which trades as a retailer, selling for cash only, obviously will not have debtors to finance. So, all other things being equal, its cycle will be quicker. To put it another way, outflows of cash for the purchase of inventory are recovered more rapidly since the customer pays 'up front' and does not expect trade credit. But the cycle is essentially the same. At the extreme end of the spectrum a business may have no inventory—most service companies fall into this category—paying out cash only for expenses, salaries and overheads, and receiving in cash as its clients are billed and settle their accounts. All businesses survive ultimately by making cash payments in the expectation that eventually larger amounts of cash will flow back to the company.

The concept of a cash-based, asset conversion cycle is described in many elementary books on finance and business but only rarely do these go on to use it to develop effective tools of analysis. The cycle is fundamental to any and every business, and success or failure depend very largely upon the efficiency of the company's management in completing the cycle. If the cycle stops, cash will cease to flow into the bank account. In these unhappy circumstances, the whole business's days are numbered.

It is sometimes claimed that there is also a longer cash cycle involving fixed assets, as though by the process of amortization or depreciation these can be turned back into cash. The popular misconception that depreciation is a source of cash encourages this view. In reality, this is not how fixed assets behave at all. A company purchases a fixed asset, uses it until it is exhausted and then scraps it. No direct cash generation occurs, the only cash flow associated directly with that asset being the outflow which arose when it was purchased. Companies do, naturally, sell fixed assets from time to time, sometimes at a profit, but that is hardly why most companies purchase them in the first place. The true purpose of fixed assets is to facilitate and create the conditions for the asset conversion cycle to take place. The purchase of a factory is simply an expense necessary if the company is to have a manufacturing process.

It is preferable to keep the focus on the asset conversion cycle. A business has constant cash outflows, not only to keep the cycle going directly but to meet taxes, executive salaries, capital expenditure and so on. The primary source of this cash, in an established business, is the asset conversion cycle, the trading operations of the company. There are other sources—loans from the bank, more equity from the shareholders and the sale of fixed assets—but none of these is inexhaustible and if the asset conversion cycle stops permanently or ceases to be adequate over a period of time the company will go out of business very quickly. Quite simply, the bank will not lend, and the equity holders will put in no further money, if they lack confidence in the asset conversion cycle to keep the cash coming in in sufficient quantity to ensure that the obligations of the business are settled in a timely way. Asset sales may prolong the company's life, but there will be a limit to what can be sold without hindering the cycle further and so compounding the problem. If a business is to survive and prosper, the management have to keep the cycle turning and generating adequate amounts of cash. All else is peripheral.

A couple of examples from the airline industry may serve to illustrate the point. In the late 1970s and early 1980s the US airline industry was brought to its knees by a combination of deregulation, a government decision to allow a 'free for all' on routes and prices, excessive competition leading to discounted fares and a depressed economy limiting the size of the market served. Airlines, by their nature, have heavy fixed costs. They have to pay, in the short term, for their aeroplanes, for fuel and for salaries whether or not the planes are full of fare-paying passengers. The difficult economic circumstances, in our terms, made it very difficult for management to complete the conversion cycle effectively and cash was often flowing out faster than it was flowing in.

A company in this dilemma, if it cannot make its cycle more effective, as was the airlines' basic problem, has the range of choices already mentioned. It could raise debt, seek new equity or sell assets. In the absence of profitability the first two are difficult, though the airlines exploited them to the full. The other possibility depended upon having assets to sell. Pan Am, one airline badly affected, survived the period by selling its crown jewels, Intercontinental Hotels and the Pan Am building in New York, as well as its Pacific routes to United Airlines. These sales brought in enough cash to keep the airline going until the asset conversion cycle could work more productively. Braniff International by contrast, had nothing to sell but its aeroplanes and there was little market for these while the industry was depressed. In any case, selling aeroplanes directly reduces the ability of an airline to complete its cycle since it prevents the airline carrying its passengers. Braniff International, as everyone knows, was reorganised, whereas Pan Am was not.

The asset conversion cycle concept gives an analyst a framework within which to examine a business's past performance and to predict the future. It also gives the analyst a way of assessing risk. Business risk means really the danger that a company may not be able to complete effectively and adequately its asset conversion cycle. Nothing more.

Examination of the accounts of Pan Am and Braniff International in the later 1970s would not have shown that while Pan Am would be a survivor in difficult times, Braniff was destined to fail. There would certainly have been clues, but traditional methods of ratio analysis would probably have missed the crucial points.

It was not the shape of the balance sheet that mattered. It was not a question of adequate working capital or of profitability, and we have seen that asset values in published accounts often, if not usually, bear little resemblance to market values. To spot the difference one needed to be aware that cash was flowing out of these companies, one had to make some assumptions about management behaviour—Pan Am can hardly have disposed of their choice assets without much soul searching—and one had to know exactly what the companies had to sell and what the assets were worth. By approaching the problem logically, starting from the asset conversion cycle, one would at least have been asking the right questions. Merely calculating ratios would have confirmed only what was obvious, that both companies were taking a battering.

A recent case in California provides a good illustration of the importance of the asset conversion cycle.

Gavilan Computer Corp was a company got together in Silicon Valley in 1982 with the aims of manufacturing and selling portable personal computers, sophisticated machines bigger than a pocket calculator but small enough to fit into a briefcase. Priced at around $4000, this was a revolutionary product with obvious and immense appeal to a wide audience, and the four computer executives who conceived the plan were under no delusions about its potential. Venture capital to the tune of $30m was soon forthcoming and by the end of 1983 the backlog of orders stood at $85m. It was a stunning machine.

The only problem was making it. It was one thing to produce a prototype, quite another to run an assembly line turning out computers by the thousand which actually worked and were free from 'glitches'. It soon became apparent that the original specification would need amending and amid various technical difficulties production slowed and deliveries ground virtually to a standstill.

While production efforts continued, nothing deterred other members of the team from pursuing the advertising or selling side of the business and the company was soon employing 300 staff. The president, attentive to the most important thing in such circumstances, busied himself (very successfully) in raising money, about $31 million in all. Orders flooded in.

It was, of course, a race against time. Gavilan Computer had to start deliveries or the market would lose patience, which in the end it did when only about 2500 machines had reached their end users. Cancellations took the place of orders and when money started to run out, lay-offs inevitably followed.

The company did eventually succeed in turning out a fault-free machine, but too late; other larger concerns had moved into the fiercely competitive market and the name Gavilan Computer no longer had the same burnish to it. Enormous debts and too small a market share finally drove the company into bankruptcy in October 1984.

What is the best way to analyse the failure of this ill-starred venture? It is easy to identify specific elements in the picture, to see it in terms of costs and revenues, economic and market forces, and so forth. All these are legitimate approaches. But observe the simplicity of the explanation in terms of the asset conversion cycle.

Gavilan Computer's asset conversion cycle had several stages. There were no supply problems in California and the materials were readily available. Similarly, there was no difficulty at the latter end of the cycle in either selling, the original concept being a runaway success with the public, or apparently in obtaining payment. The crucial weakness lay in the manufacturing process. The company took the risk that the raw components could be converted into a finished computer in a timely and efficient fashion but it proved more difficult than expected and all the while the asset conversion cycle was consuming cash.

Wages had to be paid, inventory was being purchased, and advertising and marketing expenditure was being incurred to sustain the selling part of the cycle. Management were pouring money into an asset conversion cycle which was generating virtually no cash at all.

It is not a criticism of the president that he spent much of his time raising money, an activity in which he clearly excelled. Provided cash was coming in from somewhere, the show carried on. Once the cash inflow ceased, it became impossible for management to put more cash into the cycle.

Eventually the hiatus in the cycle was bridged and regular production commenced. But by this time it was no longer possible really to keep the rest of the cycle together. Purchases of raw materials and the hiring and retaining of good quality staff became much more difficult owing to the tortured finances of the company, and selling turned hard because the company had acquired such a poor record on deliveries. Saddled as the company was with all the start-up costs, the asset conversion cycle never stood a chance of generating sufficient cash to satisfy the creditors.

The concept of profit and loss is of little help in understanding the situation, as a proper allocation of revenue and expense is virtually impossible here. Did all the start-up costs count as expenses in the initial year, or should they be spread over successive periods, that is, capitalized and then amortized?

Does it matter? In so far as Gavilan Computer was selling its product it was undoubtedly making a profit because the selling price exceeded what might reasonably be considered the net cost of production. Profit and loss analysis, though, reveal nothing about risk and it was the risk that was the company's undoing.

Let us return to our basic manufacturing example to look at business risk in more detail. Smith Ltd's cycle has several stages which are quite distinct. At each separate stage there are risks that can threaten the completion of the cycle. Like a bicycle chain, the cycle has only to stop at one point for the whole process to grind to a halt.

The first stage is the purchase on credit of the inventory. What can go wrong here? Having the cash or the credit to buy may not be sufficient. The company needs to be sure that it is possible to buy the right materials, in the right quantities, at the right price, at the right time. Depending upon the nature of the business, management may well find that obtaining the inventory that it wants is a major concern. An iron and steel manufacturer needs a secure supply of iron ore. If the company's managers assume that they can always obtain the ore merely by picking up the telephone they are taking on risk.

Ore may become unavailable because a principal supplier, say the local mine, has gone out of business. This may or may not be critical depending upon the availability of alternative suppliers or a substitute raw material. Alternatively, ore may become for some reason prohibitively expensive, being an internationally traded commodity whose price rises and falls with total market demand and supply conditions. Such a price rise might not actually cause the asset conversion cycle to stop, but it could certainly reduce its cash-generating potential.

There is a very wide range of possibilities even in this one example. The supply risks will naturally vary enormously in different types of operation and according to market circumstances. An analyst looking at a company should be attempting to quantify these risks and to assess the capacity of the company to manage if the worst happens. In the UK we are painfully familiar with the car assembly plant that lurches to a complete halt because some small local company—the only source of, say, windscreen-washers or brake linings—suffers a strike or goes into liquidation. Companies which rely on a large number of highly specialist suppliers, where the raw materials are non-commodity items and perhaps come from overseas, are especially vulnerable. By contrast, those that use raw commodities available in abundance locally are least at risk. It is not only for 'patriotic' reasons that the US Defense Department relies almost entirely on major US companies to supply its equipment and material. The Pentagon needs to be sure of supplies and does not wish to be dependent upon a flow of spare parts coming from another country over which it has no control.

In assessing the risk the analyst will note the strategies that the company has adopted to minimize that risk. Most paper manufacturers do not rely on an abundance of cheap wood being available whenever they require it; they grow their own forests instead, by a strategy known as 'backward integration'. Where this is not possible, it pays often to have a variety of sources so that, if one disappears, the company can continue its operations by making up the shortfall from elsewhere. It is worth noting that the US economy is much more self-contained than most others and is certainly better placed to withstand any breakdown in international trade or the movement of freight. British companies are extraordinarily vulnerable to possible impediments to trade, since they rely heavily on imported raw materials. A serious disruption in shipping, dock labour or haulage brings much of British industry to a halt within a few weeks. Unless we look at individual companies in the context of such risks, we may very well find that our money is in more danger than we imagined!

The second division of business risk lies in the production process. A company needs to convert its raw materials into a finished, saleable product and failure to achieve that, again will bring the asset conversion cycle to a halt. It is obvious, in one sense, that no company can stay in business if it cannot turn out its product, and of itself this observation does not get us very far. But as with the supply risk, by focusing upon what a company has to do in order to survive, it becomes relatively easy to identify possible threats or risks which need to be negotiated.

In the context of large international companies, the primary element of production risk lies with the workforce. A strike is a deadly weapon in the hands of the production workers since it brings the asset conversion cycle to a complete stop almost immediately and if prolonged will very likely destroy the company altogether. It is all the more terrible since it is extremely difficult in most situations for employers to manage or avoid this risk, particularly where the workers are unionized. If a strike occurs, it may be possible to transfer the work to other factories or even abroad, but the ill will such action provokes usually defeats the objective.

An example might be the workings of the Fleet Street printing industry. Not even the friendliest commentator could deny that this industry has until just recently been characterized by strong unions determined to maintain high levels of 'feather-bedded' employment, and weak management generally unable to introduce modern technology, one effect of which would be to reduce drastically the amount of hired printing labour needed.

The point to be made is that newspaper printing, in these

circumstances, has a high level of production risk because of the labour situation. A sudden strike in the printroom can lead within hours to the loss of an issue and, given the appalling state of industrial relations in the industry, frequent and prolonged disputes have become commonplace. There is little that management can do to minimize the risk or bring out the paper without the assistance of the printers. Attempts by *The Times* to print copies in West Germany during the 10-month stoppage in 1981 foundered on an inter-union 'blacking' agreement and the traditional hostility of all trade unions to 'strike breaking'. Certain newspaper barons are currently trying to break this union power by establishing modern presses outside of London which will not require traditional printing skills. It remains to be seen how successful the ploy will be. But in terms of production risk, the management of these enterprises is merely trying to reduce the exposure of their companies to one very serious threat to the asset conversion cycle.

Strikes occur in the docks and mines, in the steel and power industries, on the railways and, nowadays, in schools and hospitals. We virtually never suffer strikes, however, in the textile industry, in high tech manufacturing, in tourism, in banking or in other areas where the units of production are smaller, the style of management is more democratic and consultative, and there is little prospect of the employer receiving government assistance. Large-scale, particularly nationalized, industries are the usual victims of strikes.

There is little point in a strike which drives an employer out of business. The trouble is that those on strike are rarely the best judges of what the company can actually withstand and the layoffs, closures and corporate bankruptcies may follow after a period of months. Effects may be felt in other industries even more severely than in that primarily under assault. The European car manufacturers and the British Coal Board withstood the 1983 metal workers' strike in

West Germany and the 1984 coal strike in the UK: many small organizations did not. Strikes are unpredictable in their occurrence, even more so in their wider effects.

Certainly, the European bankers who lent to International Harvester, the American farm equipment manufacturer, something over US$1 billion in 1981, even while that company was virtually paralysed by a strike lasting several months, miscalculated completely the severity of the strike's consequences. The opportunity to lend to a prime US manufacturer which many foreign banks had been courting for years was irresistible, and vast sums were quickly forthcoming, just as they had been a year or two earlier when the big consortium loans to Latin American countries were assembled. Many bankers, fearing the opportunity would not arise again if they declined once, abandoned their traditional caution and fought for as big a share of the deal as they could get. 'Name lending', as it is known, has been the downfall of a goodly number of banks lately, and is always conspicuous where the credit control function is weak and the bank is dominated by hare-brained marketeers. International Harvester, it will be recalled, declared itself unable to meet its financial obligations shortly afterwards and only survived by the enforced forbearance of its bankers, who kept it going until Tenneco offered to buy a substantial part of its assets. There is no substitute for a rigorous evaluation of the risks!

Strikes are not the only element of production risk. The loss of key staff may be nearly as debilitating. This tends to occur more frequently in service and financial industries where an institution's expertise in some specialist area of, say, banking or commodity trading may be wiped out if a rival institution poaches the company's key staff. It is not unknown for whole teams of experts to leave en bloc to join a rival company, enticed away by the promise, usually, of more money and greater independence in the exercise of their skills. Again, there is little a company can do to protect itself from such poaching; the British courts are notoriously unsympathetic to 'golden handcuff' arrangements which might look like unfair shackles on the free movement of labour, and in few other non-communist countries do the employment laws encourage corporate employers to enforce their rights against existing employees, let alone against those who have left.

There is also the question of the vital resources needed for production processes, not least the availability of energy. The dependence of much modern industry on oil is well known and the British miners' strike in 1984 showed vividly that without coal it becomes hard for many unrelated operations to keep going. Heavy industries like aluminium smelting are only feasible where abundant power sources are at hand. Such is the state of competition in that industry that access to cheap hydroelectric power, as for example in Canada, is almost essential for success, and those enterprises which rely on other fuels are almost all, to some extent, in trouble. No one would now build an aluminium plant unless adequate supplies of electricity, at a moderate price, could be secured and a suitable long-term power supply contract negotiated with the authorities. A termination in supply will be fatal to the enterprise and, in the competitive milieu of today, a rise in price may slowly strangle the company. In our terms, the asset conversion cycle will cease to generate sufficient cash to keep the business afloat.

The Japanese, recognizing with characteristic acumen their total dependence on imported fuel, made a strategic decision in the mid-1970s to quit the industry altogether. Foreign competitors, less perspicacious, were left to stagnate in an industry with overwhelming macroeconomic problems.

After finishing the product it has to be sold. Herein lie a multitude of economic risks comprising what we may call 'selling risk'. It is frequently a struggle for a company to retain its market share and there is a constant danger that a product may become obsolete or that a competitor may create a rival product, perhaps better or cheaper, to entice away established customers. Companies which rely upon one or two products or a small customer base are especially susceptible to a break in the cycle at this point.

The risks of selling and marketing and the strategies employed by managers to overcome and steer around these risks are the subject of several excellent books and cannot be described adequately here. But, from the point of view of the analyst trying to evaluate the risks a company faces in successfully completing the cycle, this is an area which ought to claim detailed attention.

Selling risk is insidious and often difficult to spot because the effects of failure tend to emerge only over time. Whereas a breakdown in production causes an immediate crisis, the loss of market share in a large company happens more gradually. Annual Reports give little detail about specific products and markets, perhaps because multinationals often have thousands of different products which cannot all be explained to readers, and the definition and size of a 'market' is necessarily imprecise. Unless the reader is familiar with the different industries in which the company operates, it will be hard for him to evaluate the company's management of selling risk and the possibility that market share may be lost in the near future.

In the motor car manufacturing industry, success depends upon having a good range of vehicles available at all times and on developing a series of new models to appeal to public taste and expectations. Buying a new car is a major decision for most people and we are not easily fobbed off with one that does not match up to expectations. It seems impossible to predict which new models will catch the public imagination—who would have foretold the spectacular success of the Mini, a cramped little car of no great beauty or performance—and a new model represents a risk of significant magnitude of investment for a car manufacturer who must spend hundreds of millions of pounds on development and tooling before the first car rolls off the production line. If it acquires a reputation for poor performance or mechanical failure or if, for purely irrational reasons, the wind of fashion is blowing against it, selling will be uphill work. A succession of such failures will threaten any automaker's survival since the world market is heavily oversupplied, there is cut-throat competition for sales, profit margins are low and the costs of manufacture are largely fixed costs.

The Mini, as it turned out, never really produced any money for Austin Morris because it was always priced too competitively. Too low a price raises steeply the number of units which must be sold merely to cover the fixed costs, and in the case of the Mini this was something like 90 per cent of production capacity.

Ford's Edsel, first manufactured in 1957, was, by contrast, a failure. For an investment of US$300 million, the equivalent of several billion of today's dollars, Ford produced a veritable tank of a car which not only looked ugly and unglamorous to most prospective buyers but rapidly acquired a reputation for mechanical failure. Indeed it became something of a living legend and a severe embarrassment to its manufacturer. Edsel seems in retrospect an unfortunate choice of name although six thousand alternatives were eliminated before the company decided that Edsel, the original name given to the prototype, was the best they could come up with. Cars are things of fashion; it is hard to imagine that it makes any difference to anyone whether a new model made in Britain to a French design should be called a Talbot or a Peugeot, but evidently there are thousands of people, so it is claimed, who would buy it with the French name but not if it carried the English marker. On such trivia may hang success or failure.

It is pointless to look at the accounts of a car manufacturer without taking into account the selling risk. The past is a poor guide to the future in this area and in several industry sectors the pace of change is so rapid that failure can strike without much warning. Those who maintained that there would always be a market for a well-made buggy whip had at least a while to assess the challenge of the motor car, but those who until the 1960s were making mechanical cash registers had little opportunity to escape a sudden and cruel ruination.

In the UK such companies were an offshoot of our established engineering and metals industry. Cash registers were made in old-fashioned factories by labour-intensive methods with a predominantly unskilled workforce. The invention of the microchip, and the consequent flood of digital watches, calculators and electronic machines onto the market rendered the mechanical cash register obsolete almost overnight. Faced with the need to adopt new technology from a totally different industry, to learn new skills and to modernize their manufacturing methods to compete directly with the low-cost operators of the Far East, the makers of mechanical cash registers stood no chance. They tried vainly to produce a superior version of the old cumbersome machine, but they did not have the resources or the heart to adapt to the new conditions, and proud, once thriving companies were soon driven to the wall.

Nothing, of course, in their published accounts would have given this away in advance, indeed the management would have done anything rather than admit to shareholders that the position was hopeless. To keep going at all, they needed to maintain confidence by putting on a brave face and there was nothing to be gained by spreading despondency with forecasts of sales falling away to hopelessly unprofitable levels. And so, more with a whimper than a bang, the industry withered away.

Twenty years ago in the USA there were few better places to take a family for a meal than Howard Johnson's. The company was easily the market leader in low-priced restaurants and its establishments were renowned for cleanliness, high-quality service, good value for money and a wide if not exactly adventurous menu selection. With the expansion of the highways in the 1950s and 1960s, the orange roofs of Howard Johnson proliferated and flourished.

By the early 1980s the American public had changed its mind about Howard Johnson and the company was widely perceived as having let things slip. By the early 1980s, however, rivals like Marriot and McDonald's had seized the market leadership by aggressive investment and skilful customer targeting. While Howard Johnson was trying to improve dwindling profits through cost cutting, its customers quietly defected to the opposition.

Not everyone likes McDonald's brash style, but no one can be unimpressed by it as a business. Even in countries where there is little affection for things American, people queue to buy McDonald's hamburgers because, apart from the convenience, they like the friendliness of the staff, the hygenic surroundings, and the quality and predictability of the food—exactly the qualities that once distinguished Howard Johnson alone! But McDonald's is cheaper and, above all, that company knows what business it is in. Likewise, Marriot is a strong challenger for the more sophisticated market. Howard Johnson it seems, serve a cross-section of the community, from the family with small children to the expense account executive. The formula is less successful when each customer sector is under assault from powerful specialized competitors who can compete also on price.

The selling risks facing Howard Johnson may not have been perceived by Imperial Group, the British conglomerate, in 1979 when they bought the company for $630m. Six years later they sold it again for $300m. In fairness to Howard Johnson, it should be added that the company, now under new management, is finally fighting back hard with an aggressive advertising campaign showing the company's revamped hotels and restaurants and parading the slogan 'This is Howard Johnson!'

Selling risk is absolutely crucial to any analysis and the analyst should always address the question. Can the company sell its products successfully in the future? Are some products obsolescent? Is there a threat from a competitor? Is the pricing and marketing strategy correct? Is sufficient being spent on advertising or on research and development? In short, what are the components of selling risk in the company and how well can the management handle them? These are hard questions which call for intimate knowledge of the company's industry and place in the economy and on which precise information can be hard to obtain.

US companies produce a filing known as a Form 10-K which often gives some valuable hints. For other companies one has to rely on published studies and especially on the newspapers. Nowadays, economic developments around the world are exhaustively analysed by experts and their views can be had for the price of a subscription to a financial newspaper. Much of this information is available on databases or in standard reference books. Rating agencies also publish industry and company data although the price of the subscription tends to be prohibitive except to large institutions. There are no easy answers to corporate analysis. It is a process of digging to establish the true position. Vast amounts of material are available, of varying qualities. The problem lies in sifting and evaluating it.

Finally, it is not sufficient just to sell the product. The company has to be paid for the cycle to be complete. Debtors are an asset on a balance sheet but their only value lies in the cash that those debtors eventually pay. All businesses, except those selling only for cash, extend credit from time to time to customers who default. It is a fact of business life that companies sometimes collapse and the best credit procedures will not weed them all out. For small companies, often reliant upon one or two major customers, this credit or collection risk can destroy the asset conversion cycle.

It is common for the failure of a large company to involve the demise of other smaller ones, especially since in addition to any credit loss it may be hard for the smaller companies to find alternative customers. Large companies usually have a diversity of customers and expect to lose only a small proportion of their sales through bad debts, seldom much more than 1 per cent. It is, though, a point to watch where there is heavy reliance on a few, possibly weak, customers.

Collection risk is far more serious for those companies whose principal business is the creation of financial assets—banks, that is, which have debtors arising from the direct lending of money. Why should banks, who are supposed to be experts on credit, be more at risk to bad debts than, say, food distributors? Do they not after all do business with some of the same organizations?

The short answer might be that food distributors tend to fight shy of lending to Latin American countries on a long-term basis and it is certainly a factor that many a bank has some appallingly irresponsible credit decisions to live down. To be fair, though, the natures of the two types of business are totally different. Food distributors are usually well capitalized, being in large measure funded by the owners rather than by the lenders. They have comfortable margins which can absorb some losses and their exposure to customers is short term, rarely more than two or three months. By contrast, banks are normally lending their depositors' money. They have to do this because the margins they get on lending are very fine and for the shareholders to make a profit a generous element of leverage or debt finance is unavoidable. Loans made by banks are often large in proportion to their equity and are longer term. Banks simply cannot afford to lose multimillion dollar loans because they simply do not have the equity base to withstand those losses. Food distributors can absorb normal trade losses or bad debts as a cost of doing business.

One might suppose that the historical debt loss experience of a company would be a vital piece of information in the assessment of collection risk. Were it possible to ascertain the correct number for the amount of debts written off, it undoubtedly would be, but the double entry system treats these losses in a complicated way and few modern presentation formats give any prominence or recognition to the actual level of write-offs.

Before we go on, a little needs to be said about debits and credits. Although pregnant with moral overtones in everyday parlance, these words are quite unambiguous in accountancy. A debit is just an entry on the left, and a credit an entry on the right. That is all. Their etymology from Latin verbs meaning respectively 'to owe' and 'to believe', much quoted in the textbooks, does not render the system easier to understand and is best forgotten about.

To avoid complication, we shall work our examples by employing T accounts, whereby the T supports the name of the account and the debits are entered on the left and the credits on the right. Closing balances will be indicated beneath a second horizontal line thus:

	Name of Account		
Debits	4	2	Opening balance
	5	6	Credits
	8	4	
		3	
Closing balance	2		

We do not follow the convention of showing the balancing items also above the line, on the opposite side as a carry forward. That practice is highly confusing except to accomplished bookkeepers, and greater clarity is to be achieved by ignoring it. In analysing company accounts what matters is to grasp the dynamics of double entry, not the observance of the detailed day to day rules of bookkeeping.

All that one needs to know to comprehend the essential

workings of the double entry system through the T accounts method can be briefly stated. A balance sheet is a list of the closing balances on the T accounts. Because it is inadmissible to pass other than matching totals of debits and credits, the sum of the debits must equal the sum of the credits and for that reason a balance sheet always balances. An income statement is a partial summary of the entries over the 'profit and loss' account and would be a complete statement of the entries passed over the equity account were it not that changes in equity not directly associated with trading tend to be omitted. A cash flow statement is a full summary of all the entries over the cash account. There is no limit to the number of T accounts that may be employed in an analysis.

To return to the question of credit losses, imagine that a company reported on its balance sheet trade receivables or debtors of £200 (this year) and £300 (last year) net of 'provision for doubtful accounts' or some such phrase of £25 and £30 respectively.

Neither the amount of the income statement charges, nor the actual written-off amount, is given. This scenario corresponds roughly to what is normally available in an Annual Report.

On our T accounts, we can represent these numbers thus:

	Receivables			Provision	
Opening balance	225			25	Opening balance
Closing balance	330			30	Closing balance

Debts are written off not by direct debit to the income statement but by debit to the provision account, and at the end of the year a double entry is passed, Dr. Income Statement Cr. Provision, to 'top up' the provision account to what is deemed an adequate balance to accommodate likely losses on the outstanding receivables. If any bad debt number is given, it will be this topping-up entry which is a direct charge to income.

Suppose that the income statement provision was £15. From our T accounts we might jump to the conclusion that bad debts written off were in fact £25 + £15 − £30 = £10. Thus,

	Receivables			Provision	
Opening balance	225			25	Opening balance
	330	215	10	15	
		10			
Closing balance	330			30	Closing balance

Cash		Income statement	
215		15	330

This will be true only in the most straightforward case. The provision account will in practice be affected not only by the two entries given above, but by other entries made during the year to cover the writing back of specific provisions no longer needed, the recovery of debts previously written off, foreign currency adjustments, adjustments due to consolidation or deconsolidation of subsidiaries and so on.

The most interesting number here is undoubtedly the cash receipt figure of £215. This compared with the £225 of receivables at the beginning of the year tells us exactly what we want to know about the asset conversion cycle and collection risk. Unfortunately, this number is never published and is often virtually impossible to calculate. The £15 charge on the income statement is essentially a compound number affected, even in this simple example, by the actual level of bad debts, any growth in the overall receivables total and any change in the level of provision perceived by the company to be necessary and appropriate.

As if this were not bad enough, there are the usual pressures on a company to 'tinker' with the number; a larger provision reduces profits and (generally) taxes and a smaller debit has the opposite effect. On the one hand, no company wants to provide more than is absolutely necessary, so as to maintain profits; on the other there is a natural desire to be conservative and make excess provision to avoid taxes. Tax authorities around the world are well aware of the problems and many lay down rules to prevent abuses.

The upshot of all this is that analysis of a company's bad debt experience is, in complicated cases, hard to perform with any confidence.

Assessing the risk of bad debts is almost impossible. Even where we can unravel the historical numbers, this analysis will not, of course, tell us much about the future, although large variations will be cause for comment. American banks and financial institutions have good disclosure practices in this area, provided one can understand the disclosure. Multinational companies usually control their receivables well. They do not allow their customers to take excessive credit and their receivables are often protected by credit insurance, particularly in relation to exports, or by retention of title arrangements, a legal device which allows the seller to retain ownership of the goods until he has paid for them, notwithstanding the collapse of the customer. Service companies and most particularly financial companies are rather more exposed to the dangers inherent in collection risk. The greatest danger lies where a company has one major customer who takes extensive credit.

In thinking about risk there is a useful distinction to be drawn between *transactional business risk* and *strategic business risk*. The former embraces the specific risks which, in the short term, threaten to interrupt the asset conversion cycle. It is a useful exercise to list them and consider how well the company is placed to handle them if they actually arise. One might well conclude that a given company is in severe danger of a major stoppage. On the other hand, it may be that the company's managers have perceived the threat and are well positioned to negotiate the obstacle.

Strategic business risk refers to the longer-term problems that a company faces, broadly speaking, in adapting its products to a changing economic and competitive climate. As already observed, almost all companies need to maintain or increase their market share, an objective which calls for ingenuity and strategic planning. The appropriate strategy will depend upon the nature of the market, the entry and exit barriers, the number and strengths of the competitors, the methods of manufacture and selling and a host of similar factors.

IBM, the world's leading computer company, does not need to lead the field in innovation or to be the cheapest supplier. Customers are prepared to wait and to pay more in the knowledge that they are unlikely to be disappointed in the product or the quality of service. IBM's strength and reputation, the size of its market share and its financial strength, allow it to avoid the riskier areas of activity in the computer industry.

A small software company has to play the game very differently. To succeed it must have a constant stream of new products, it needs dynamic salesmen and it needs to be competitive in price. Software companies are legion and the entry barriers are low—all it takes is a couple of boffins and a few thousand pounds. It will be hard to retain any customer loyalty and at least initially such a company will be running fast just to survive. The business risks in this latter case lie, transactionally, in recruiting and retaining the best software writers, in the struggle to obtain reasonable contracts, and in the possibility that even a single example of faulty work will damage the company's reputation irreparably. Finally, in that the company's customers will be predominantly at the smaller and financially weaker end of the scale there is also a credit or collection risk. Not getting paid on a big contract could wipe out the whole show.

Strategically, the question is whether a small software company has a future at all. It may be that this is the type of market where only large players can survive, or that specialist software houses are a passing phenomenon. An unrealistic scenario, perhaps, but whole industries can disappear in a quite short period if the markets turn unfavourable; witness the demise earlier this century of the once mighty British cotton-spinning industry.

The study of Annual Reports is not overly helpful in the assessment of business risk. Annual Reports are, in the financial sense, always backward looking and while most are sanguine about future prospects, detailed projections are virtually never published by the companies themselves. New products are described with relish, but 'risk' is a word normally conspicious by its absence. The financial data, in fact, can create a totally false sense of security. Profitable operations and a healthy asset and capital base tell us only that the company has prospered in the past. There is the implication that progress will continue, but that presupposes that management can cope as effectively with the new challenges arising as they have with those already encountered.

The examination of the past is logically the wrong place

to start. If we want to know how the company will do in the future, we should be asking what it is the company must do and do well in the future. Then we should consider what obstacles it has to surmount and what resources are available to it in the endeavour. Of these, the two most important are probably the quality, experience and adaptability of the management and the skills and dedication of the workforce, neither by any means to be taken for granted. The financial resources are obviously important too, but not even the strongest can survive if their businesses become fundamentally and economically unviable. At best, a strong financial position is only a cushion to soften the blow if markets turn unfriendly and the asset conversion cycle slows or stops. A healthy balance sheet may buy time to manoeuvre but no more.

We should not overstate the case. It is possible to predict the future in practice only by reference to the past and historical statements have to be the starting point. The danger lies in the crude assumption that past trends can be extrapolated into the future; often the assumption is valid but we should not blind ourselves to other, perhaps less favourable, possibilities. Companies which are going to fail, particularly large ones, generally give certain muted signals beforehand. These signals are not infallible harbingers of doom, merely danger signs, indications of possible trouble in the making. An analyst must observe and monitor these signs as his aim is to sense the storm while it is still beyond the horizon. Equally, there are trends which point to a well-managed company, not of course a sure sign of future prosperity, but encouraging to the investor who may feel relatively comfortable that the management is of a quality to handle risk effectively.

If we assume naïvely that a successful company will continue uninterrupted in that success, we discount or ignore the question of risk. 'What are the business risks and how will they be negotiated?' is what we should be asking, not: 'Will profits now rise faster or slower than they have done over the last five years?' The concept of the asset conversion cycle is a peg on which to hang an evaluation of business risk and by concentrating on the separate stages of the cycle one can always identify a variety of risks, some perhaps serious, others relatively minor. Financial data really only help with an understanding of financial risks. The process by which a company makes money has economic, social and human dimensions that are at least as important as the financial aspects. We ignore these at our peril!

4

How to measure a cycle—
And why it matters

And the end of all our exploring
Will be to arrive where we started
And know the place for the first time.
T. S. Eliot, *Four Quartets,*
'Little Gidding', 240–242

Cyclicality is part of the order of the universe. When it appears to us that groups of people, cities, countries remain the same over a period of time, we are looking at an illusion. Although the sum of the parts may not alter too drastically on a superficial level, the individual components which make up the total are changing endlessly, unpredictably too, as each of them passes through the cycle of birth, marriage and death. London and New York are not the same places now as they were a year ago. You cannot step twice into the same river.

This is not an idea that many people find comfortable and we prefer on the whole a more upbeat view of society and of ourselves, one which emphasizes the elements of progress and achievement. The natural tendency for any institution to decline over time is seen primarily as a challenge to the members of that institution to press onwards to higher goals and levels of excellence. By constant innovation, determination, courage and hard work, so we believe, continued prosperity is within our grasp.

In their celebrated book *In Search of Excellence*, Peters and Waterman tried to identify US companies which exemplified just this notion. Find the truly excellent companies, those that have been successful over a long period, through all the vicissitudes of the changing corporate scene, those which have grown ever stronger and bigger while others were failing, and examine how they did it. Identify the common elements in their management style and behaviour, and categorize them into a blueprint for universal success. Then others can follow in the same path, the straight and narrow path which leads to excellence.

Anyone wanting to learn how to succeed in running a multinational company may, of course, learn a good deal by examining the history of other successful companies. General Motors and Procter & Gamble have done much that is right in conducting their affairs and something of the inherited wisdom and tradition that endures in such organizations must be of value to others. However, the underlying premise that an organization can continue to flourish indefinitely by practising the precepts of excellence laid down by such research is, in the long term, plainly wrong.

Since the publication of *In Search of Excellence* a number of the corporations held up as models have run into serious problems and would certainly not now appear quite so excellent as once they did. In November 1984, *Business Week* ran a cover story following up the 'excellent companies' and showing that several of them had not lived up to their prior excellence over the previous two years. Some 14 of Peters and Waterman's 43 excellent companies had to some degree tarnished their image. There was no common cause readily discernible. It might have been that the underlying research was not thorough enough and that the characteristics of excellent management were not identified with sufficient precision, but the truth of the matter is that *nothing succeeds for ever*.

Most of the modern multinational corporations started from modest origins many years ago. They are the survivors from countless other enterprises which failed, or were absorbed into other concerns or which never broke out of being small businesses. The reasons why some small businesses grow into multinationals, while others stay small or fail, are complex, but as a generalization we may say that growth was achieved by having the right products, in the right place, at the right time and at the right price, and further, that management were sufficiently astute to handle the change in form and dynamics that any small company experiences as it moves from the one-man entrepreneur structure characteristic of a new company, to the highly complex, layered society that is found in a corporate giant.

None of Peters and Waterman's 'excellent' companies will last for eternity, because no society comprised of human individuals ever does. Some companies and indeed some countries have achieved a solidity and momentum which makes it hard to believe that they will ever disappear. However, just as the Romans found that their empire declined and fell and the British that the sun did not shine on theirs for ever, so one day the great nations and economic formations of our own time will disappear to be replaced by others.

How does all this help us to analyse companies? First of all, analysts should be aware that past success is not a guarantee of future prosperity. Large companies do not fail very often but it does happen and it will continue to happen. Business does not take place in a vacuum and the milieu in which any company operates is subject to a degree of cyclicality. General economic activity and world trade show recurring cycles of growth and expansion followed by decline and depression that governments are virtually powerless to control, and in recessionary times and during the subsequent recovery, many companies are driven over the brink. The losses incurred by countless otherwise successful manufacturers in 1982 said much more about the prevailing climate than about the individual companies.

Coming down to the micro level, the same principle of cyclicality operates within a company as it trades. Annual Reports tend to portray companies as sources of profit with the strong implication that this profit stream will go on getting richer and faster every year. This implication is part of the propaganda of business. Profit is merely a crude measure of growth in a business and there is nothing inevitable about a business being profitable or growing. Indeed, the legal immortality conferred by incorporation should not blind us to the essential mortality of even the most successful companies. If an analyst assumes that a company will grow in the future as it has in the past he will, more often than not, be disappointed. The mistake can be avoided by asking about the nature of the company's activity in terms of cycles. What wealth or resources is the business consuming, what is it generating and how is it placed to cope with cyclical fluctuations in its economic environment?

We have observed that the heart of a business is its asset conversion cycle. In evaluating and assessing a business it is this cycle which should form the focus of the investigation and an analyst therefore needs a tool of analysis which addresses and measures this cycle and tests it for efficiency. One such tool is the concept of Net Trading Investment.

The asset conversion cycle is a cash-based cycle. It starts with cash being paid away and comes full circle when cash is received by the business. In the intervening stages the business is 'out of cash'. It has money 'tied up' in the assets on the balance sheet and since businesses have money tied up almost all the time in inventory and debtors, every business faces the task of financing those assets. In terms of double entry, the question would be: 'What are the corresponding credits?' The answer is that the cycle is to some extent self-financing because not all the cash outflows have to happen at the same time that the assets are purchased. It is usual for a company's suppliers to allow a measure of trade credit and as some expenses will be included in the value of inventory we may include with trade creditors the value of expenses accrued. By adding together the stated amounts of inventory and debtors and subtracting creditors and accrued expenses we arrive at a number which we may call Net Trading Investment, a number which indicates the amount of money tied up, at the balance sheet date, in the asset conversion cycle.

Net Trading Investment = debtors + inventory − creditors
− accrued expenses

Take the following balance sheet:

	£		£
Cash	5	Short-term borrowings	15
Debtors	30	Creditors	20
Inventory	45	Accrued expenses	5
Fixed assets	20	Long-term borrowings	35
		Equity	25
	100		100

Net Trading Investment = £30 + £45 − £20 − £5 = £50

We have made some scathing comments about accountants and analysts for the naïvety of certain of their assumptions, so we will point out straight away that there are some theoretical objections to be weighed. First, the figure for debtors includes an element of profit. It could be argued that, when inventory is sold and the cycle moves on a stage, as the amount credited to inventory will be smaller than that debited to debtors, the calculation gives the misleading impression that extra cash is tied up in the cycle. There is no cash flow associated with a credit sale and it is therefore questionable whether it is accurate to say that more cash is tied up in the cycle as a result of the transaction.

Secondly, we are assuming that inventory is valued at a reasonable current cost, probably FIFO. A company on LIFO often has its inventory heavily undervalued. Thirdly, the accrued expenses may include items which are not strictly part of the conversion cycle, possibly accrued executive salaries or taxes where these are not given separately. And fourthly, where we are looking at consolidated accounts, the assets and liabilities of a number of separate companies will have been combined. In reality these will have separate and perhaps quite different trading cycles. The significance of net trading investment may in these circumstances be diminished. Theoretically, all these arguments are valid and should be borne in mind.

Because of the nature of the material available, the analysis of large corporations cannot be an exact science. In any case, lenders and investors are not too interested in precise numbers; they are interested in reducing a highly complex picture to one of manageable dimensions and in perceiving and understanding the crucial underlying trends. With a little imagination it is comparatively easy to identify what should and should not be included in Net Trading Investment (or NTI as we shall call it from now on) even if the effort involves a certain degree of juggling, like, for example, adding into inventory the LIFO reserve, if that is appropriate. The point is to be consistent and to calculate the number in the same way for a period of years. In this instance, the historical cost convention helps the analysis since the values for the components of NTI are closely related to cash flows, which is primarily what we are interested in when we consider the asset conversion cycle.

Experience shows that in most manufacturing companies there is a close correlation between the levels of sales and NTI and one can reasonably express NTI as a percentage of sales. A figure of 20–30 per cent might be considered normal, and would indicate that for every pound of annual sales the company has tied up an amount of 20 to 30 pence in NTI. It follows that if the relationship between sales and NTI is to remain roughly constant, an increase in sales of any given amount or percentage should have a corresponding effect on NTI. A 10 per cent increase in annual sales will lead, all other things being equal, to a 10 per cent increase in NTI. An absolute increase in annual sales of £1000 will cause NTI to go up by between £200 and £300. Declining levels of sales will usually cause NTI to fall in exactly the same way.

A further way to look at what is happening lies in the concept of the net trading cycle. Suppose in our example that annual sales are running at £200. Dividing NTI by sales and multiplying the result by 365 days we arrive at the number of days in the net trading cycle; in this case $50/200 \times 365 = 91.25$ days. This number expresses NTI as a number of days' sales and tells the analyst that the company has an external financing need equal to 3 months' turnover. For the reasons given above, one should not use this type of calculation uncritically, but it is a useful device generally to express balance sheet accounts as a number of days' sales as this does give a comparatively good idea of the speed at which the different parts of the asset conversion cycle work.

The quotient of inventory divided by sales multiplied by 365 days tells us roughly how long a time elapses between the arrival of the inventory at the factory and its sale as a finished product. If this period is seen to be lengthening it suggests the process is becoming less efficient. There are several other possible explanations; it may be that inventory is piling up because of deliberate or inadvertent over-stocking. Alternatively, some of the inventory may not be really saleable owing to obsolescence, damage or some other cause. In theory, the auditors should not permit the over-valuation of inventory, but it normally takes a while for management to screw up the courage to write down part of the inventory from cost to a market value perhaps near zero, a process that can reduce profits dramatically. Burgeoning inventory is often the prelude to a spectacular write-off.

In consolidated accounts, a change in the 'business mix' of the underlying companies may have a similar effect. A company selling fresh fish tends to turn over its inventory every day. One selling grand pianos will expect its inventory to move once or twice a year. A conglomerate selling both will have a consolidated inventory which consists partly of fish, partly of grand pianos, and if the relative proportions of the two arms of the business change, the cycle will be seen to lengthen or shorten depending upon whether the company is expanding on the fresh fish side or the grand piano side!

Inventory write-offs should be viewed with great concern by an analyst since they suggest a profound structural inability on the part of the company to complete its asset conversion cycle. Whereas a debt written off may just be unfortunate, an inventory write-off may be an indication that the business is not actually viable. It is saying, in effect, that the cycle no longer works. If there are other product lines unaffected, the situation may not be irreparable, but the onus must be on the company to demonstrate its continued viability. When a company starts writing down its inventory, there is a real chance that it is no longer viable. Be ultra wary of small write-offs buried in the notes.

A similar calculation performed by dividing debtors by sales and multiplying by 365 days produces the figure for 'credit given', the number of days which the company allows its customers to settle for purchases. Again, there are factors cautioning us to view the result with circumspection, not least the practices of selling receivables, factoring and transferring trade receivables to captive finance companies. Discounting, selling for cash and the establishment of hire purchase facilities can all distort the number. Any one of these could explain a sudden change, or indeed a gradual improvement or deterioration, in the length of credit apparently given.

Discounting for a moment all these objections, we can add the days' debtors turnover to the days' inventory turnover to find the length of the gross asset cycle, the number of days between the arrival of the raw material at the factory and the receipt of payment. This number, in so far as it is accurate, reveals something about the efficiency of the company in manufacturing, selling and debt collecting, important areas each of them, and any substantial deviation from what might seem to be the norm will require investigation, in case some change has occurred in the fundamental workings of the business. Change in the nature and functioning of the cycle suggests additional risk, the whole focus of our analysis.

Expressing creditors and accruals in days' sales give a rough idea of the length of credit taken by the company, and substracting the number of days' credit taken from the length of the gross trading cycle gives us the net trading cycle. This number is a compound and represents not so much the length of time it takes for anything to happen, as the length of cycle requiring outside finance. Effectively, we are saying that the production, selling and collecting process takes so many days and that during that time the company is out of funds. However, cash is not paid out on the first day of the cycle since inventory and labour are bought on credit. External finance is needed to cover the period between the expiry of the trade finance and the completion of the whole asset conversion cycle. A longer gross cycle, less credit taken and, of course, a sales increase occasioning higher levels of NTI will all call for more finance and cash will be consumed by the cycle. A shorter gross cycle, more credit taken and a reduction of NTI will reduce the amount of finance needed, and cash will be liberated from the cycle.

We have seen that as sales increase in a company, the amount of cash tied up in the cycle tends to increase roughly proportionately. This increase in NTI has inevitably to be financed in some way and a growing company is very often short of cash as a consequence. This is a fact well known to bankers who handle the accounts of small businesses, although it is often a mystery to a small entrepreneur why, when his company is trading profitably and he expands, his overdraft gets bigger rather than smaller. It is quite simply because more cash is needed to finance and run the asset conversion cycle.

Two observations stand out from this discussion. First is that any increase in the absolute level of NTI amounts to a financing need for the company. The company may raise the cash in various ways, including profitable trading, but growth implies higher NTI and unless that growth is both profitable and at a modest rate some external finance will be required. Secondly, the relative levels of NTI and sales are a function of efficiency. If NTI rises and falls in line with sales (that is, the percentage is constant) it indicates a cycle of unchanging length. If NTI rises faster than sales then the cycle is getting longer and the company has to finance not only the growth but also the slack in the cycle. Conversely, if NTI rises more slowly there is a trade-off between the rate of growth and the more efficient cycle, growth tending to consume cash, efficiency in the cycle tending to release it.

It is a little-known phenomenon that declining companies with falling sales tend to generate cash mountains. This is particularly true when a profitable company is being wound down and the assets liquidated in an orderly manner. The same tendency can be seen in companies whose markets collapse relatively suddenly with profits turned into losses, although in these instances the losses and the restructuring costs tend to consume the cash within a year or two. From the point of view of risk, declining companies are rather less risky than growing ones for the investor or banker, as anyone who has dealt with small high-tech companies will appreciate. Growth usually requires more money tied up in the cycle, and indeed in other assets, and rapid growth often necessitates extensive borrowing. The more money tied up in NTI and in other assets, the greater the risk that cash will not be liberated, and the cost of a breakdown in the asset conversion cycle will be all the more painful.

NTI is not the same thing as working capital even though the two are often confused. When we refer to NTI we have in mind the net investment in assets required by a company to keep its asset conversion cycle turning. It should be thought of as on the debit or asset side of the balance sheet. Conversely, working capital belongs on the credit or liability side.

NTI is an expression of the need for liquidity. As NTI grows, more money needs to be found. Working capital is really a measure of the long-term funding, debt and equity, that a company has managed to raise to finance its investment in NTI.

The usual definition of working capital is 'current assets minus current liabilities'. This is a definition that suggests that assets are the core of the matter. In practice, the concept of working capital is often used in this way by lenders who are seeking a measure of liquidity in their corporate customers.

To view working capital as a quantitative means of liquidity is dangerous and begs vital questions. The assumption is that the current assets are liquid and will be turned into cash to pay the current liabilities, an unrealistic attitude in most types of business and certainly mistaken when there is any danger of the asset conversion cycle ceasing to revolve. The difference may seem academic but it is not. Receivables are not always collected in full. If inventory rises much more quickly than sales, there is a distinct probability that some of this inventory is unsaleable. In other words, liquidity can be an illusion. Remember that working capital never paid off a cash obligation!

Assume that the build-up of unsaleable inventory goes on for some time and that short-term debt is used to finance this bloated asset holding. Traditional analysis shows that 'liquidity' is unchanged, the growth in current assets being matched by a corresponding growth in current liabilities. Our approach leads us to the true answer for bank borrowing is excluded from the calculation of NTI. NTI will rise steeply in these circumstances and the proportion of it financed by working capital will get smaller. A much greater amount of NTI will be supported by short-term debt which we know to be inappropriate as a long-term funding source. Alarm bells start to ring!

As the very term implies, working capital is more correctly conceived as non-current liabilities (including equity) minus non-current assets. It is the amount of long-term or permanent finance employed by the business in assets which are not fixed, that is, in working or circulating assets. To put it another way, in most businesses the bulk of the equity and long-term liabilities cover or finance the long-term assets; the remainder is working capital, which finances the asset conversion cycle.

How is this second definition more useful than the first? Is the distinction worthwhile or meaningful? We should not be so confident of long-held beliefs here that we let slip the significance of a different approach. By identifying working capital as a liability rather than an asset we can use the concept to help us understand the asset conversion cycle better. If the level of NTI indicates to us the extent of the asset investment, the level of working capital tells us something about the manner in which that investment is financed.

In a manufacturing company, NTI will almost invariably be a positive number. Finance for the investment may come, broadly, from one of two sources, long-term funds designated as working capital, and bank debt or short-term funds. A comparison of the respective levels of NTI, working capital and short-term borrowing tells us the extent to which NTI is funded by the two different sources. This information, in turn, tells us something about risk.

High numbers for NTI are found in companies with a long manufacturing cycle which keep heavy stocks of inventory and allow generous trade credit. Most types of metal-based manufacturing and engineering fall into this category. Companies that engage in long-term projects inevitably have considerable resources tied up in their asset conversion cycles, though they will usually collect stage payments from their customers to ease the strain on the cash flow.

To ease the strain on the balance sheet, such stage payments are normally shown as a deduction from work in progress rather than as deferred income on the liability side. One cannot quarrel with this practice, but an analyst should be aware of the contingent liability effectively masked by this treatment; failure to complete the project to a satisfactory standard may result in the need to repay some if not all of those stage payments. Failure to complete a major long-term project can be catastrophic.

Current assets other than cash have a value only if they can be turned into cash eventually, and current assets which cannot be so converted are essentially indistinguishable from losses or expenses. Long-term contracts imply a prolonged investment in work in progress, usually on a substantial scale, with full conversion back into cash delayed until the very end, perhaps years after the contract was undertaken.

NTI will be much lower in companies which sell for cash or have a rapid manufacturing process. Clearly, these do not have much money tied up in current assets and are consequently less risky to do business with. Service companies fall into this category and NTI may even be negative if trade credit is taken. Supermarkets and hotel chains usually show negative NTI. A company with a low investment in inventory and debtors is intrinsically less risky than one with a heavy investment, because the asset conversion cycle is shorter and therefore less vulnerable to disruption.

There is also a funding risk to be considered and negative NTI should be regarded with caution. If trade credit exceeds the total of inventory and debtors, it follows that trade creditors may be effectively financing long-term assets, a potentially destabilizing funding mismatch. Another way of looking at this is to say that there will be little liquidity to service the trade creditors and there may be an acute shortage of cash if trade credit were to be shortened for any reason. Low NTI is also suspicious if it is unexpected. It may not represent a smaller investment in the asset conversion cycle. An alternative cause may be a higher than normal dependence upon trade creditors and the accrued expenses—quite probably unstable funding sources.

Most companies produce their annual accounts as at 31 December each year, the end of the calendar year being as good a time as any. By coincidence, just after Christmas is for most businesses a relatively quiet time when the investment in NTI is likely to be at or near its lowest. When a manufacturing or retailing company is stretched to its limit, say before the Christmas rush, the level of NTI inevitably rises steeply as the amounts tied up in debtors and inventory are increased. Such seasonal investments are often, and legitimately, financed by an overdraft or some other form of short-term borrowing instrument. But, at the low point of the year, the seasonal excesses of NTI have been liquidated and the short-term funding repaid. Consequently, one would not expect to see large amounts of short-term borrowing on a published annual balance sheet for a manufacturing or retailing company. Company managements are very sensitive to this. When a company has a low point at the end of the summer, if at all possible the accounts will be drawn up as at 30 September or 31 October, partly, as management sometimes claims, because closing the books is easier at a time when resources are not already overstretched by peak trading, but partly because no manager wants to show the world a balance sheet heavily reliant on short-term borrowings.

It should be assumed, on the whole, that the level of NTI indicated in the published balance sheet is essentially permanent. During the trading year the level may rise but it is unlikely to fall below the figure indicated by the published statements. The same may be said of the overdraft or short-term borrowings.

The concept of NTI is a useful tool in forecasting funding needs. Increasing sales may lead to higher profits but will it lead to higher cash generation? In other words, will the expected growth lead to unacceptable levels of borrowing? If a company has sales of £1000, a net profit margin of 3 per cent and NTI is historically 25 per cent of sales, a 20 per cent spurt in sales may cause a problem. Consider; if sales rise to £1200, NTI will increase from £250 to £300. Net profit for the year should improve from £30 to £36. Even if all the year's profit is retained and no dividends are paid, extra borrowing is likely to be needed to support the extra investment in NTI, and that leaves out of consideration the likely need for a further purchase of capital assets to generate the additional sales.

A company looking at declining turnover might expect to

see lower profits or even a loss. Its funding problem and cash flow may, however, benefit from the reduction in NTI. To get a clear idea in any specific case, of course, more detailed projections would have to be done, involving full balance sheet and income statements.

One curious property of working capital is that it can only be created in a limited number of ways. An increase in long-term liabilities will obviously do it, as will the retention of profits or a new issue of equity. The sale of fixed or long-term assets is about the only other possibility. None of these options can be easily manipulated to fit the day to day demands for finance of the asset conversion cycle. Short-term debt, by contrast, is an ideal medium for the financing of short-term NTI requirements.

Bankers do not worry as much as they should about their short-term lending policy. In the USA, short-term lending is evidenced by a 'note payable'—a promissory note signed by the borrower. This note has a repayment date on it and traditionally a bank takes a dim view of a company which seeks to extend or roll on the stated maturity. Such a system works effectively in ensuring that short-term bank borrowing means what it says.

In the UK, the time-honoured method of bank financing for short-term needs is the overdraft. The borrower is allocated a credit limit and is allowed to run his account into debit up to that ceiling. While a banker would not be at all happy to see an overdraft constantly near its limit, a 'hard-core overdraft' as it is called, there is usually no specific repayment schedule. The advantages of the overdraft are its flexibility and its relatively modest cost. There are next to no formalities associated with its creation and the borrower pays interest only on what he uses.

Little attention is ever focused on the shortcomings of this manner of financing business. It is widely known that overdrafts are rarely seen in the USA (although they are not completely illegal as is often suggested), but we rarely stop to wonder why the Americans can do without a tool which has for decades been the principal lending mechanism in the UK. The answer lies in the word 'control'.

Under the 'notes payable' system, an American banker knows immediately a note has to be extended, or cannot be repaid on time, that there is a short-term financing problem. Failure to repay a note on time indicates, prima facie, a disorder in the asset conversion cycle which calls for immediate investigation. His British counterpart, whose management of the account extends only to checking each day that the limit is not exceeded, does not have this level of control. He will certainly be watching for the problem of hard-core borrowing, principally by checking the maximum and minimum levels of borrowing each month, but it may be several months before the tendency to greater reliance on the overdraft becomes apparent, especially if the pattern is complicated by seasonal trends. By the time the company's difficulty has surfaced in the 'max and mins', the company's asset conversion cycle may well be in some trouble.

Many smaller companies have a tendency to 'overtrade'. This curious and paradoxical term is applied to a company, usually profitable, which tries to increase profits by boosting turnover without having adequate working capital or long-term finance to support the increased investment in NTI. Entrepreneurs are often unaware of the underlying lack of balance in their operations and have eyes only for the most obvious symptoms of overtrading, an acute shortage of cash. As overtrading companies are seldom loss making initially, they are often granted overdraft facilities which they proceed to use to expand the business, inevitably generating thereby a hard-core overdraft.

The cures for overtrading are either the injection of long-term money to reduce the dependence on the overdraft, or a scaling back of trading levels. The former may be difficult for a small bu. 'ness, the latter rarely appeals to entrepreneurial types. So the overtrading tends to be chronic. Does this matter? And how should the bank respond?

It matters for several reasons and it will be argued that the banks do not always respond correctly. Excessive reliance on short-term money is potentially harmful to the company because it imports unnecessary risks. There is first the interest rate risk as overdraft rates move in line with bank base rates in the UK and an unexpected rise in those rates may reduce or eliminate the profitability of the asset conversion cycle. By funding with either fixed rate debt or equity this risk is avoided. Using longer-term debt at floating rates there is at least the chance to lock in the rate for 6 months between rollovers. Secondly, the funding is not secure. Overdrafts are repayable, in theory, on demand. To the bank, an overdraft is a current asset, and is funded by the bank's own demand deposits. If a company relies on an overdraft for long-term funding, it risks the bank demanding its money back at short notice and liquidating the company if it does not get it. Banks in the UK do not make reckless demands on overdrafts as a matter of policy, but the divergence between the legal situation and the underlying reality points out the shaky basis of overdraft lending.

The result is that all bank branches have a measure of hard-core, permanent overdraft lending on their books. Provided they do not perceive the risk as excessive, they have no desire to call it in since their overdrafts are earning assets. What they do not perceive is that they are being robbed!

Hard-core borrowing is really long-term debt and should certainly command a higher 'reward' because of the increased risk. Managers do sometimes charge split rates on overdrafts to reflect this difference. But on a stricter view, it can be said that hard-core overdraft lending is really equity because it is virtually certain not to be repaid.

The bank is being robbed because, while the official equity holders are earning perhaps 25 per cent on their investment each year, the bank is getting, say, 3–4 per cent. From the risk standpoint, the banks are not quite as exposed as the equity holders since the latter will lose all their money first, before the bank loses a penny, but anyone lending long term to a business is exposed to the business risks inherent in that business and should be rewarded accordingly.

To mitigate the extent of this risk, the UK banker's standard ploy is to take security on the assets of the company, typically by a combination of fixed and floating charges. While this will undoubtedly strengthen the bank's position, it does not attack the root of the problem, the dependence of the company upon short-term money. And it generates a good deal of ill will into the bargain. As already mentioned, the bank will be paid in advance of the shareholders. The taking of security in no way strengthens the bank's position *vis-à-vis* the shareholders. What 'collateralizing', as the Americans say, does is to put the bank ahead of the trade and other creditors in the liquidation pecking order.

When a company fails and is liquidated, there is an order laid down, broadly the same in most countries, as to what is paid first. Top of the list will be the liquidator's expenses, taxes and possibly unpaid wages. Next will come secured creditors, followed by unsecured creditors, and if there is anything left it will be returned to the shareholders. Each class of claim will be paid in full before the next gets anything. By taking security, the bank pushes itself towards the top of this list, to the detriment of the company's suppliers and others who have innocently allowed the company credit.

The taking of security is resisted by shareholders and directors because of its impact on trade. Charges have to be registered and are therefore public knowledge. Suppliers and potential unsecured creditors may be scared away from giving credit to a company subject to a floating charge, with consequent detrimental effect on the asset conversion cycle. One can understand the banks wishing to protect themselves but it is hard to justify that protection coming at the expense of the unsecured creditors.

The real problem lies in the use of overdraft financing in inappropriate ways. If short-term lending were restricted to just that, there would be much less need to take security to ensure the safety of overdraft lending. If the bank manager's response to a potential overtrading situation was to look at the asset conversion cycle and suggest ways of tightening it up, rather than the claiming of security over all the company's assets, many company failures might not happen at all. It is the age-old dilemma in banking. The banker wants to lend money and do business, yet he cannot absorb a heavy risk. Security is not a universally equitable or appropriate means to square the circle.

It should not be thought that all short-term lending appearing on a published year-end balance sheet is somehow suspicious. One explanation for heavy short-term indebtedness at the year end, supposedly the low point, is that it represents legitimate permanent or semi-permanent funding for NTI. Many Japanese companies have a symbiotic relationship with their banks and for cultural and historical reasons are constant and heavy short-term borrowers. This is normal and certainly does not mean that disaster is looming. In a Western context one would be more sceptical as many, particularly smaller, companies are reliant upon short-term borrowing to a dangerous extent.

When we look at the consolidated accounts of multinationals there are other possibilities. The notes will rarely if ever tell you the true answer, but be aware of some of the options. Short-term debt may be a permanent overdraft run by an overseas subsidiary, guaranteed by the parent company. By keeping the borrowing in the same currency as the assets being financed, the group as a whole can hedge its risk as well as, in some cases, take advantage of low interest rates. Such arrangements are very common in Latin America and Europe.

Much short-term bank debt may represent finance for specific short-term trade transactions. Even the strongest and most liquid of companies regularly ask their banks to finance exports, the loan being repaid from the money paid by the importers. This may be to allow the company the benefit of cheap money under government sponsored export credit schemes, as, for example, those made available by ECGD, the US Export-Import Bank, Coface or Hermes. Usance letters of credit and bill-discounting arrangements also amount to short-term borrowing in many cases.

Again, short-term debt may be merely bridging finance, set up to accommodate the acquisition of a new investment or asset pending more permanent long-term finance. There are numerous other ways in which this item may arise on the year-end balance sheet. A high number may indicate excessive dependence on short-term bank borrowings in support of NTI, or it may not.

This chapter has tried to give some idea of the scope of the problem and to build up our methodology based on risk. When we analyse companies and their performance, it is not sufficient to play with the numbers. Even if these numbers were reliable, which they are not, ratio analysis will get us only part of the way. We have to have regard for the underlying substance, the real world position of which the numbers are a pale, distorted reflection. Risks have to be identified and assessed, weighted for seriousness, dissected and considered in aggregate. We should not accept unthinkingly the traditional tools of analysis, largely designed for a simpler environment we have now left behind. If necessary, we have to design our own tools and apply them to the information available to reach an informed and intelligent solution.

The concept of the asset conversion cycle, flawed and imperfect though it may be, is a better tool with which to approach most modern businesses than that of working capital. It may not be feasible to decipher much about the cycle from the consolidated accounts of a group with interests in meat processing, insurance and mining but by thinking about the very different cycles natural to these different businesses we shall at least be asking the right questions. If the numbers are not helpful, we shall know that we need other ways of grasping the nature and extent of the risks.

5

Cash flow—A source of life and a cause of death

Ready money is Aladdin's lamp.
Lord Byron, *Don Juan*, Canto 12.12

Just a few years ago, in 1982, a young analyst named James Chanos, barely out of college and working for an obscure, unknown and very small securities house in Chicago, created a sensation in the US financial markets. Using what *The Wall Street Journal* described as 'a well-known but tedious technique called cash-flow analysis' Chanos investigated the standing of Baldwin-United Corp. and concluded that, despite the company's burgeoning profitability and boldly advancing share price, Baldwin-United was heading for bankruptcy. Baldwin-United had originally been a piano manufacturer in Cincinnati (on a modest scale) but in latter years had branched out into insurance and financial services, ending up as one of the leading companies in the Midwest, a corporate giant quoted on the New York Stock Exchange. It was this company that Chanos took on for his first assignment.

Deciding that a major corporation is on the verge of the abyss is one thing; telling the world about it is another, and Chanos's employer Gilford Securities, Inc. bravely put out a circular recommending the stock as a 'sell'. About a year later, Baldwin-United filed for voluntary reorganisation under chapter 11 of the US Bankruptcy Code, to near universal consternation and bewilderment. By contrast, the young James Chanos rose to sudden fame and fortune and was made a partner in record time.

It is comparatively rare for so substantial a company as Baldwin-United to fail, though major corporate failures are more common now than they have been at any time since the 1930s and the Great Depression. For such a profitable company to fail suddenly, almost without warning, is even rarer, most big companies heralding their eventual demise by a series of crippling losses. Yet it does happen, in defiance of traditional analysis which says, virtually, that companies survive so long as they can make profits.

Why the discrepancy in some cases? How can a 'successful' company collapse? The answer lies in the true meaning of profitability and success. Profitable companies do tend to continue in business simply because their very profitability is a measure of their success. But partly, the prophecy is self-fulfilling in that profitable companies find it relatively easy to raise new money either in debt or in equity and there is nothing like an influx of cash from whatever source to keep an enterprise on the road.

Because profitability and success tend to go together, one readily imagines there exists no distinction. 'A company is profitable', so the argument runs, 'and therefore it continues to trade.' This may be true in our experience, but the conclusion does not necessarily follow from the premise. More apt is surely the logic that states, 'a company is profitable and therefore it attracts lenders and investors. Because it has a supply of outsiders injecting money into it, the company continues to perform.' Granted that may not be the whole story, at least there are no missing steps in the argument! Now we can see, too, how profitable companies can fail—the lenders and investors may perceive something other than the company's profitability which causes them to withhold their money!

There is no surviving in business without cash flow. It

takes no deductive thought process to see that any trading company has constantly to make payments, usually by asking its banker to effect those payments on its behalf through the cheque-clearing system. Suppliers, shareholders, lenders and other sundry creditors all have to be paid. No banker will be willing to continue making payments unless he receives regular reimbursement, unless money is flowing from some source into the company's bank account. It may be that the banker will grant an overdraft or loan and allow the company to make payments in excess of the sums deposited. It may be that funds on deposit will be sufficient for regular payments to be made for some time in the absence of new deposits. But ultimately external payments have to flow into the account to replenish it, or the banker's patience will be exhausted. At that point, the game is over and the company's creditors will start proceedings to have the company liquidated. Once the cash dries up, down go the shutters.

The principal source of cash, by which we mean here money in the bank rather than notes and coin, is the asset conversion cycle which, as we have seen, both consumes or ties up cash and also generates it. On balance, more cash must come out of the cycle than goes into it if the business is to flourish, since all the other potential sources of cash will be finite unless the asset conversion cycle is contributing a reasonable proportion of the cash needs. It is necessary to say 'on balance' because temporary shortfalls do regularly occur and there is nothing untoward about a company seeking temporary finance for a short-term or seasonal investment in a higher level of NTI, perhaps just before Christmas or over the summer. When NTI rises, it means that more money is tied up in the asset conversion cycle and it may be that the cycle will at that time be absorbing more cash than it is providing and so creating illiquidity.

Our approach in this book is to identify the most fundamental ways in which a business functions, and then to develop tools of analysis that enable us to measure the efficiency of the basic underlying mechanism. According to traditional analysis, the main tool for measuring the efficiency of the trading pattern is the notion of profitability. To arrive at a profit figure, an accountant adds up all the revenues which he considers belong to the relevant accounting period, and from that total subtracts the sum of the expenses attributable to the same period. Various profit figures may be struck depending upon the inclusion or exclusion of interest, taxes and extraordinary or non-recurring items. Whether nor not the cash payments associated with those revenues and expenses occurred within the accounting period is irrelevant!

It is this last point which renders profit an inadequate basis on which to found an analysis of cash flow. During any accounting period some of the cash flows actually occurring will be allocated by the accountant to preceding or subsequent periods. The net amount of cash actually received will inevitably be either greater or less than the stated figure for profit.

Mention cash flow to most analysts and they will tell you that cash flow is net profit plus depreciation. Ask again how depreciation can add to cash flow when, as everyone knows, no cash flow is associated with it—in accountants' jargon it is a 'non-cash item'—and the answer may well be something not too coherent.

Let us begin by clearing up some common misunderstandings. Depreciation is not in any real sense a source of cash even though it is often so described; a small example proves the point. Suppose that the following is the income statement of a manufacturing company:

	£
Sales	1000
Trading costs	(500)
Depreciation	(100)
Profit	400

What is the cash flow? Adding back the depreciation charge to the profit gives us £400 + 100 = £500. The same result could have been obtained by deducting the trading costs from the sales: £1000 − 500 = £500. In other words, depreciation being a non-cash and indeed non-operating item needs to be excluded from the profit figure to bring that profit figure nearer to the cash flow figure. What we are really saying by this calculation is that sales (cash) minus trading costs (cash) gives the net cash flow figure.

The inadequacy of this well-known and much-used formula is immediately apparent. Sales is not a cash number; it is the value of sales attributed to the accounting period in question. Similarly, trading costs is not necessarily or even probably the same as the cash expended for trading; it is the sum of the outflows attributed to the accounting period. In following the old formula, all we have done is to make one adjustment to the profit figure and blithely assume that all the other components of the income statement may be equated to cash flow. This is nonsense. A further shortcoming is that we have worked from the net profit figure which is conventionally struck after interest and tax, not items we want to allow to muddy our picture of the cash-generating properties of the asset conversion cycle.

In theory, and quite correctly, cash flow is a measure of a company's ability to fund its capital expenditure and debt repayment out of its own resources. No company can expect to finance these outflows exclusively from external sources, asset sales, new borrowings or increased equity. The trouble is that the figure for 'cash flow' obtained by this method is often so wildly inaccurate that to use it at all is positively dangerous. Net profit plus depreciation is, of course, always a larger number than net profit and tends to feature in an analysis only when profitability is poor and depreciation a relatively large number. Such statements as 'Profitability was much reduced, but the company generated an improved cash flow' are to be found from time to time even in the most reputable financial newspapers.

The formula is most inaccurate and confusing precisely when it is most crucial that accurate cash flow information be available. A growing or expanding company needs a larger NTI to support its growing sales volume. Higher sales lead, in the expectation of the shareholders, to higher profits, otherwise there is little point in growing. But what shareholders and managers often forget is that growth also consumes cash. A lot of it. Rapidly growing companies may be highly profitable; however, they rarely generate cash. Just to take the profit and add back the depreciation is ludicrous since the result is to make a cash starved company look like a cash cow! Growth is often a dangerous enough process because of the many stresses to, and changes in, production methods, management style, distribution patterns and so forth that accompany it, without the company's watchers coming to utterly the wrong conclusion about the basic financial pattern such a company must display. With a little effort, ideally backed up by a small home computer, it is perfectly feasible to do a great deal better. Cash flow is not the same thing as profit even allowing for depreciation. Cash flow in the widest sense is the sum of all the company's receipts and payments. The most perfect cash flow statement we could devise would be based not on the published accounts but on the bank statement.

Entries in a bank statement are listed chronologically, but suppose that we made a list, by category, of all the inflows and outflows (debits and credits as the bank calls them), separated those that were directly related to the asset conversion cycle, and then compared that total with the other non-operating outflows for interest, capital expenditure and the rest, before adding in the external financing raised so that ultimately we could reconcile the change in the cash balance from the beginning to the end of the year. That would really tell us something about cash flow! Do that for five consecutive years and there would not be much doubt as to where that company stood and was going!

Bankers have for years worked with their smaller business customers on cash flow forecast statements, better known as cash budgets. Many budding entrepreneurs have little idea what their cash requirements will be as their new businesses develop and grow, seeing only the profit to be made by selling their product in ever greater quantities. A prudent businessman will draw up, month by month or week by week, a plan of all payments and receipts going through the bank account from which he will see how much he may need to borrow, how long he will need it for and on what timescale he can repay. His 'friendly' bank manager will be interested to see this projection and discuss it with him, possibly pointing out likely variations or doubtful areas, and this discussion will form the basis of an agreement about what, if any, borrowing facilities the businessman's company needs and what, if any, the banker is willing to furnish.

Crucial to this type of statement is that nothing should be excluded from it. If major payments or receipts are missed out the budget will be worthless. It does not matter how individual inflows and outflows are classified since the effect on the bank statement will be identical, but everything must be included for the budget to have validity and value. Such accounting dilemmas as whether or not to classify some expenditure as an expense or an investment, or how to show some extraordinary item, do not arise. If there is a cash flow expected it has to be in the budget because it will eventually hit the bank account. *Depreciation, write-offs, revaluations and the like will never be seen in a cash budget because there is no cash flow associated with or derived from them.*

In looking at much larger companies, we should be adopting the same approach. So far as possible we want a complete picture of the cash receipts and payments, complete and undistorted by the vagaries of accounting convention and presentational manipulation.

Such an ambition might seem far-fetched, but it is not. Some compromises do have to be made since the bank accounts of a major multinational, which might do business with upwards of a hundred banks in many different countries and currencies around the world, will contain countless thousands if not millions of entries. But we are not concerned with each and every entry. We cannot handle that type of data and, even if we could, we would have untold problems deciding upon the classification of the individual entries. In any case, large companies do not publish their bank statements and it is most unlikely that any one bank would have the whole picture, or indeed, more than a tiny part of it.

What a company does publish is an Annual Report, a balance sheet and income statement and, in most countries, a funds flow statement of some kind. While none of these statements can truthfully be considered cash based, constructed as they all are in accordance with the accrual concept, they are all the product of the double entry bookkeeping system which in essence is cash based. Provided that the statements reconcile and balance, we can discover much more about cash movements within the accounting period covered by those statements than the company expects or wishes readers of its report to know. The figures can actually be made to reveal secrets which the company's managers might well prefer kept under wraps.

Extracting these secrets is quite easy, when you know how to do it. The trick is to understand precisely the relationship between cash and profit, and also the way in which the double entry system hides and disguises the pattern of cash inflows and outflows. We will begin by illustrating some very straightforward bookkeeping from an unusual angle (that is, the *cash* angle!)

Let us suppose that last year WB (Manufacturing) Inc. received $1000 in cash as a result of its selling activities and the liquidation of its receivables. That is not the same thing as supposing that sales in the accounting sense amounted to $1000. What would be the accounting treatment of such a result? We need to look more closely at the interaction between double entry and the accrual system.

In theory, a business need not bother with the double entry system at all and could record all its financial transactions solely in a cash book, entering receipts as debits on the left of the page and payments as credits on the right. Entries in the cash book would have to be passed to match or, more precisely, to mirror the entries made by the bank over the company's account in its books. No consideration would be given to accruals, deferrals, nor indeed to anything except actual realized cash flows. At the end of the year, the company would produce a report showing a summary of payments and receipts broken down by category, the difference between payments and receipts being necessarily the change in the level of the cash balance since the end of the previous year.

Would such a statement be satisfactory? No matter where the company was incorporated, if that were all it produced, that company would undoubtedly be in pretty serious breach of the law. There is no law anywhere prohibiting the disclosure of unadulterated cash flow information in an uncomplicated format, but this is not the way accountants work and accountants around the world have over the years established accounting conventions (and sponsored laws!) encouraging a quite different approach—the accrual approach.

Accountants would, of course, soon be out of a job without the accrual concept since the recording of cash flows takes no accounting skills whatever. The only possible room for judgement would lie in the classification of cash flows by type and, that apart, there is no conceivable way to vary the numbers so as to influence the presentation for better or worse, or to make any adjustments. By the end of the year, the cash flows are a matter of history, objective facts which are not susceptible to adjustment without outright falsification. Compare the profit figures companies produce where a host of assumptions underlie the numbers, which would themselves be quite different if the underlying assumptions were to change.

Taking the process one step further, we can restore the double entry system without adopting a full accrual system, merely by opening a second account to track the effect of the cash movements on the owners' equity. Thus, when cash is received, to balance the debit to the cash account we would pass a matching credit to owners' equity to reflect the increased value of the company to its shareholders. Credits to cash would be matched by equal and opposite debits to owners' equity.

Although in theory it would be possible to keep the books of even a large multinational in this way, to the extent that the cash account would always balance with the equity account, it is impractical in reality to maintain the books of anything larger than the very smallest club or society on this basis. The accrual concept is actually integral to the whole process of accounting to a surprising extent, and few people realize that its influence is not confined to the income statement. Accountants are not in danger of becoming redundant as a consequence of the ideas in this book and accrual cannot be dismissed out of hand as a fraud and a fiction!

One principal objection to a totally cash-driven accounting system is that it will not generate a balance sheet. Under the double account method just outlined, all cash flows are effectively accounted for as revenues and expenses. Some cash flows cannot in fairness be forced into these two categories. Borrowing money certainly increases the cash account debit balance, but it cannot be said to increase directly the value of the owners' investment.

Likewise, the purchase of fixed assets intended to contribute to the company's activities over a long period cannot fairly be considered as reducing the value of the company by the purchase price at the moment when it is paid. To get around this problem, instead of passing the balancing entry to owners' equity, we open another account and pass the balancing entry to that.

These considerations do not affect the entries made to the cash account, which will remain the same however many and varied are the balance sheet accounts which are opened to accommodate the balancing debits and credits. The equity account, however, will be affected in that the greater the complexity and proliferation of the balance sheet accounts, the greater the number of cash entries which do not touch the equity account. The two accounts for cash and for equity, which originally were mirror images of each other, become quite different.

If the entries over the cash account run as follows:

	Cash	
Opening balance	1000	740
	100	150
	50	85
	75	10
Closing balance	240	

the equity account, if it were the only other account, would be the reverse of it:

	Equity	
740	1000	Opening balance
150	100	
85	75	
10	50	
	240	Closing balance

It makes no difference what labels we give to any of the entries. The equity account cannot be any different from that shown above. Allow the use of the balance sheet accounts and the picture might become:

	Equity		
Costs	740	1000	Sales
Interest	10	75	Commissions
		50	Other income

	Fixed assets	
Factory	150	

	Borrowing		
Repayment	85	100	Bank loan

and we can now draw up a balance sheet and income statement:

	£		£		£
Cash	240	Borrowing	15	Sales	1000
Fixed assets	150	Equity		Costs	(740)
		(profit)	375	Commissions	75
	390		390	Other income	50
				Interest	(10)
				Profit	375

For the sake of keeping the example as simple as possible we have not only used small and unrealistic numbers but have also eliminated the complexities of detailed book-keeping, and in particular, all types of suspense accounts.

Notice that the cash account is unaffected by the creation of the balance sheet. The cash flows are fixed and given and cannot be allocated to other accounts. By contrast the equity account, in this instance effectively the income statement (which is only ever really a summary of the 'operating' entries over owners' equity) is directly affected by the extraction of certain items for 'capitalization'. If it had been decided to put more or fewer items on the balance sheet, the income statement would have been different. There is a choice as to whether each cash flow should go on to the income statement as a revenue or expense item or on to the balance sheet as an asset or a liability. The difference between an asset and an expense and between a revenue item and a liability is fundamentally only a matter of judgement.

So far, so good. The trouble is that once one admits the validity of opening balance sheet accounts it becomes automatically possible to pass debits and credits where neither entry touches the cash account. There is no rule that requires one half of the double entry always to pass to cash. Until now all entries were dependent upon cash movements, and since cash movements are an objective reality there has been limited scope for the exercise of discretion; in fact, the only opportunity has been in the allocation of the balancing entry.

Consider now the treatment of depreciation or an asset revaluation. Both of these affect owners' equity and one half of the double entry must be applied to that account. However, neither depreciation nor asset revaluation affects cash in any way and the balancing entries will be passed to accumulated depreciation or the actual asset account as is deemed appropriate. Again, this is an area where the treatment is determined by accounting practice and convention. The more entries of this type a company makes, the harder it becomes to use the statements to track the flows of cash, since it becomes progressively less true that changes in the balance sheet accounts are evidence of actual movements of cash.

Unfortunately for our purposes, the treatment of the asset conversion cycle in the accounting world is not cash driven. By that is meant that it is not the payment or receipt of cash which primarily determines the passing of the accounting entries, it is the desire of the accountant for correct allocation of revenue and expense under the accrual concept. Sales are 'recognized' not when cash is received, as in our example above, but usually when the goods are shipped, and the entries are not Dr. Cash, Cr. Owners' Equity but Dr. Receivables (debtors, assuming a credit sale), Cr. Sales (i.e. the income statement). The cash payment is recognized when it is received by entering Dr. Cash, Cr. Receivables. It is easy to see from this that the difference between cash receipts and sales recognized lies in changes occurring in the balance on the Receivables account.

To go back to our question raised earlier, how to account for cash receipts of £1000 arising from sales, the answer depends upon what has happened to the Receivables account. Assume that it has risen by £45 over the year and the sales figure must be £1045. The company shipped £1045 worth of goods and was paid for £1000 worth. The £45 remaining was owed by the company's customers. In fact, it will be a little more complicated than this since we have assumed an opening balance on the Receivables account of zero. If the opening balance had been, say, £100 and the closing £145, what really happened was that the £100 outstanding at the opening of the period was received during that period, the company shipped £1045 worth of goods for which it received £1000 in cash and was at year end awaiting payment of the remaining £145. The relationship between the cash and sales numbers may be expressed in a formula, thus:

Sales = cash receipts + increase in receivables

or more generally, and much more usefully:

Cash receipts = sales − increase in receivables

Should the increase be negative, that is, if receivables are reduced during the period, the implication is that cash receipts exceed stated sales and the decrease in receivables should be added to the sales figure to arrive at the cash receipts.

By a very similar process it is possible to go from the cost of sales figure to the actual amount of cash purchases. When inventory is bought by the company, there is either an immediate cash outlay or, more likely, an increase in payables if the supplier is prepared to grant trade credit. Assume for a moment that we are looking at a company that buys its supplies for cash. What is the relationship between the cash purchases and the cost of sales?

Well, cash purchases increase inventory pound for pound. Cost of sales is the cost price of the inventory considered to have been sold during the period. If inventory rises over the period it follows that less was consumed than was purchased. Conversely, if inventory falls, consumption must have exceeded purchases. The cost of sales figure is in fact determined by reference to the assessed value of inventory at the balance sheet date by the formula:

Cost of sales = purchases + opening inventory
− closing inventory

or more simply

Cost of sales = purchases − increase in inventory

We can again reverse this formula in our attempt to find out about cash flows and read:

Purchases = cost of sales + increase in inventory

Notice that the year-end inventory valuation is of crucial importance to the cost of sales figure since any variation resulting either from inaccuracy or difference in the method of valuation has a pound for pound impact on the profit level. It makes no difference whatever to the purchases figure which is a matter of objective history, as any error in the inventory valuation is exactly cancelled out by an equal and opposite error in the cost of sales. As already stated, accounting methods have no power to influence historic cash flows.

A moment ago, we assumed that all purchases were for cash settlement. This is an unrealistic assumption in most businesses and we need to examine what happens when purchases are made on credit. Not surprisingly, the picture is a mirror image of what happens when sales are made on credit! The difference between accrued purchases and cash purchases is reflected in the change in the balance on the payables or creditors account. A cash purchase is a credit to the cash book, but a credit purchase is a credit to payables. If the debt is settled during the accounting period no overall change will arise in the payables balance.

Any change which does arise in the payables balance would seem to derive from a difference between the purchases figure used in the computation of cost of sales and the actual cash purchases figure.

At first sight, it is slightly hard to grasp what is going on here, so we need our example. Let us suppose cost of sales was £800 and inventory and payables rose over the accounting period by £25 and £45 respectively. Summary entries would run as follows:

Income Statement (Owners' Equity)	
800	

	Inventory	
825	800
Increase 25	

Payables	
780	825
	45 Increase

Cash	
	780

Cash payments must have amounted to £780. Purchases for cash and credit were £780 + £45 (the increase in payables) and cost of sales was £780 + £45 − £25 (the increase in inventory). To put the whole matter into a useful formula again:

Cash purchases = cost of sales + increase in inventory
− increase in payables

Decreases in inventory or payables will be treated as negative increases and added in the case of inventory and subtracted in the case of payables.

By performing these calculations we have managed to uncover some information about a company which that company probably did not wish us to know: the amount of cash received, and paid away as a direct consequence of the manufacturing process. A 'successful' manufacturing company is likely to report a reasonable gross profit with sales revenue well in excess of cost of sales. Adjusting for the balance sheet changes in receivables, inventory and payables may show that there is little or no liquidity in this gross profit. Such is the likely outcome if holdings of inventory have risen steeply, debtors are taking longer to pay or the suppliers are demanding prompter settlement.

Notice, too, that this type of illiquidity arises naturally from the trading cycle and can easily happen without management even being aware of it. Companies and some analysts tend to describe the process in terms of a profitable company making an additional investment in 'working capital' (by which is usually meant NTI). While management may consciously decide to increase NTI, they do not do so 'out of profits' in any real sense. It is done by leaning more heavily on the bank account, so that money flows in slightly more slowly or out slightly more quickly.

Can we build these simple techniques into an analytical method for investigating complex companies? Indeed we can. We have seen that our primary source of information about a company's real cash flow, by which is meant the totality of its cash payments and receipts, is the income statement. In addition, we know that the income statement is a misleading guide because the entries on it do not tally exactly with the cash account entries as a result of certain entries being passed to the balance sheet. An entry may be made to the income statement and the corresponding debit or credit may go to a non-cash balance sheet account; or the pattern may be of a cash entry matched by an opposing entry to a non-cash balance sheet account. Various permutations are possible. Not all double entries are for equal and opposite amounts and a series of debits may be matched by a series of credits with any number of items in each series, provided only that the totals of both series are identical. Lastly, entries may be made across two balance sheet accounts neither of which is cash. Usually this would occur when some reclassification is considered appropriate.

All this might be too confusing to unravel were it not for the invariable fact that each year the balance sheet balances and that it is almost always possible in published accounts to reconcile the income statement with the change in the owners' equity. The latter exercise often calls for some juggling with the numbers in the footnotes, but is rarely unduly taxing, bankers and investors tending to exercise extreme wariness in dealing with companies where this reconciliation eludes them.

Consequently, the change in the cash balance between the beginning and end of an accounting period may be defined by reference to the totality of all the other changes which took place in the balance sheet over the same period. Put another way, the increase, if such it be, in cash is equal to the increase in the total liabilities side of the balance sheet minus the increase in the total asset side of the balance sheet excluding the cash account. The sum of the individual increases on the credit side and reductions on the asset side will tell us about increases in the cash account, and conversely the sum of individual increases on the asset side and decreases on the credit side will shed light upon decreases in the cash account.

It will not, of course, be this simple since we know that there will not necessarily or even probably be an exact unitary relationship between individual balance sheet changes and cash flows. However, we shall have a series of numbers that add up correctly and which may form the basis of quite a detailed cash flow if certain adjustments— balancing adjustments, naturally—are made. Chief of these adjustments will be to replace the figure for the increase in owners' equity, better known as retained profit, by the individual components of the income statement which add up to the same figure.

The procedure will become much clearer by illustration. Below are the figures published by Avnet, Inc., a US electronics company, for its first quarter to 28 September 1984. All numbers represent millions of dollars.

In presenting these figures some liberties have had to be taken with the original (see Exhibit 2). Avnet published figures in round thousands of dollars, a level of accuracy

Income statement		Balance sheet		
	9/84		6/84	9/84
Sales	432.4	Cash and marketable		
Other revenue	2.0	securities	92.1	76.1
Cost of sales	(310.7)	Receivables	285.4	289.1
Depreciation	(3.2)	Inventories	410.7	439.8
Selling, general		Other assets	10.1	15.3
and adminis-		Property, plant and		
trative expenses	(78.2)	equipment	73.1	75.7
Interest	(2.9)	Intangibles and other	39.4	42.9
Income tax	(19.5)	Total assets	910.8	938.9
Dividend	(4.4)			
Retained profit	15.5			
		Short-term borrowings	3.1	2.9
		Accounts payable and		
		accrued expenses	182.8	194.4
		Dividends payable	4.4	4.4
		Current portion of		
		long-term loans	3.2	3.3
		Long-term debt	113.9	114.0
		Shareholders' equity	603.4	619.9
		Total liabilities and		
		equity	910.8	938.9

which serves only to clutter the page with six- or seven-digit numbers. The above format recognizes that for a company of this size nothing under $100 000 is worth worrying about. Various subtotals have been omitted as being irrelevant to our analysis and a small rounding error caused by the reformatting of the numbers has been accommodated over the 'intangibles and other' account. The dividend figure in the income statement has had to be calculated from elsewhere since it is not supplied anywhere in the First Quarter report, the published statement ending with net income. Also, the charge for depreciation has been broken out of the figure for cost of sales; it is common practice in the USA to amalgamate the depreci-

Consolidated Statements of Income
Avnet, Inc. & Subsidiaries

First Quarter Ended	Sept. 28, 1984	Sept. 30, 1983
(Thousands except per share data)	(Unaudited)	
Revenues:		
Sales	$432,431	$355,458
Other, net	2,031	4,058
	434,462	359,516
Costs and expenses:		
Cost of sales	313,948	259,479
Selling, shipping, general and administrative	78,228	62,925
Interest	2,912	1,037
	395,088	323,441
Income before income taxes	39,374	36,075
Income taxes	19,477	17,393
Net Income	$ 19,897	$ 18,682
Earnings per share	$ .56*	$ .53
Average shares outstanding	37,518*	35,363

*Average shares outstanding include common equivalent shares attributable to the convertible debenture issued in October, 1983. For purposes of calculating earnings per share, interest on the debentures, after income taxes, has been added back to the net income shown above.

Consolidated Balance Sheets
Avnet, Inc. & Subsidiaries

	Sept. 28, 1984	June 30, 1984
(Thousands)	(Unaudited)	
Assets		
Current Assets:		
Cash	$ 9,280	$ 4,290
Marketable securities	66,829	87,754
Receivables	289,127	285,366
Inventories	439,758	410,662
Other	15,331	10,076
Total current assets	820,325	798,148
Property, plant and equipment, net	75,722	73,066
Intangibles and other assets	42,837	39,557
Total assets	938,884	910,771
Less liabilities		
Current Liabilities:		
Short-term borrowings	2,931	3,116
Accounts payable and accrued expenses	194,431	182,756
Dividends payable	4,412	4,404
Current portion of long-term debt	3,253	3,180
Total current liabilities	205,027	193,456
Long term debt	113,998	113,912
Total liabilities	319,025	307,368
Shareholders' Equity	$619,859	$603,403

NOTES:

1. In October, 1983, the Company issued 8% Convertible Subordinated Debentures due October 1, 2013 in the aggregate amount of $100 million. The Debentures are convertible into Common Stock of the Company at a conversion price of $52 per share.

2. During the first quarter ended September 28, 1984, a total of 865 shares of preferred stock (75 shares of $1.00 Cumulative Convertible Preferred and 790 shares of $2.50 Cumulative Preferred, Series C), were converted into a total of 9,034 shares of Common Stock, resulting in an aggregate increase of $8,169 in Avnet's stated capital and a like decrease in Avnet's capital surplus.

Exhibit 2   Reproduced by permission of Avnet, Inc.

ation figure rather than show it separately, though the depreciation charge is easily identifiable from the statement of changes in financial position.

For some reason, accountants abhor minus signs, preferring to use any one of half a dozen typographical devices to indicate deductions. Usage even of these tends to be inconsistent and an analyst needs to look carefully to see what is being added and what substracted. To avoid this confusion all debits to the income statements, deductions on the

balance sheet and cash outflows will be shown in parentheses.

The technique outlined so far suggests that our cash flow
statement for Avnet should contain the following entries:

Receivables	(3.7)
Inventories	(29.1)
Other assets	(5.2)
Property, plant and equipment	(2.6)
Intangibles and other	(3.5)
Short-term borrowing	(0.2)
Accounts payable and accrued expenses	11.6
Dividend payable	—
Current portion of long-term debt	0.1
Long-term debt	0.1
Shareholders' equity	16.5
Cash increase (decrease)	(16.0)

Of the $16.5m increase in shareholders' equity we know
from the income statement the origin of $15.5m. The differ-
ence of $1.0m we will assume to represent a raising of new
equity. Combining the cash flow derived from the balance
sheet as above with the income statement, and omitting
accounts where there is no change, our full cash flow
becomes:

Sales	432.4
Other revenue	2.0
Cost of sales	(310.7)
Depreciation	(3.2)
Selling, general and administrative expenses	(78.2)
Interest	(2.9)
Income tax	(19.5)
Dividend	(4.4)
Receivables	(3.7)

Inventories	(29.1)
Other assets	(5.2)
Property, plant and equipment	(2.6)
Intangibles and other	(3.5)
Short-term borrowing	(0.2)
Accounts payable and accrued expenses	11.6
Current portion of long-term debt	0.1
Long-term debt	0.1
Shareholders' equity	1.0
Cash increase (decrease)	(16.0)

From now on we need only to make certain adjustments and to decide upon a format which displays with the greatest clarity the full significance of these numbers.

First, the adjustments. The apparent cash outflow in respect of depreciation must be an illusion. It is beyond doubt that Avnet did not write out a cheque for $3.2m payable to depreciation but that having debited this sum to the income statement a corresponding credit was passed to the account for accumulated depreciation. This being only a quarterly statement, that account is not disclosed separately but has been netted against the account for property, plant and equipment, which account increased by $2.6m over the quarter. The clear implication is that the capital expenditure of the company was $2.6m + $3.2m = $5.8m, the apparent cash flows relating to depreciation and property, plant and equipment being added together. At the beginning of the quarter the fixed asset account stood at $73.1m. The depreciation charge reduced it by $3.2m to $69.9m and capital expenditure of $5.8m increased it back to its closing level of $75.5m. Because our cash flow statement balances correctly, it follows that any error or mis-allocation (as in the case of depreciation) must be matched by a balancing error, in this instance in property, plant and equipment.

How to treat 'current portion of long-term debt' is a tricky question. The current portion of long-term indebtedness is not a separate type of financing. It is merely that portion of the long-term debt which is due for repayment in the next 12 months. As we are dealing here with a quarterly statement it makes sense just to combine the apparent cash flow in respect of current portion of long-term debt with that indicated by the change in long-term debt. The objection to this is that the cash flow will not in this event show how much new borrowing was taken and how much repaid, exactly the sort of information a cash flow statement might be expected to provide. An argument could be made for saying that the opening balance on current portion of long-term debt is the cash actually expended during the following year and should be so shown on the cash flow; the closing balance is merely an allocation of long-term debt and should be added back to long-term debt before the year to year difference is calculated. Thus, for example, a company might show:

$m	Year 1	Year 2
Current portion of long-term debt	100	150
Long-term debt	800	1000

The cash flow could read either:

Current portion of long-term debt	50
Long-term debt	200

or, under the argument just given:

Repayment of long-term debt	(100)
Long-term debt raised	350 (i.e. 1000
	+ 150 − 800)

The net effect is, of course, the same in either case. While the latter method is attractive it will certainly not work with quarterly statements since they are not a full 12 months apart and there is no saying when settlement of the current portion shown at the opening of the year takes place. A further difficulty is the common practice of rolling-on loans as they mature. There is no cash flow effect if a loan is renewed or extended and, although banks like to regard this sort of transaction as the repayment of one loan and the drawing of another because this creates the impression that their loan book is current, to depict it on a cash flow statement in this way might be considered misleading. The funding arrangements of multinational companies tend to be extremely complicated and debts are constantly being renewed or amended to an extent an analyst will find it impossible to track accurately.

We can now address the matter of format. Our analysis is being done for our own private purposes and there is no external constraint on the way in which we organize and display the numbers. On the other hand, a logical approach is essential if the statement is to have any validity and here we should go back to our discussion of the asset conversion cycle. The purpose of cash flow analysis is to examine the cash-generating properties of the asset conversion cycle and from there to ascertain the adequacy of the resultant cash flow to meet other cash outflows both obligatory and discretionary. It is no help to have just a list of sources and then a list of uses or applications of cash, since that will tend to cloud over the importance of the asset conversion cycle in the overall pattern of the cash flow. The format recommended is therefore by no means the only legitimate one but it is an enlightening one, which is all that really counts:

Operating/asset	Sales	432.4	
conversion cycle	Receivables	(3.7)	
items	Trading receipts		428.7

	Cost of sales	(310.7)	
	Inventories	(29.1)	
	Payables	11.6	
	Cash purchases		(328.2)
	Cash from asset conversion cycle		100.5
Quasi-operational items	Selling general and admin. expense	(78.2)	
	Other revenue	2.0	
	Other assets	(5.2)	
	Income tax	(19.5)	
	Cash from quasi-operational items		(100.9)
	Cash after quasi-operational items		(0.4)
Financing costs	Interest	(2.9)	
	Dividends	(4.4)	
	Cash financing costs		(7.3)
	Cash after financing costs		(7.7)
Discretionary flows	Capital expenditure	(5.8)	
	Intangibles and other	(3.5)	
	Discretionary cash flow		(9.3)
	Cash after discretionary flow		(17.0)
Financing	Short-term debt	(0.2)	
	Long-term debt	0.2	
	Equity	1.0	
	Total financing		1.0
	Increase (decrease) in cash		(16.0)

In summary, cumulative subtotals on the right:

Cash from asset conversion cycle	100.5	
Cash from quasi-operational items	(100.9)	(0.4)
Financing costs	(7.3)	(7.7)
Discretionary flows	(9.3)	(17.0)
Financing	1.0	(16.0)
Decrease in cash	(16.0)	—

Now some interesting and important features of Avnet's performance over the quarter begin to emerge, details of which are by no means evident from a cursory glance at the figures the company published. First, we can see that the asset conversion cycle is cash generating notwithstanding quite a steep rise in inventories. Trading is sufficiently profitable at the gross profit level (depreciation, of course, being excluded) to finance that increase. An increase in the amount of trade credit taken by Avnet also contributed. Remember, though, that the changes in receivables, inventories and payables do not constitute distinct cash flows on their own; the only actual cash flows so far examined relate to the purchase and sale of the company's product and the cost of direct factory labour.

The asset conversion cycle does not operate in a vacuum and sundry other items arise more or less directly from it. 'Quasi-operational items' is a blanket term used to cover the secondary cash flow deriving from the asset conversion cycle and also included here are some miscellaneous cash flows which may or may not have anything to do with it. These flows together consumed $100.9m leaving a deficit to be financed of $10.4m. Avnet does not appear to be paying its way quite so well as the income statement suggests.

Cash flow analysis often shows up startling results and a word or two of caution is necessary to prevent us leaping to possibly unfounded conclusions. Avnet is a very substantial and complex organisation, but its figures do not really reflect that complexity. There are pitfalls to be avoided and one of them is to imagine that the use of the balance sheet changes and the income statement items inevitably leads to the correct answer. In this instance it would, for example, be sensible to treat the tax figure, taken straight from the income statement, with some circumspection. This figure is naturally the tax reckoned by the company as accrued on the quarter's business activity and it is most unlikely to be the amount actually paid to the US and other tax authorities. Taxation is an enormous subject that defies any sort of full explanation here, but it is worth knowing that US companies usually pay tax quarterly at a rate agreed with the tax authorities and largely based upon the previous year's results, any shortfall or overpayment being made good after the end of the fiscal year. The Texas Instruments example in Chapter 2 demonstrated that taxes are not paid on reported profits in the USA but on tax adjusted profits, and that enormous discrepancies may exist between tax accrued for a period and tax actually paid.

Once again the double entry system comes to our assistance. If tax accrued and tax paid are not the same, the difference between the two must of necessity be reflected in a balance sheet account and will, therefore, be picked up in the cash flow analysis. If part of the tax charge is deferred and cash payments are less than the accrued figure, a credit for the deferral is passed to the deferred tax account on the liabilities side. This increase in a credit side balance sheet account becomes an inflow of cash on the cash flow statement. Of course, there is no real inflow, but if we net the apparent outflow of cash suggested by the income statement with the apparent inflow suggested by the balance sheet, the result will be the actual cash expended. Avnet's tax deferral (or indeed prepaid!) balance sheet accounts seem to be combined into the 'other' category and we cannot pursue the question further.

It is also important that the sections into which the cash flow statement is divided are, to a degree, flexible. Separating precisely those cash flows which reflect the asset conversion cycle from those which do not is an impossible task and there will always be gray areas. Annual Reports are the end result of a large simplification process and that simplification is done with a specific purpose, to present the accounts in accordance with established requirements and management's own desire to communicate (or not) with the shareholders. If we try to use the figures in a totally different way, we may expect to find that a good deal of critical detail eludes us.

In the next section come the cash financing costs that Avnet incurred, in other words the financial costs of being in business. The lumping together of interest and dividends in this fashion is revolutionary and quite distinct from the income statement approach. Interest is regularly perceived as a cost of doing business and is just about everywhere tax deductible. Dividends count as a cost only in books about corporate finance, the rest of the world seeing dividend payments as a distribution of profits. In the Avnet quarterly statement the number for dividends had to be calculated from the notes; it was not shown on the income statement. Cynics might observe that the directors of a company do not like to show the dividends they pay as weakening the company by reducing the equity and that the alternative scenario, of profits accruing to the shareholders being partly paid out in dividends, partly 'reinvested', is a more congenial one. Business law, in the UK and elsewhere, also perceives dividends as a profit allocation rather than an expense and, partly for that reason, restricts the distribution of dividends in excess of a company's accumulated profits.

While the traditional view is arguable, there is a powerful case for viewing dividends as a financing cost. No company has to pay a dividend by law, but the legal aspect is not the point at issue. Companies face compelling pressure from market makers and shareholders to maintain dividend levels, even in the absence of current profits, and cutting the dividend payment is perceived universally as an admission of serious trouble, rightly or wrongly. Most public companies will go to almost any lengths to avoid this horrible embarrassment and the collapse of the share price that goes with it. Only in the most extreme conditions is the payment of a dividend really optional or discretionary.

Not infrequently one sees on the balance sheet an account for dividends accrued or interest accrued arising, as usual, from a difference between the accrued value of these items in the income statement and the cash actually expended during the relevant accounting period. In preparing a cash flow, a difference on the corresponding balance sheet accounts will be treated identically to the way in which deferred taxes are handled. The apparent cash flow suggested by variations between opening and closing balances on these accounts should be added into this section so that the cash as opposed to the accrued value of interest and dividend paid stands revealed. Lack of detail prevents us doing this here and we cannot therefore be too confident of the numbers. It looks, though, as if during the quarter in question Avnet's funding costs were not met by operational cash flows and had instead to be financed externally.

The calculation of capital expenditure has been explained already with reference to the apparent depreciation cash flow. Quite what to make of the $3.5m outflow categorized as the change in 'intangibles and other' it is difficult to say. It is inherently unlikely that the company went out and acquired goodwill, patents or some other intangible asset in isolation. Much more probable is that the figure of $3.5m represents only a part of a bigger transaction. Evidently Avnet purchased something, an investment or a new subsidiary, and probably it paid more than $3.5m; the additional cost is reflected somewhere else in the cash flow, perhaps in capital expenditure, perhaps in the outflows attributed to the increases in receivables and inventory. On this occasion, there is absolutely no way to telling. The existence of this admittedly relatively small apparent cash outflow alerts the reader that a much larger error may have crept unseen into our analysis. Unfortunately, the mystery is not capable of resolution at this stage, so we have to be content with the figure as it stands and note that discretionary cash out-flows of $9.3m were a further drain on the company's bank account and had to be financed. Aspects of the business included up to this point in the cash flow consumed $17.0m of cash, a drain which had to be covered in some way for Avnet to remain in business.

Little need be said about the actual financing. The $1.0m equity increase was deduced from the difference between retained profits for the quarter and the increase in equity on the balance sheet and changes in short- and long-term debt are taken straight from the balance sheets, the change in the current portion of the long-term debt being accounted for as part of the change in long-term debt itself.

Finally, and providing there are no errors in the arithmetic, the change in the cash balance emerges as the bottom line. Cash holdings fell by $16.0m over the quarter and it was this cash reduction which basically financed the net cash outflows resulting from the payment of financing and discretionary outflows during a quarter in which the asset conversion cycle and operation generally yielded no positive cash flow at all.

Is this pattern of cash flow good or bad? And, if it is bad, how bad is it? Furthermore, what kind of pattern of cash flow should one expect to see in a healthy, successful manufacturing company? In the next chapter we shall look at the shortcomings of the analytical method, the process by which the numbers are obtained. Some hints have been given already that the numbers we have calculated, although they balance and cast correctly, may not be strictly accurate.

It is our own experience that when analysing multinational companies, the inaccuracies yielded by the income statement and balance sheet changes method are so extensive that they cannot be overlooked. The format, however, used in the cash flow analysis of Avnet makes perfect logical sense. In effect it is a cash-based income statement, one with all the accruals stripped out, and provided the numbers are accurate it tells precisely what the analyst wants to know about the subject company's cash flow. So, how does one interpret the Avnet statement shown above, assuming that the figures are correct?

If the figures produced by Avnet for the one quarter were typical the company would, from a cash flow point of view, eventually run into trouble. The asset conversion cycle was not sufficiently cash generating during this quarter to pay the financing costs let alone any portion of the discretionary flows, and that is not a pattern which could continue indefinitely. *On balance, a company must generate sufficient cash from the cycle to finance the cycle itself, to pay its taxes and other quasi-operational items, to meet its financing costs and debt repayments and to contribute to capital expenditure.*

It is easy to see the broad truth of this by considering the reverse side of the coin. On balance, external parties, lenders and shareholders will not put money continuously into financing a cycle which consumes more cash than it produces, nor will they willingly contribute cash to pay taxes or financing costs. They may do so on a temporary basis or on occasions. But, as a fundamental rule, these payments have to be funded from internal sources if the company is to remain viable, and attractive to investors and lenders alike.

The repayment of maturing indebtedness and the funding of capital expenditure are more problematic. Older textbooks are strongly influenced by the notion that debt should be reduced until it is all repaid and that it should not be 'refinanced'. Such an attitude may be on the side of the angels, but it does not accord with modern business practice which tolerates more or less perpetual indebtedness in a company so long as the debt level is within the demonstrable or perceived corporate debt capacity of the company and debts are adequately serviced and repaid on their appointed maturities. Similarly, it is hard to be dogmatic about the funding of capital purchases, although a measure of internal funding must be highly desirable; a strong and successful company should be growing from within—and exhibiting the tendency of such companies, if they cease to grow, to replace debt with equity (see Chapter 7 on Sustainable Growth Rate for further discussion of this topic).

What is really more important than rigid rules is the trend. The key question to ask is, 'At what point does the cash flow turn negative?' Below that point, expenditures call for external funding and the lower on the statement that point occurs, the stronger generally the cash flow. With several years of cash flow statements one can observe the cash flow coverage trends and see whether the cash flow is strengthening or weakening.

The next point to make is that it is fruitless to attempt any sort of an analysis on the basis of one set of quarterly results. It is the patterns and the trends that matter and one is not justified in assuming that the type of cash flow shown by Avnet in one quarter is necessarily the one which the company will display in all successive quarters. Multinational companies are enormous organizations, often employing more than 50 000 people in 20 or more countries, and frequently engaged in a variety of businesses some of which may be quite unrelated. Not a few of the largest corporations are tantamount to independent economies greater than those of some countries. General Motors Corporation's sales in 1984 were nearly $84bn, roughly the same as the gross national product of Belgium and nearly three times that of Greece. Even at number 46 in the Fortune 500 list of leading US multinationals, the sales of Coca Cola Corporation at $7.4bn comfortably exceeded the gross national product of Paraguay!

When organizations of this size and complexity are reduced to a handful of numbers much of the detail will almost certainly have been forfeited and one should remember that the apparent accuracy of amounts given to the last dollar or cent derives only from the discipline of the bookkeeping process.

Three years' figures should be the minimum requirement for any serious analysis of a company's performance and even then there are the usual problems of establishing a basis for comparability. In the course of a year or two changes take place in a company's structure, in the number and location of its subsidiaries and associates, possibly even in the range of products manufactured or sold. From one year to the next a company may well have changed to such an extent that two successive sets of statements cannot be compared in any worthwhile or meaningful way.

Cash flow analysis is not exempt from these difficulties since it is only as good as the numbers on which it is founded. It does to some extent cut across many of the foibles of accounting practice by stripping out the accruals with which the accountants have adjusted the cash figures and to that extent it is illuminating. What it does not do is to reconstruct, in all cases and all circumstances, all that we might wish to know about the actual flow of cash.

In the discussion so far it has been assumed, for the sake

of explanation and simplicity, that all the balance sheet changes are the direct result of the routine application of the double entry bookkeeping system to a normal style of selling. This is a larger assumption in the case of major international companies than it is safe to make and in the next chapter we shall explore its validity in some depth.

6
Cash flow and funds flow—
Romping through the maze

Ah, take the Cash and let the Credit go,
Nor heed the rumble of a distant Drum!
Omar Khayyám: Rubaiyat XIII
(trans. Edward Fitzgerald, 4th edition)

Cash flow analysis of the type described in the previous chapter is not a new technique and has indeed some claim to antiquity. A German banker once claimed to us that German banks were using it in the last century, a boast which prompted a French colleague present to exclaim that the French had been using it well before the Revolution! As both France and West Germany have accounting conventions of such complexity that a balance sheet driven cash flow analysis is virtually impossible without a drastic restatement and simplification of the figures, we may be forgiven a measure of scepticism, even as we acknowledge that the measurement and control of cash flow are, and must be, as old as business itself. Cash flow analysis is, in fact, primarily an American technique, and certainly little used outside of the USA for the evaluation and credit assessment of significant companies.

Financial analysis as an art, a science and latterly an industry is largely a twentieth-century phenomenon and it has grown and developed in response to the needs of a rapidly changing and expanding financial market. Modern lenders and investors demand more information than their forebears, and as the required data have been wrung out of companies, sharper skills and more sophisticated techniques have been required to process it.

Serious interest in cash flow has been growing since the 1950s and it received its first acknowledgement from the US accounting bodies in 1963 when a pronouncement known as APB 3 called on companies to publish a 'Statement of Source and Application of Funds' in conjunction with their other financial statements. The new statement was not mandatory and companies that did publish it could choose whether or not to have it audited.

APB 3 was a milestone but it did not signal any revolution in attitudes. The earliest 'funds statements' were little more than catalogues of balance sheet changes which anyone could have calculated for himself, and the statement simply relieved the analyst of some dull number crunching. Little help was given by APB 3 on the key question of format, with the predictable result that there arose considerable variation; most published statements adopted the obvious but uninformative device of listing first the sources of funds and then the applications.

A further step in the acceptance of the concept followed 8 years later in 1971 when APB 19 was promulgated, a new accounting standard which made the publication of a 'Statement of Changes in Financial Position' mandatory and required it to be subject to audit certification along with the other statements. Apart from the variation in the name of the statement and the imposition of the audit requirement, this standard did little more than clarify the prescribed treatment for such awkward transactions as the conversion of debt into equity and the rescheduling of borrowings. It also made clear that the purpose of the statement was to contribute to the understanding of the other two principal statements and that, so far as possible, the entries on the funds flow statement should be capable of reconciliation with numbers elsewhere in the Annual Report.

'Financial position' is a curious concept of ambiguous interpretation. APB 19 deliberately left companies the choice of whether to adopt cash or working capital as the balancing figure, a decision that did not indicate any real desire to see proper cash flow statements. 'Financial position' appears to mean, in this context, the whole balance sheet and the perceived aim of the funds flow statement was to explain how the balance sheet had changed from one reporting date to the next. The injunction of APB 19 to show conversions of debt into equity and debt reschedulings as both sources and applications in the full amount of the transaction when, by the very nature of such transactions, no cash flow actually occurs, lends credence to the belief that the 'Statement of Changes in Financial Position' was not intended to be a cash flow statement at all, but an inane explanation of balance sheet changes.

It does not actually matter very much what the funds flow statement is supposed to be about since it is an open secret that virtually no one ever gives it more than a cursory glance; certainly, few bankers or investors could claim even to have derived anything of use or importance from the study of one of these statements. In theory, the statement is supposed to be giving shareholders critical insights into how capital expenditure and debt repayments were funded, what happened to the proceeds of debt and equity issues, how the company managed to increase working capital and pay a dividend in spite of recording a loss and other such weighty matters. In practice, it is not at all easy to answer even these questions from a published funds flow statement and, to crown it all, these are not the questions that intelligent shareholders should be seeking to answer from the funds flow statement anyway.

All in all, confusion reigns supreme, the accounting bodies have retained the air of mystique which surrounds their profession and fees while the public are kept politely in the dark. A hurried, fleeting look, and one turns the page in search of something more enlightening!

A published funds flow statement is actually a cash flow statement, not unlike that prepared for Avnet in the previous chapter. The format does not much resemble the cash flow format adopted in this book but much of the same information is there, if one knows how to extract it.

In the format we customarily see published, that beginning with profit of some sort followed by the adding back of depreciation, the supremacy of the income statement is acknowledged and confirmed. Profit earned is represented as the primary source of funding for a successful company. This is not exactly untrue but it is a fundamentally misleading and confusing way to describe the process which in this book we have tried to illustrate with the concept of the asset conversion cycle. The expression 'asset conversion cycle' is never to be found in an Annual Report nor does even the idea feature in the commentaries companies publish to accompany the financial data. We do encounter the word 'operations' frequently in Annual Reports. Unfortunately, while 'operations' has something in common with the asset conversion cycle, the two are not at all the same thing.

Cash flow analysis is a powerful tool. It is powerful because it almost unfailingly succeeds in exposing the key mechanism by which a company lives or dies. Cash flows cannot be manipulated by accounting convention and there is virtually no way in which a company can hide significant flows from an analyst who knows how to use cash flow analysis skilfully, except by outright fraud. Cash flow analysis is for these reasons not much liked by companies or their accountants and there is considerable hostility to it in most published work on corporate finance.

The funds flow statements we see in Annual Reports are a relatively recent development and they have seen the light of day only because of pressure from investors, beginning in the 1950s and 1960s. If the international accounting profession had wished to give true and helpful information about corporate cash flows, they would have derived a statement starting not with net income (as in the USA) or profit before tax (as in the UK) but with trading receipts, from which would be deducted trading outgoings. It would, in other words, have been a summary of cash movements and the numbers would have borne only a passing resemblance to those given by the income statements and balance sheet changes method. Such a statement would have been readily comprehended by ordinary investors and would have rendered the job of the analyst much less demanding.

In preparing funds flow statements, the principal objective would seem to be to come up with numbers which can be checked by reference to the other statements, the clear implication being that the funds flow statement is intended to explain changes in the balance sheet. There is no other convincing explanation for the convoluted construction of funds flow statements. The finished product is in practice well nigh incomprehensible to the lay person as few readers can perform the mental gymnastics necessary to understand how the numbers work. Published funds flow statements are a near complete waste of time except in so far as they can be rearranged to tell us what we really want to know, how much cash the business is generating from internal sources and how adequate it is to meet compulsory and discretionary outgoings.

Let us consider an actual example of a funds flow statement and use it to address two issues which we shall be exploring for the rest of this chapter. How can the information given in the statement be rearranged to make it more informative, and is the exercise worth doing at all as we already know how to construct a cash flow by the technique demonstrated with Avnet?

We shall use the latest figures published by a highly

Consolidated profit and loss account

For the year ended 31 March 1985

Electrocomponents plc

Note		1985	1984
		£000	£000
2	**Turnover**	164,024	129,300
	Cost of sales	(100,948)	(78,983)
	Gross profit	63,076	50,317
	Distribution costs	(8,364)	(6,395)
	Administrative expenses	(25,745)	(22,218)
	Other interest receivable and similar income	1,090	873
4	Interest payable and similar charges	(470)	(353)
5	**Profit on ordinary activities before taxation**	29,587	22,224
7	Tax on profit on ordinary activities	(13,087)	(9,890)
	Profit on ordinary activities after taxation	16,500	12,334
	Extraordinary items	—	(598)
		16,500	11,736
	Minority interests	(153)	42
8	**Profit for the financial year**	16,347	11,778
	Dividends paid and proposed	(5,351)	(4,076)
	Retained profit for the financial year	10,996	7,702
	Retained profit at beginning of year	34,496	26,794
	Retained profit carried forward	45,492	34,496
9	Earnings per share	16.0p	12.1p

The notes on pages 17 to 27 form part of these accounts

13

Exhibit 3(a)   Reproduced by permission of Electrocomponents plc

Consolidated statement of source and application of funds

For the year ended 31 March 1985

Electrocomponents plc

	1985 £000	1985 £000	1984 £000	1984 £000
Source of funds				
Profit on ordinary activities before taxation and extraordinary items, after minority interests		29,434		22,266
Adjustments for items not involving the movement of funds:				
Depreciation and amortisation	1,858		1,297	
Revaluation deficit	152		—	
Surplus/(deficit) on sale of tangible fixed assets	17		(7)	
Profit/(loss) attributable to minority interests	153		(42)	
Exchange adjustment	54		15	
		2,234		1,263
Funds generated from operations		31,668		23,529
Funds from other sources				
Proceeds of sale of tangible fixed assets	125		99	
Government grant	—		3,600	
Increase in creditors:				
amounts falling due after more than one year	—		194	
		125		3,893
		31,793		27,422
Application of funds				
Purchase of fixed assets	5,078		9,737	
Tax paid	7,965		7,260	
Dividend paid	4,383		3,362	
Decrease in creditors:				
amounts falling due after more than one year	34		—	
Purchase of additional 5 per cent share of subsidiary	—		27	
		17,460		20,386
Increase in working capital		14,333		7,036
Components of increase in working capital				
Stocks		8,213		6,740
Debtors		6,690		8,120
Creditors: amounts falling due within one year		(844)		(2,610)
Movement in net liquid funds:				
Increase/(decrease) in cash at bank and in hand	1,463		(3,582)	
Increase in overdraft	(1,189)		(1,632)	
		274		(5,214)
		14,333		7,036

Exhibit 3(b)   Reproduced by permission of Electrocomponents plc successful British company engaged in a similar range of business, Electrocomponents plc. This company's statement of source and application of funds will serve us well since its layout is fairly representative of those currently being produced by British companies in the wake of the 1981 Companies Act, and with only a few minor adjustments the layout would not look out of place in a US multinational's Annual Report. Exhibit 3 shows the consolidated profit and loss account for the year to 31 March 1985 and the consolidated statement of source and application of funds for the same period.

Look first at the section entitled 'Source of funds', a series of entries whose sum is given next to the subsequent subheading 'Funds generated from operations'. One might expect to find a list of operating sources but in fact one finds nothing of the kind; the principal source is said to be 'Profit on ordinary activities before taxation and extra-ordinary items, after minority interests', a curious concept which does not even appear on the profit and loss account. It is derived from the 'Profit on ordinary activities before taxation' less 'Minority interests' (29 587 − 153). The other sources listed are not in fact sources at all but 'Adjustments for items not involving the movement of funds', that is, non-funds entries made to the profit and loss account and, in this case, all deducted from income before the figure of 29 434 was struck. As these non-funds entries have already been deducted, they have to be added back to the profit figure to give us the funds content of the profit, the amount of the profit figure which represents funds flow.

We have used the word 'funds' in the last paragraph because that is the word that the statement uses. A glance lower down the statement shows that funds means no more or less than 'working capital' and, as these two expressions are not normally synonymous, it is hard to avoid the impression that the word 'funds' is employed because to the uninitiated it suggests 'cash'. If companies came out openly and published statements of source and application of working capital, it would not perhaps be long before even the most unbusinesslike of shareholders began to wonder why anyone should be the least bit interested in where the working capital came from or went to.

The presentation of the 'source of funds' is another obfuscation. Only one of the adjustments (minority interests) can be matched to an entry on the profit and loss account, so we have little idea of the extent to which each entry on the profit and loss account is a 'funds' or a cash number. It is rather like the old parlour game of putting a couple of dozen objects on a tray and then, when everyone has had a minute to look, surreptitiously removing a few objects and leaving the assembled company to guess from what is left which objects have been abstracted. Except that in the parlour game one finds out the answer at the end; with funds flow statements one stays in the dark!

Apart from the figure for 'Depreciation and amortisation' which could quite reasonably have been broken out separately on the profit and loss account, none of the adjustments is of the slightest interest in itself and readers would have been much better served by a funds adjusted version of the profit and loss account totalling to the same figure 31 668. This might have looked something like this:

Turnover	164 024	
Cost of sales	(99 090)	(i.e. −100 948 + 1858)
Distribution costs	(8 364)	
Administrative expenses	(25 745)	
Other income	1 313	(i.e. 1090 + 152 + 17 + 54)
Interest expense	(470)	
	31 668	

Such numbers are altogether more comprehensible and informative. There is now no adjusting or adding back, simply a list of funds flows we may use to investigate the asset conversion cycle, our main objective in studying cash flow data.

'Funds from other sources' need not detain us long since the only entry is for the proceeds of tangible fixed assets. Alert readers will have noticed that there was a surplus of 17 on the sale of these fixed assets. The question immediately arises of whether 125 was actually what the company received in cash from the sale or whether it was $125 + 17 = 142$ or even $125 - 17 = 108$ as one might be forgiven for concluding.

Actually, 125 is the correct figure. The loss on the sale is essentially included no less than three times in the statement and it needs a keen eye to avoid confusion. The 17 loss is already there in the top line of 29 434 and is added back as an adjustment, both entries being non-funds. The sale proceeds figure of 125 includes, therefore, the 17 loss and we may be tolerably certain that the book value of assets disposed of was in fact 142.

It should not be assumed that the quoted funds figure is always correct. Had the adjustments not been made in the 'Source of funds' section, it would have been necessary to show the loss in with the proceeds of the sale and the figure of 142 would have been quoted, possibly but not necessarily with a caption indicating that this was the book value of the assets disposed of.

Total funds generated come to 31 793, and the remainder of the statement is just a list of the uses or applications to which these funds were put. The order of capital expenditure, tax, dividend, creditors and then working capital items is neither logical or informative and, as often, care has to be taken with the use of the parentheses to indicate negatives. Although it does not say so specifically, the 'Application of funds' section is deducted from the sources to yield the 'Increase in working capital'. All the items in the section are outflows and would under our scheme be marked as negatives.

Similarly, the 'Components of increase in working capital' are highly confusing in that the positive numbers for stocks and debtors represent increases in those accounts and therefore outflows of cash, while the negative figure for 'Creditors: amounts falling due within one year' represents a decrease in working capital and hence an increase in the liability and a cash inflow. Likewise the increase in the overdrafts and the increase in cash balances is shown as positive. All this is arithmetically correct, and the statement balances with footings of 14 333 which is the increase in working capital over the year.

As a final shot, we may observe that it is impossible to derive the figure 14 333 from the balance sheet (see Exhibit 4) since the apparent change in working capital is not 14 333 but $44 928 - 37 058 = 7870$. The funds flow figures for changes in stocks and debtors are the same as the balance sheet changes but the same is not true of creditors and the note explaining the breakdown of creditors (see Exhibit 5) gives us no help at all.

It is quite extraordinary that shareholders are expected to make sense of a statement which purports to explain the sources and application of funds (that is, apparently, working capital) when the stated increase in working capital is nearly twice the amount that one would expect by looking at the balance sheet! No wonder that source and application of funds statements receive so little attention.

The Electrocomponents statement of source and application of funds tells the reader that profit adjusted for depreciation and a few other insignificant items was virtually the only source of funds or working capital during the year, and that slightly over half of these new funds went on capital expenditure, taxes and dividends. Working capital increased by 14 333 and that was essentially accounted for

Consolidated balance sheet

At 31 March 1985

Electrocomponents plc

Note		1985 £000	1985 £000	1984 £000	1984 £000
	Fixed assets				
10	Tangible assets		17,960		14,976
	Current assets				
12	Stocks	36,647		28,434	
13	Debtors	39,043		32,353	
14	Investments	26		26	
	Cash at bank and in hand	5,588		4,125	
		81,304		64,938	
15	**Creditors: amounts falling due within one year**	(36,376)		(27,880)	
	Net current assets		44,928		37,058
	Total assets less current liabilities		62,888		52,034
16	**Creditors: amounts falling due after more than one year**		(160)		(194)
17	**Provisions for liabilities and charges**		(3,359)		(3,732)
	Net assets		59,369		48,108
	Capital and reserves				
18	Called up share capital		10,192		10,192
	Share premium account		2,976		2,976
19	Other reserves		294		191
	Profit and loss account		45,492		34,496
20	Minority interests		415		253
			59,369		48,108

These accounts were approved
by the board of directors on 10 June 1985
R A Marler
J L Robinson
Directors

The notes on pages 17 to 27 form part of these accounts

Exhibit 4   Reproduced by permission of Electrocomponents plc

Notes to the accounts   continued

15   Creditors: amounts falling due within one year

	Group		Company	
	1985	1984	1985	1984
	£000	£000	£000	£000
Bank loans and overdrafts	3,055	1,866	165	43
Trade creditors	11,563	10,431	—	—
Amounts owed to group companies	—	—	242	142
Other creditors including taxation and social security	15,886	9,988	2,406	1,936
Accruals and deferred income	2,152	2,843	39	—
Proposed dividend	3,720	2,752	3,720	2,752
	36,376	27,880	6,572	4,873

Trade creditors comprises:				
Capital projects	293	983	—	—
Other	11,270	9,448	—	—
	11,563	10,431	—	—

Other creditors including taxation and social security comprises:				
Corporation tax	13,507	8,012	2,406	1,836
Other taxes	1,854	1,768	—	—
Social security	172	186	—	—
	15,533	9,966	2,406	1,836
Other creditors	353	22	—	100
	15,886	9,988	2,406	1,936

16   Creditors: amounts falling due after more than one year
Group

	1985	1984
	£000	£000
Term loan	141	160
Other creditors	19	34
	160	194

The term loan represents amounts repayable after more than one year at an interest rate of
2 per cent above the inter bank base rate. The loan is secured by an equitable deposit of the title
deeds to the leasehold land and premises located in the Republic of Ireland.

Exhibit 5   Reproduced by permission of Electrocomponents plc

by the increases in stocks and debtors. There were some relatively minor movements over creditors, cash and overdrafts accounts. All in all, we are little the wiser!

Happily, our predicament is not hopeless. It is quite easy, especially with such an uncomplicated statement, to rearrange all these numbers in the format we devised in the last chapter. This format, it will be recalled, was specifically constructed to illustrate the working of the asset conversion cycle and to establish the adequacy of cash generated by operations to meet the other cash expenditures of the company during the year.

What the statement of source and application of funds does give the analyst is a list of cash inflows and outflows and these he is at liberty to rearrange into a more informative and enlightening pattern. Electrocomponents' cash flow for the year to 31 March 1985 would look like this:

Operating/asset conversion cycle items	Turnover	164 024	
	Debtors	(6 690)	
	Trading receipts		157 334
	Cost of sales	(99 090)	
	Stocks	(8 213)	
	Creditors	844	
	Cash purchases		(106 459)
	Cash from asset conversion cycle		50 875
Quasi-operational items	Distribution and administrative costs	(34 109)	
	Other income	1 313	
	Tax	(7 965)	
	Cash from quasi-operational items		(40 761)
	Cash after quasi-operational items		10 114

Financing costs	Interest	(470)	
	Dividends	(4 383)	
	Cash financing costs		(4 853)
	Cash after financing costs		5 261
Discretionary flows	Capital expenditure	(5 078)	
	Long-term creditors	(34)	
	Disposals	125	
	Discretionary cash flow		(4 987)
	Cash after discretionary flow		274
Financing	Overdraft		1 189
	Increase in cash		1 463

In summary with cumulative subtotals again on the right:

Cash from asset conversion cycle	50 875	
Cash from quasi-operational items	(40 761)	10 114
Financing costs	(4 853)	5 261
Discretionary flows	(4 987)	274
Financing flows	1 189	1463
Increase in cash	1463	—

This statement, although we have reason to believe that not all the numbers are entirely accurate, is much more useful than the published statement and the strength of Electo-components' cash flow is now clear for all to see. All the subtotals are positive and cash generated by the asset conversion cycle was sufficient to meet all the quasi-operational items, the financing costs and the discretionary flows. There was some additional overdraft borrowing which added directly to the cash account. For a young and fast-growing company whose sales had shot up to £164.0m from £129.3m the previous year, this is a remarkable performance. Provided Electrocomponents can continue this pattern it is most unlikely to find itself having debt servicing problems and new money will probably be available in abundance to finance further expansion plans.

Reference has been made several times to our uncertainty about the accuracy of the numbers we are working with and some words of explanation are in order here. Two methods of cash flow construction have been illustrated, both producing in the end a cash flow statement in the same format, one based on the income statement and the balance sheet changes (the Avnet example), the other on the income statement and the published funds statement.

The two methods invariably give different results for the same company and both cannot be right since a company's cash flow over a period is a matter of objective reality not susceptible to retroactive manipulation without downright falsification. It is our experience from looking at hundreds of cash flow statements from multinational companies that the spreading of funds flow statements as just described yields greatly superior results in almost all cases. The balance sheet changes approach, which is well known at least among US analysts, works tolerably well for relatively simple companies that do not have extensive overseas activities or a complicated network of subsidiaries engaged in a range of diverse activities. It does not work well for multinationals. The buying and selling of subsidiaries or their reclassification as investments valued at cost or under the equity method wreaks havoc with the balance sheet changes method. As most multinational companies are, to some extent, in a constant state of corporate reorganization, the technique becomes severely limited in its application.

The balance sheet changes method starts from the premise that there is a close link between individual balance sheet changes and cash flow. So far we have assumed that, if receivables increase over the period, the change represents the difference between purported sales and cash receipts, and that in preparing our cash flow statement the apparent cash flow associated with the change in receivables is an operational item to be placed near the top of our cash flow format.

This assumption breaks down in the face of the realities of modern business and accounting and there are at least two common occurrences which render it invalid. The first is a movement in foreign currency exchange rates. An exporting company almost inevitably has monies owing to it in foreign currencies and such receivables have to be valued in the domestic currency for incorporation into the published figures. This valuation is done normally at the exchange rate prevailing at the end of the period and that rate will not be the same for successive periods. If the US dollar is appreciating over time, an American company with a constant volume of foreign currency debtors will show a progressively smaller dollar value for that asset and the published accounts will indicate a falling level of receivables. This 'unrealized translation loss' will be passed to a special reserve fund in the equity section of the balance sheet and will not, as in earlier times, be debited to the profit and loss account. The balance sheet changes method will pick up the reduction in receivables as a cash inflow and the reduction in equity as a cash outflow. Both are, of course, fictitious and should cancel each other out.

Information will not, however, be available to the analyst to effect this cancellation since the amount of the change in the receivables account attributable to foreign exchange factors will not be disclosed. The total foreign exchange translation gain or loss will be calculable, but the composition of that number, the individual balance sheet accounts to which it relates, will not be disclosed and there will be no way to tell what portion of it relates to receivables rather than to inventory, fixed assets, cash balances, borrowings or other assets or liabilities.

The funds flow statement, if it has been prepared properly, will have made this adjustment. Instead of the balance sheet change for receivables as an inflow and an equity adjustment as an outflow, the change in receivables shown should be the true operational change and the apparent change in equity should not appear at all. In other words, the balance sheet changes method and the funds flow method would yield identical results if sufficient information were provided to make all the adjustments necessary to the balance sheet changes figures. That method produces a 'raw' statement containing a number of non-cash errors which should cancel out one against the other. In the funds flow statement some, though never all, of these cancellations have been effected and the cash flow derived from the funds flow will, to the extent that non-cash errors have been eliminated, yield a superior analysis.

Unfortunately, there is resistance among accountants to making too many of these eliminations, because the further one goes along this route the less closely one can reconcile the funds flow statement with the balance sheet. The 'Statement of Changes in Financial Position' is regularly perceived not as a cash flow document but as an explanation of the changes which have taken place in the balance sheet, and if that is the chief object of the statement, investors are likely to be upset at finding that none of the numbers in it can be reconciled to the actual changes in the balance sheet.

Just as the sources of funds presentation is dominated by the figure for income, to which sundry non-cash adjustments are made, so much of the rest of the statement is dominated by the balance sheet. Published funds flow statements are an uneasy compromise between a desire to present true cash flow information and a persistent and rather inglorious clinging to the accrual driven numbers of the older traditional statements. Popular attention still focuses on these statements and funds flow can only be allowed to add further insight and illustration. The funds flow must not be allowed to challenge and suggest inadequacies in the balance sheet and most certainly should not be seen to undermine the profit calculation!

APB 19 is quite specific on this point when it says:

> The amount of working capital or cash provided from operations is not a substitute for or an improvement upon properly determined net income as a measure of the results of operations and the consequent effect on financial position .... The Board strongly recommends that isolated statistics of working capital or cash provided from operations, especially per share amounts, not be presented in annual reports to shareholders.

Consolidation and deconsolidation of subsidiaries is a very thorny problem for exactly the same reason. When a company acquires an investment of more than 50 per cent in another company, the usual practice is to consolidate the two entities by adding together their assets and liabilities into one consolidated balance sheet. This practice, which is now enshrined in the laws of most industrial countries (with the exception of West Germany where only domestic subsidiaries are consolidated), became common only in the 1930s and was specifically intended to prevent a company hiding its true position by showing only investments on the balance sheet as the sole token of what might be an extensive business empire. To show a holding in another company as an investment at cost or under the equity method, as is usual when the holding is less than 50 per cent, also of course keeps the inferior company's borrowing off the balance sheet and reduces the apparent level of gearing. Full consolidation is supposed to give a clearer picture of the comprehensive state of a company's affairs.

In cash flow terms, when Company X acquires some portion of Company Y, there is a cash outflow equal to that portion of the purchase price which was for cash settlement. If settlement is by shares, warrants, debenture loan stock or some other non-cash method, there may be no cash flow at all. Sadly, the honest truth seems to be an embarrassment to many companies who cannot bring themselves to show on their funds flow statements the actual amount of cash paid for the new acquisition. Indeed, it is not unusual to see a different amount, substantially lower, representing only part of the acquisition, as though in buying the new operation the separate parts of the balance sheet were purchased individually.

The key to this anomaly lies in the consolidation process. Acquisition of a new consolidated company boosts the levels of all the working capital accounts as the receivables, inventory and payables of the two companies are combined. These increases will be picked up in the construction of a balance sheet changes driven cash flow as operating flows, something we know full well they are not. It is impossible to reconcile the tension between the two aims of a funds flow statement, to list the balance sheet changes and to show the actual cash flows accurately. Either one retains the actual year to year balance sheet changes on the funds flow statement, in which case the purchase price of the new company will be incorrect as shown, or one shows the correct acquisition price and confuses investors with numbers for changes in balance sheet working capital accounts which do not correspond to the actual changes. An unenviable choice!

Yet a further complication lies in the treatment of goodwill and the capital assets acquired. Goodwill is merely the difference between the book value of assets purchased and the actual amount paid. The extra cost is an embarrassment to the double entry system; as there is understandable reluctance to charge it to income it gets put on to the balance sheet as an asset. Accountants justify this by claiming that it represents an 'intangible asset'—the reputation and name of the company taken over—and the same argument is handy in resisting pressure for rapid amortisation of goodwill, a process that obviously reduces reported profits in the early years after an acquisition. The *Financial Times* reported in October 1985, in a Lex article entitled 'Bad news on goodwill', that the shares of a leading company had fallen in value on the London Stock Exchange in response to the announcement of the new 'tougher' accounting policy requiring all goodwill to be written off to income over a fixed period.

Evidently some investors and market makers did not understand that although reported profits clearly would be lower, the effect on the actual operations of the company itself would be precisely zero; the entries passed would be purely book entries and the amortization of goodwill is not an expense allowable for tax in the UK.

The purchase of goodwill is often shown on funds flow statements for all the world as if the company had one day decided that it was a commodity they could use in greater quantity and had bought some over the phone! It appears, of course, only as a consequence of the principles governing the construction of funds flows. The purchase price of a company is effectively divided, like all Gaul, into three parts: the cost of the working capital purchased is included in the working capital reconciliation, the cost of the fixed assets (less the long-term liabilities assumed) is included in capital expenditure, and the balance, for which nothing tangible has been obtained, is said to represent the purchase of goodwill.

It is not necessary to enter into the complexities of what happens when subsidiaries are sold. Suffice it to say that the treatment in published funds flow is similarly complicated.

A rather better funds flow statement than that published by Electrocomponents is shown in Exhibit 6. National Semiconductor Corporation's funds flow is far from perfect, as we shall see, but once again, the blame can hardly be laid at the door of the company because management is constrained by the accounting rules governing presentation and format. The techniques for converting this statement into our own format are exactly the same as before, the usual care being required to distinguish inflow from outflow and to eliminate non-cash items.

The first line of the sources is 'Earnings (Loss) before

Consolidated Statements of Changes in Financial Position
(in millions)

Years ended May 31,	1985	1984	1983
Operations:			
Earnings (Loss) before extraordinary credit	$ 34.4	$ 56.2	$ (14.2)
Items not requiring the current use of cash:			
Depreciation and amortization	143.3	115.1	102.2
Deferred income taxes — noncurrent	23.1	33.3	(23.4)
Total generated by operations before extraordinary credit	200.8	204.6	64.6
Extraordinary credit	8.8	7.8	—
Total generated by operations	209.6	212.4	64.6
Changes in items affecting operations:			
Receivables	19.7	(73.4)	20.8
Inventories	(0.3)	(49.1)	28.3
Prepaid expenses	(10.7)	(2.4)	(0.9)
Deferred income tax benefits — current	(33.1)	(14.8)	(4.8)
Accounts payable	(43.1)	72.8	(7.9)
Accrued expenses	(17.1)	18.6	0.3
Income taxes	(1.6)	7.8	2.3
Deferred income on shipments to distributors	6.7	29.5	6.4
Other current liabilities	5.9	(1.0)	(2.2)
Other noncurrent assets and liabilities	(9.1)	(1.9)	7.5
Cash generated by operations	$ 126.9	$ 198.5	$ 114.4
Investments:			
Purchase of property, plant and equipment	$(400.6)	$(278.1)	$(110.5)
Retirements of property, plant and equipment at net book value	16.6	11.8	9.4
Acquisition of Data Terminal Systems	—	—	(48.6)
Cash required by investment activities	$(384.0)	$(266.3)	$(149.7)
Financing:			
Net short-term borrowings and current portion of long-term debt	$ 20.8	$ (15.9)	$ (27.2)
Net short-term borrowings reclassified as long-term	200.0	9.8	28.0
Long-term borrowings	9.7	0.6	24.8
Long-term debt — decreases	(8.0)	(125.3)	(11.5)
Issuance of common stock under employee benefit plans	19.0	21.8	13.2
Net proceeds from common stock offering	—	197.6	—
Cash generated by financing	$ 241.5	$ 88.6	$ 27.3
Total cash generated (required)	$(15.6)	$ 20.8	$ (8.0)

See accompanying Notes to consolidated financial statements.

Exhibit 6(a)   Reproduced by permission of National Semiconductor Corporation

Consolidated Statements of Operations

(in millions, except per share amounts)

Years ended May 31,	1985	1984	1983
Net sales	$1,787.5	$1,655.1	$1,210.5
Operating costs:			
Cost of sales	1,258.5	1,146.3	928.4
Research and development	204.6	158.5	114.7
Selling, general and administrative	264.9	247.6	167.2
Plant closing costs	—	—	9.0
Total operating costs	1,728.0	1,552.4	1,219.3
Operating income (loss)	59.5	102.7	(8.8)
Interest, net	7.7	1.3	14.1
Earnings (Loss) before income taxes and extraordinary credit	51.8	101.4	(22.9)
Income taxes (credit)	17.4	45.2	(8.7)
Earnings (Loss) before extraordinary credit	34.4	56.2	(14.2)
Extraordinary credit—tax benefit resulting from utilization of operating loss carryforwards	8.8	7.8	—
Net earnings (loss)	$ 43.2	$ 64.0	$ (14.2)
Earnings (Loss) per share:			
Earnings (Loss) before extraordinary credit	$0.38	$0.66	$(0.20)
Extraordinary credit	0.10	0.09	—
Net earnings (loss)	$0.48	$0.75	$(0.20)
Weighted average common and common equivalent shares	89.8	85.3	70.6

See accompanying Notes to consolidated financial statements.

Exhibit 6(b)   Reproduced by permission of National Semiconductor
Corporation

extraordinary credit', a post-tax profit subtotal, as laid down by the US accounting standard APB 19. The amount is taken straight from the income statement. To this are added back the usual adjustments in respect of depreciation and deferred taxes. The latter adjustment tells us that although the company suffered a tax charge of $17.4m in fiscal 1985; it passed a credit of $23.1m to the deferred tax liability account and would therefore appear to have received back from the IRS the sum of $5.7m. In fact, this is not the whole story since there are further tax items on the statement which must all be added together to find the amount actually paid in cash. The fact that no less than five entries on the income statement and funds flow statement relate to tax is an indication that the actual sum paid is considered of no importance whatever, the focus of attention being on at least partially reconciling all the different balance sheet tax accounts.

This word 'funds' is happily absent from the funds flow though its absence almost shrieks out from the expression 'Total generated by operations.' Most interestingly, NSC acknowledges that the changes in working capital items are for the most part true operating items and they are included above the line 'Cash generated by operations', but whereas the changes in the balance sheet ought truly to be said to derive from the operations of the business, the statement implies that the numbers in some way affect the operations, witness the phrase 'Changes in items affecting operations'. The apparent hubris might seem a small matter, but it betrays the way many people view accounting numbers.

In the 'Investments' section, the disposals of fixed assets are shown at book values, an admission that any profit or loss has been quite shamelessly included in the earnings figure and not adjusted for. By no stretch of the imagination is a gain on the sale of a factory an operational item.

Finally, under 'Financing' it is evident that again balance sheet reconciliation is the driving force rather than the exposition of actual cash flow. Changes in the current position of the long-term debt are not cash flows in their own right for reasons already explained, and the reclassification of short-term borrowings as long term has no cash flow associated with it at all.

NSC's statement is fairly typical of those now being produced by US multinationals though there is considerable variety of detail in the format. Whereas very strict and complicated rules govern the writing of the income statement to prevent the manipulation of net income, little guidance or instruction is given on the formatting of funds flow statements. One readily concludes that this is purely because no decisions are made on the basis of the numbers and more particularly the subtotals in that statement. It is rare to see even the cash flow operations figure quoted on the highlights page of an Annual Report and, when it does appear, sometimes it includes the changes in working capital items and sometimes it doesn't!

There is a more complex example of a funds flow statement given in Chapter 8, where we have examined Revlon, an ailing giant of the cosmetics industry that recently fell prey to corporate predators. It is recommended that readers work through the analysis in detail, not so much for what the analysis reveals about Revlon, as to learn at first hand how even when the accounting conventions have been scrupulously followed the result can be extremely difficult to understand and analyse. It is also an illustration of how patient and relatively uncomplicated analysis can shed light on an otherwise incomprehensible forest of numbers.

Some readers may be concluding by this time that analysis of companies via the funds flow statement is a fundamentally flawed procedure, so complex as to be not worth the effort. That would be a defeatist attitude and not justified by some broad truths and by recent developments. First of all, the quality of published funds flow statements has improved enormously in the last 5 years, both in the UK and the USA. Additionally, companies in many other countries are starting to find that, if they wish to raise money internationally, it is easier if they produce the kind of numbers that British and particularly American lenders and investors are used to seeing, and that includes funds flow statements. Standards of disclosure are, by American standards, extremely low in many countries, not least those where the published figures form the basis of tax assessments, but times are changing and even in such places as West Germany, Denmark and Japan, where funds flows were never published before, the larger companies are starting to concede the point.

Books written quite recently advise that relying on the funds flow statement is always dangerous and naïve, and they often recommend a much more laborious method of cash flow analysis commonly known as 'transaction analysis'. The essence of this technique is to construct a worksheet showing the opening and closing balances on all the balance sheet accounts, and then to try to reconstruct all the entries made during the year by working through the income statement and the notes. While this is an impressive and incisive technique wholly in the spirit of this book, it is of little practical value for several reasons.

The main difficulty is that it is vexing and time consuming. Each year has to be done separately and it takes quick wits and a sharp pencil to do one year of a large company's accounts in under an hour. The advent of the 1981 Companies Act, which has relegated even more information to the notes, has made the process more difficult for British companies and we believe that this approach can in practice only be an academic exercise, so difficult have the accountants made it to effect transaction analysis quickly and efficiently.

By complete contrast, the spreading or 'runnering' of funds flow statements and their adaptation into a more suitable form for sensible analysis is easy to computerize, and once the program is set up it is no problem to learn how to put in the numbers. The computer should be programmed merely to rearrange the entries and to add the subtotals in line with the format recommended, or any other format which the user feels is helpful in illustrating the workings of the company under review.

Exhibit 7 shows an input form which could be used for the purpose. This, or a similar model, can be built on a worksheet business analysis program such as Multiplan or Lotus 1−2−3 and the analyst has only to put in the numbers from the income statement and the funds flow, more or less as he finds them, and the computer will do the rest. Care should be taken to show inflow as positive and outflows as negative numbers and to ensure that the sum of all numbers input, excluding the totals, is equal to zero. It will not matter if some items do not fit the frame but these have to be accommodated in the most suitable place so that they are shown correctly on the final cash flow. The program should obviously add together all the tax-related lines, and so to that extent it makes no difference on to which of the tax-related lines any particular tax number is put.

The product of a program of this type will not be perfect until the quality of published funds flow takes a quantum leap forward, and the problems associated with foreign exchange and consolidation will remain problems so long as accountants permit the confusion to persist. Almost inevitably there will be items which do not fit easily on the statement; very often there are non-cash items which properly do not belong on the statement but alert us that other supposedly cash numbers on the funds flow are actually corrupted by accruals. Other peculiarities may result from something incurred in the nature of the business. Beware particularly of extraordinary losses. Write-offs of plant and inventory are not cash flows and if the loss appears on the funds flow there must be a corresponding fictitious cash inflow, possibly concealed in the reconciliation of inventory or in the catch-all 'others' category. Sales of fixed assets, if deemed to generate extraordinary loss, are in all cases cash inflows unless the company actually pays another party to relieve it of the subject assets, which is not a common occurrence. The difficulties can be exaggerated, however. Analysts have become inured to dealing with published statements containing large doses of assumption and surmise, and they do not normally reject the basic statements because they are partial, limited and possibly distorted. The same should apply to cash flow analysis. It is the insight which the analysis gives that is important and total accuracy is not usually essential. Inaccuracy is natur-

Spread Sheet
For Statements of Sources and Application of Funds

NAME:

CURRENCY:

BASE YEAR:

SOURCES OF FUNDS   YEAR

SALES					
COST OF GOODS SOLD					
DEPRECIATION - PLANT					
AMORTIZATION/DEPLETION					
OPERATING EXPENSE (SGA)					
DEPRECIATION - OTHER					
OTHER INCOME					
INTEREST EXPENSE					
OTHER EXPENSE					
TAXES					
DEFERRED TAXES					
MINORITY INTEREST					
Adjustments - plant					
Adjustments - investments					
Extraordinary Gains					
Extraordinary Losses					
•					
•					
NET INCOME					
DEPRECIATION/AMORTIZATION					
DEFERRED TAXES					
GAIN/LOSS ON SALE OF FIXED ASSETS					
EQUITY IN PROFIT OF ASSOCIATES					
MINORITY INTEREST					
Other non - cash items					
•					
•					
DISPOSAL OF FIXED ASSETS					
INCREASE IN LTD					
INCREASE IN COMMON STOCK					
INCREASE IN PREFERRED STOCK					
Decrease in other assets					
Increase in other liabilities					
Other sources					
•					
•					
•					
TOTAL SOURCES OF FUNDS					

Exhibit 7(a)

ally misleading and should, within reason, be minimized for the best results to be attained.

How should the information garnered from cash flow analysis be put to the service of lenders and investors?

NAME:

USES OF FUNDS	YEAR				
DIVIDENDS - COMMON					
DIVIDENDS - PREFERRED					
PURCHASE OF FIXED ASSETS					
INVESTMENTS					
REDUCTION IN LTD					
CONVERSION OF DEBT					
PURCHASE OF TREASURY STOCK					
Increase in other assets					
Decrease in other liabilities					
Other uses					
•					
•					
•					
TOTAL USES					
INCREASE (DECREASE) IN W/C					
CHANGES IN WORKING CAPITAL					
CASH					
NEAR CASH ITEMS					
ACCOUNTS RECEIVABLE					
INVENTORY					
PREPAYMENTS					
NOTES PAYABLE					
CPLTD					
ACCOUNTS PAYABLE					
ACCRUED EXPENSES					
DIVIDENDS PAYABLE					
TAXES PAYABLE					
Other working capital items					
•					
•					
•					
DECREASE (INCREASE) IN W/C					

Exhibit 7(b)

Putting the funds flow through a computer is only the first step and one should no more be mesmerized by the result than one should take off one's hat to the literal meaningfulness of the balance sheet and income statement. Cash flow analysis is a tool and a means to an end and it does not necessarily supplant other analysis.

Supporters of cash flow sometimes go overboard in their enthusiasm, and the academic industry, no friend to revolutionary criticism of the accounting profession, has on occasions attacked the technique because too much is claimed for it. A favourite target is the claim sometimes propounded that cash flow numbers give a better indication than the traditional profit figures of those companies likely to outperform the market or alternatively to fail and go bankrupt. Weighty statistics involving hundreds of companies are regularly rolled out by both sides in their attempts to resolve this bone of contention; for more is at stake than might appear.

It will be clear from earlier pages that cash flow is a tool of analysis which allows a company watcher to gather insights in an incisive and logical way, and to penetrate beneath the layers of accrual accounting, to ascertain the efficiency of the key process of a business, the asset conversion cycle. We have said that a company not generating cash from its cycle will eventually fail because sources of external finance are limited and the suppliers of it are demanding.

It is also beyond dispute that the crunch comes for any company when its sources of cash dry up. Inability to meet maturing obligations spells immediate bankruptcy unless more money can be found. In these situations profit is quite irrelevant except that a profitable company will almost always find it easier to raise funds than an unprofitable one. Bankers' perceptions have a crucial role in the survival of troubled companies, since it is usually the bank that has the unenviable task of deciding whether to put yet more money into a troubled organization with no great expectation of getting it back, or liquidating the company often with almost certain heavy losses crystallizing immediately. The death throes of many a spent company are extended by a curiously selfish mercy that bankers lavish upon the dying!

A cash-consuming asset conversion cycle does not necessarily indicate weakness. It is characteristic also of growing companies. The point they both have in common is that they are risky companies, entities soaking up money from outsiders whose financial integrity is predicated on the tide eventually turning and the money starting to flow out of the company. If the risk pays off, the investment has been worthwhile and probably will be handsomely rewarded; if it doesn't, lenders and investors will be substantially the poorer. Cash flow on its own does not distinguish winners from losers. It does identify with devastating clarity companies with a recurring need to be propped up with money from outside.

Liquidity is another factor to consider. A company can consume cash for as long as it has cash to spend and a cash-rich company is not going to collapse, whatever its book losses, until that cash is exhausted. Many wondered what GEC, the British electronics company, planned to do with its 'cash mountain' of more than £1bn. Would they buy another major organization, or perhaps repurchase a substantial portion of their equity? £1bn is a colossal sum of money but GEC for several years showed no sign of spending more than a small part of it, apparently in the belief that plentiful cash kept the options open and gave the company a flexibility it would not otherwise have.

This is admirable logic. A lesser company with much of its balance sheet liquid would be a juicy takeover target, and it is naturally an expensive luxury to hold cash, even if it is invested in marketable securities to earn interest. If money cannot be invested more profitably in the company's own operations there is little point in being in business at all! But for GEC, the costs were evidently of secondary importance to the benefits of being able to take a few risks without endangering the whole operation. GEC's surprise bid for Plessey in December 1985 appeared to be the culmination and justification of this strategy, until the Monopolies and Mergers Commission disallowed it. GEC's 7-year

itch to dispose of part of its cash was relieved with its
recent venture with Philips in high-technology medical
systems.

To use cash flow figures as a substitute for profit figures
without taking other factors into account is futile and
bound to be disappointing. The two approaches should be
seen as complementary, neither telling the whole story and
both suspect—profit because it is open to manipulation and
is based on unstated and not necessarily justifiable assumptions, cash flow because it is not the whole story of a
business's success or failure.

It is fair to say that cash flow is a better tool for the
analysis of weak companies, and of less interest for strong
ones; a small to moderate sized company in trouble will be
acutely short of cash and the management's attention will
be keenly focused on possible sources. Rather like sex, cash
flow concentrates the mind wonderfully in its absence. At
the other end of the scale, multinationals often have their
own treasury departments and act rather like banks. The
focus will not so much be on sources of supply, which will
be numerous if the company is a successful one, as on
minimizing funding costs and obtaining the optimum
return on deposits.

The main shortcoming of the cash flow analysis demonstrated so far that it is entirely historical in outlook, a
limitation shared with conventional profit-driven analysis.
By the time the Annual Report appears, months will have
passed and there are obvious dangers in assuming that the
future can be extrapolated from established trends. The
past is studied only because it is a guide to the future and
the future may not deliver true to form. Anyone whose
investment in a company is expected to be long term, by
which is meant here longer than a year, should ideally be
projecting forward to try to see what the company will look
like during the whole life of the investment, and to satisfy
himself that cash flow difficulties are not likely to show up.

Sophisticated techniques exist for projecting financial statements, but the basic approach is not difficult. Decide what the sales level is expected to be in future years and scale up (or down) proportionately all balance sheet and income statement items that might be expected to move in line with sales. Then choose appropriate numbers for depreciation, capital expenditure, long- and short-term interest rates and make any other adjustments that seem justified. Finally, balance the statements over the cash and borrowing accounts. Some juggling is necessary since until the projection is completed the amount of borrowing cannot be ascertained, but without the level of borrowing the cost of interest payments is also unknown.

Once a feasible projection scenario has been mapped out it can be tested for sensitivity. What happens if the sales fall instead of rising, if the capital asset expansion is postponed, if interest rates rise unexpectedly? Either separate projections can be prepared for each of these eventualities, or different combinations of them, or shorthand routes can be taken to gauge merely the rough effect on profits, borrowing, cash or whatever. Manually this is a laborious process, but with a computer countless variations can be tested very quickly, as this is just the kind of number crunching at which computers excel.

The pity of it is that analysts are reduced to playing such guessing games. Investors rarely get to see much projected analysis since companies never publish their projections, and analysts' reports tend to go to little further than indicating expected levels of turnover and profitability. These numbers are eagerly watched by stock markets and an amended prediction by a respected analyst can send a share soaring or reeling on the market.

The huge sensitivity of the market to profit figures precludes companies making public their own internal forecasts. In the USA a disappointed shareholder has an extraordinary propensity to phone his lawyer, and it is tantamount to commercial suicide for a company to put out information that can be demonstrated to be erroneous. Company managements certainly indicate directly and indirectly when major breaks are expected in the earnings pattern, but they will not quote numbers in advance of the publication of official results. In Europe, managers have long been used to giving much less than their US counterparts and are even less forthcoming about future prospects.

One important exception deserves mention. When a company comes to a major stock exchange for the first time, it must issue a prospectus containing quite detailed forecasts for the benefit of potential investors. There will not, though, be any analysis of the sensitivities or suggestions of possible variations; rather, there will be a conspicuous disclaimer absolving the directors and their advisers from any responsibility for their accuracy!

How accurate could one expect a forecast to be? Not surprisingly, it largely depends upon the industry the company is in. Solid, unspectacular industries like food retailing, tobacco, textiles or light engineering are relatively easy to predict and competent analysts are usually close to the mark, at least in the short term. For banking, oil and commodities trading, insurance, high tech and shipping, all volatile industries, predictions are regularly wider of the mark.

It is no secret that since the Latin American debt crisis, the profitability of major international banks hinges in no small measure on the level of provisions made for 'doubtful' or 'non-performing' loans (to use the current euphemism). Provisions are debits to the income statement and there is understandable reluctance to provide more than is absolutely required by the authorities. Consequently, those banks whose Latin American exposure is well in excess of their net worth have generally provided for only about 1 per cent of the total. Banks with virtually no exposure have provided for as much as 75 per cent and banks falling between the two extremes have provided whatever they think they can afford! No wonder banking profits are so unpredictable!

For investors, who are risking their own money in the expectation of above normal returns, the uncertainty of the future is one of the hazards of the game, and until the investing public forces the corporate world to say more about expectations, individual investors will have to trust whatever analysis they can perform or obtain and their own intuition. That is what risk taking is about. Bankers and long-term lenders are in a quite different position and are now beginning, belatedly, to seek much clearer indicators of expected progress from their long-term customers. Bankers have long since abandoned what influence they may once have had on the terms of accounting standards and formats. They have been content to accept Annual Reports, designed to impress the shareholder and focusing on areas of quite secondary importance to lenders, as their principal source of the information they need to make a lending decision. Now they are having to think again.

Why bankers have been so pusillanimous in this regard has to do partly with an attachment to some old-fashioned methods of doing business. Bankers are innately conservative people. A second factor is that the level of competition in banking has tilted the balance of power in the customer–banker relationship towards the customer. Strong customers nowadays bestow information on their banks on a grace and favour basis, while many multinationals with dozens of banks refrain from giving material other than their Annual Report to any bank, quaintly pleading that they wish to keep all their banks on an equal footing. In other cases, internal management information is available only to a select few banks that have dealt with the company over many years. There are many banks today with lending running to tens of millions of dollars out to companies whose income statement has never been disclosed, let alone any kind of cash flow.

On occasion, though, the bank has the upper hand and

some very interesting cash flow information is starting to be seen, all in strictest confidence, inside the banks. The best examples come from oil and gas project deals and from leveraged buyouts, two classes of business united by the common thread that banks provide the vast bulk of the money at risk. In a leveraged buyout, a group of investors, often the managers of the business, borrow nearly the total of the company (often vastly more than the book value) to take it over from the existing shareholders. Of course, the resultant balance sheet shows minimal equity and horrendous debt levels, but the idea is that, as the business prospers in the coming years, debt is gradually replaced by equity or redeemed from asset sales, the banks are repaid, perhaps over 10 to 15 years, and the entrepreneurs become extremely rich. Unless, that is, interest rates rise steeply, asset sales fail to materialize, profitability and cash flow fall or unforeseen capital expenditure needs cripple the company, in any of which cases the entrepreneurs may lose everything and the banks will face a summary bloodletting. It is too soon yet to know which of these is the most likely outcome of the recent spate of such transactions in the USA, but the Federal Reserve's determination to curb the issue of 'junk bonds' to finance buyouts indicates that that institution, if no other, has started to think hard about the risks.

Banks have correctly insisted that they will not lend money for long periods to companies whose balance sheets are highly leveraged without a clear repayment schedule and without demonstration from the company that that repayment schedule is plausible and achievable. The perfect tool for satisfying the banks is, of course, a projected cash flow statement or cash budget showing precisely the amounts of cash generated by operations and consumed by interest, dividends, debt repayment and capital expenditure. Exhibit 8 is an example taken from information supplied to certain banks a few years ago in respect of an oil

OIL EXPLORATION COMPANY

CONSOLIDATED CASH FLOW STATEMENT

US$ 000's	1983	1984	1985	1986	1987	1988	1989	1990	1991	1992	1993	1994	1995
CASH FROM FIELDS A-C	470	3140	6754	6600	23089	24264	19374	12160	8542	6421	5598	5394	5419
CASH FROM FIELD D	3300	1456	975	754	996	1153	1016	748	463	385	186		
TOTAL OIL REVENUES	3770	4596	7729	7354	24085	25417	20390	12908	9005	6806	5784	5394	5419
DEVELOPMENT CAPEX	-1540	-3907	-10874	-1887	-13472								
ADMINISTRATION EXPENSE	-2578	-1456	-2547	-2200	-2200	-2200	-2200	-2200	-2200	-2200	-2200	-2200	-2200
EXPLORATION EXPENSE	-7600	-9000	-6500	-6500	-1600	-1600	-900						
DIVIDENDS (GROSS)	-1367	-1367	-1367	-1367	-1367	-1367	-1367	-1367	-1367	-1367	-1367	-1367	-1367
OTHER ITEMS	-139												
TAX	-209							-1280	-2036	-1016	-150	-184	-250
NET CASH FLOW BEFORE FINANCING	-9661	-11134	-13559	-4600	5446	20250	15923	8061	3402	2223	2067	1643	1602
INTEREST EXPENSE	-730	-1150	-2650	-4275	-4576	-3751	-1850	-463					
REPAYMENT OF EXISTING DEBT	-8500												
INTEREST INCOME	844	32	35	26	86	79	95	105	485	736	970	1260	1549
INCREASE IN NEW LOAN	2000	14000	16000	8000	13000								
REPAYMENT OF NEW LOAN					-13000	-17000	-15000	-8000					
CHANGE IN CASH	-16047	1748	-174	-849	956	-422	-832	-297	3887	2959	3037	2903	3151
OPENING CASH BALANCE	16286	239	1987	1813	964	1920	1498	666	369	4256	7215	10252	13155
CLOSING CASH BALANCE	239	1987	1813	964	1920	1498	666	369	4256	7215	10252	13155	16306
CUMULATIVE LOAN OUTSTANDING	2000	16000	32000	40000	40000	23000	8000						

NPV CALCULATIONS (PRE-TAX)

	1983	1984	1985	1986	1987	1988	1989	1990	1991	1992	1993	1994	1995
FIELD A, NPV PRE-TAX	5635	6755	7054	7965	8910	10005	6873	2754	754	90			
FIELD B, NPV PRE-TAX	46189	52365	55432	60837	58034	46729	31785	25494	19752	15690	11742	7429	4287
FIELD C, NPV PRE-TAX	13876	14675	10754	6643	3687	1639	164	95	64	12	7	4	
FIELD D, NPV PRE-TAX	7184	4708	4076	3790	3427	2485	2074	1203	639	351	174		
TOTAL	72884	78503	77316	79235	74058	60858	40896	29546	21209	16143	11923	7433	4287
LESS TAX, NPV	-1745	-1879	-2756	-2894	-2761	-3173	-3895	-3981	-3187	1316	-428	-639	
NET GROUP, NPV	71139	76624	74560	76341	71297	57685	37001	25565	18022	17459	11495	6794	4287
NET GROUP, NPV / LOAN OUTSTANDING	35.57	4.79	2.33	1.91	1.78	2.51	4.63						

Exhibit 8

financing. The numbers have been changed to preserve the company's anonymity.

The first thing to notice is that we have none of the quite unnecessary problems that arose in creating a cash flow schedule from a historical funds flow statement. Instead of the usual convoluted format with sources shown as profit plus depreciation and other non-cash adjustments, we see the simple number for cash revenues. An oil exploration company's receipts are simply the amount of oil sold multiplied by the selling price. From the cash inflows have to be paid the various expenses of operating the rigs, capital investment, dividends, taxes and, of course, debt repayment. It makes not the slightest difference how the double entries are made, what profit the company makes, or what the balance sheet looks like since all cash outflows are treated as deductions from the cash pool. The 'bottom line' is not the profit earned but the change in the cash balance, and if there is a shortfall, more borrowing or equity will be needed.

From a banker's point of view, this cash flow budget is an invaluable tool in the making of the lending decision even if its format is less than ideal. It matters not one iota whether there will be adequate working capital over the life of the loan or what the debt to equity ratio is or what any financial test may or may not reveal, for none of the standard techniques sheds any light on repayment. Repayment comes from the cash flow and all that the banker needs to supplement this statement is an idea of the sensitivities to which the cash flow is subject. In the oil industry, exploration loans are usually structured so that the net present value of the cash flow expected from proven reserves at all times exceeds borrowings by a stipulated margin, and that is the significance of the last row on the schedule. Two crucial variables would be the rates of interest prevailing over the life of the loan and the market price of a barrel of oil. With a computer it is a straightforward exercise to rerun the numbers with different assumptions to establish whether the loan is still viable in the most adverse circumstances envisaged.

Conventional historical analysis of this kind of situation is a complete waste of time. In the early years there will be no revenues or profits and any balance sheet will be meaningless. The historical cost approach just gives no indication of the worth or likely success or failure of an oil exploration project because historical costs are about past cash flows, not future ones. Historical accounts are the wrong tool for the job. It could be argued that oil exploration is a special case, indeed that project finance generally is different from 'normal' lending. In truth, the only thing that is different in 'projects' is the mentality of the participants. Much bank lending today falls into the category of 'cash flow lending', a term describing longer-term loans that are expected to be repaid from operational cash flows, not from the liquidation of assets. A banker who makes a cash flow loan relying mainly on published historical data tends to be relying implicitly on the asset backing in the balance sheet. Whether the loan will be repaid by the cash flow generated by the operations of the borrowing company, or if there is in fact heavy reliance on the availability of refinancing at maturity, is a question regularly overlooked.

Cautious and prudent bankers are today reluctant in most circumstances to lend unsecured, that is, without some defined asset protection, to a company where it is obvious that repayment in, say, 5 years' time depends upon an alternative lender taking over the exposure. In many cases, though, the bankers never realize that this is what is happening. They lend to a 'successful' growing company, with a repayment schedule and perhaps covenants in place, blissfully unaware how fast the borrower is consuming cash and trusting that strong profit performance in the future will guarantee servicing and repayment of the loan. Often the bankers will get away with it, as successful companies do not lack for rival importunate bankers knocking at the door, chequebooks in hand, ready to establish undisciplined facilities. However, if the expected success fails to materialize, alternative sources of finance will dry up and the repayment of the supposed cash flow loan will become a problem of asset liquidation.

This is no way to run a railroad! A demonstrable repayment pattern is vital to a lending proposition, and future repayment is only really clear and visible if the company provides a cash budget. It is possible to develop projections from published statements and to deduce cash flows from them, but the techniques have a wide error margin and to a large extent the bankers and analyst are working in the dark. At the root of the difficulty is that lenders have usually to rely primarily on the published statements, documents prepared for a quite different purpose, namely to satisfy the shareholders' aspirations and to fulfil legal and accounting requirements. As bankers no longer attempt to influence accounting standards except when those standards affect the banks' presentations of their own accounts, and with the shift in emphasis, particularly in international banks, away from 'balance sheet backed' finance, published statements are becoming progressively less relevant to lenders.

Bankers individually do not have much power over their larger corporate customers, and if a banker were to ask General Motors for a projected cash flow budget along the lines of the oil company's he would almost certainly be shown the exit without more ado. As a consequence, bankers have largely given up trying to extract the information they really need from borrowers and contented themselves with what the shareholders, with the law on their side, have extracted from the management.

There is no intrinsic reason why this should be so. Investors over the last 50 years have fought for the information that companies now provide. Company managements have conceded it reluctantly and piecemeal, in formats that often hide its true import. Bankers and indeed investors could and should join forces to make managements produce more worthwhile data better suited to their requirements. This does not mean using the power of the purse to extract more information, but favouring companies and managers which produce the right information—and standing back from those who do not. Accounting standards should also, in this context, become a target for change. There are obvious difficulties in requiring the universal disclosure of cash budgets, and for a manufacturing or financial company the figures would be more complex than those of the conventional 'project'; but there is absolutely no reason why a company borrowing medium- to long-term should not be expected to produce a cash flow statement detailing how the bank will recover its money. Public companies are not allowed to hoodwink their shareholders by giving them only periodic bland assurances and lenders should never have allowed themselves to be fobbed off, as they have been in the main, with purely historical data little suited to their purposes.

Techniques of analysis exist to enable an analyst to make reasonable estimates about the future on the basis of the past. In a world which changes ever more rapidly, the value of most standard techniques is now quite limited. These techniques would not be necessary at all, let alone relied upon so desperately, if companies told lenders and investors, first, what they really need to know about future cash flows and the company's likely ability to service its debt and pay dividends, and what, realistically, the assets are worth.

A great banker was once asked the secret of his success. He replied that he had two questions he had always asked of every borrower and he had insisted on a straight answer: 'How are you going to pay me back?' and 'What are we going to do if your plans fail to work out?' Not many bad loans got past an inquisition like that.

7

Some weapons in the armoury—And how to deploy them

'I am inclined to think'—said I. *'I should do so'* Sherlock Holmes
remarked impatiently.
Sir Arthur Conan Doyle, *The Valley of Fear*

A number of so-called 'tools of analysis' have
achieved wide popularity in analytical circles, particularly
in the USA. Common to all of them is the idea that a few
key numbers can be manipulated to reveal important trends
in performance, or insight into the likely success or failure
of a company. Fairly rudimentary forms of these tools are
frequently used in practical analytical work and there is no
doubt that in skilful hands they can be made to work
splendidly. Conversely, much of the literature describing
them is highly technical and draws upon advanced statistical knowledge that is rarely to be found in the fraternity of
commercial business analysts as distinct from their
academic counterparts. There is no shortage of textbooks to
expound the virtues and applicability of these techniques,
and our intention here is not to argue for their more
widespread acceptance, but rather to consider as to whether
they do or do not achieve what they are supposed to, and to
point out their true advantages and shortcomings. In doing
this, we shall not resort to statistical examination of large

volumes of data or rely upon stock market reactions to validate or refute the argument, but will merely make some common-sense observations founded on elementary principles of business and accounting.

The du Pont Formula

The US chemical producer known grandly as E.I. du Pont de Nemours pioneered in the 1950s a whole system of management control which has, for the most part, now sunk into oblivion. One calculation, however, which was only a tiny part of the whole, has become immortal:

$$\frac{\text{Income}}{\text{Sales}} \times \frac{\text{Sales}}{\text{Assets}} = \frac{\text{Income}}{\text{Assets}}$$

What this says is that the return on a company's assets is the product of the margin on sales and the rate of 'asset turnover'. Obviously, the sales figure cancels out in the equation and is in no way intrinsic to the calculation of the return on assets (ROA). Assume, though, that ROA has been increasing over a period of years. Some indication can be gained as to the reason for the change by plotting the movements in the margin and turnover ratios. ROA could be changing for one or both of two possible reasons. Either the company is more profitable than it was, or it has begun to operate on a smaller asset base relative to sales. Thus on the following figures:

$m	1980	1981	1982	1983
Net income	5.4	5.7	6.3	10.8
Sales	100.3	110.4	120.7	133.0
Total assets	83.1	84.0	83.3	80.4
Margin	5.38%	5.16%	5.22%	8.12%
Turnover	1.207×	1.314×	1.449×	1.654×
ROA	6.49%	6.78%	7.56%	13.43%

The du Pont formula tells us that the improvement in the ROA over the years arose principally out of the ever better rate of asset turnover. This number has increased each year while for the first 3 years the margin remained fairly constant. In 1983 the margin leapt steeply and that break-through combined with the further improved turnover nearly doubled the ROA.

An additional refinement is to multiply the ROA by the leverage formula assets/equity to produce the return on equity (ROE), otherwise obtainable just by dividing income by the balance sheet equity. If the equity is now built into our example, we can examine the influence of leverage on the ROE.

	1980	1981	1982	1983
Equity	32.1	35.8	40.1	48.2
Leverage (assets/ equity)	2.589×	2.346×	2.077×	1.668×
ROE	16.801%	15.906%	15.704%	22.402%

Now it is clear that between 1980 and 1982 ROE was declining because the company was progressively less leveraged and more reliant upon equity funding. This trend continued in 1983, but the improvement in ROA was so dramatic that there was still a big jump in ROE.

The series of ratios in the multiplication sum can be extended considerably further if desired, the next stage perhaps being to multiply ROE by dividends/income, the dividend payout ratio, to calculate the dividend yield on book equity. And so on.

How valid is this approach? The first point to make is that this type of reasoning can be very incisive and it is particu-larly valuable for illustrating the fundamental mechanics of different kinds of operations. A supermarket chain, for example, inevitably operates on low margin and higher turnover with perhaps moderate use of leverage. The critical factor in a supermarket's success is a rapid rate of sales without which ROE is bound to be depressed. On the other hand, a furniture retailer or a heavy manufacturing company will not be able to use turnover to drive ROE but must rely on higher margins. Commodity traders and financial institutions of all varieties have fine margins and substantial assets, and for them leverage is essential if they are to achieve a respectable ROE. There is nothing whatever wrong with the conceptual foundation of the du Pont formula and return on book equity is undeniably a function of margin, turnover and leverage.

The difficulty, as so often, lies in the validity of the numbers themselves, numbers which come straight from the Annual Report and which have been produced by the double entry bookkeeping system. It may be mathematically accurate to account for the movements in ROE between 1980 and 1984 along the line already indicated, but the ratios are ultimately only as good as the numbers on which they are based.

Consider first net income. Any unusual or extraordinary item included above the income line will obviously distort the figure and such distortion will carry directly on into ROA and ROE. Profit can be manipulated in the short term by innumerable factors and the concept of margin is in any case wide open to misinterpretation. The improved 'margin' in 1983 is obviously real in one sense, since we are defining the margin as net income divided by sales. It might be, though, an unwarranted assumption that the business had suddenly moved to a higher margin as the term is normally understood—if the change came from an unusually high level of 'other income', perhaps interest during that year. All that the formula really tells us is the mathematical truth that one component in the ROA or ROE is the quotient of income divided by sales. It does not tell us anything about what determines the relationship between income and sales. To find that out, we need other tools.

Similarly, the relationship between sales and assets is an ill-defined one. It is supposed to be a measure of efficiency of how fast a company 'turns over' its assets in the sales figure; the faster the rate, the more efficient the company, though some types of businesses characteristically turn over assets faster than others. From another perspective, a company may be said to require a certain level of assets for each dollar of annual sales and, other things being equal, the smallest possible asset support will be the optimum. Naturally, however, there is no way a car manufacturer can control assets to the extent that an advertising agency can.

The asset figure used in our example was the year-end book value of the assets and, unfortunately, there is a real danger in assuming that that represents the true value of the assets held by the company during the year. While it would be a refinement to use average assets calculated as the mean of the year's opening and closing balance sheet footings, that expedient does not get over the problem that the assets are not valued at anything approaching their real 'value' but are recorded at some derivative of historical cost. Book assets, as we have seen, are in large part merely unexpired costs and different accounting procedures would throw out different numbers for the same company. A particularly blatant example of this is the British practice of deducting current liabilities from current assets and calling the results net current assets, a figure which is added to the other asset balances to produce footings which understate total assets by the amount of current liabilities.

So far as the true assets are under or over valued in the balance sheet, the error is carried dollar for dollar into the equity section of the balance sheet which, because it is always smaller than total assets, suffers a proportionately greater distortion. Companies are not in real life valued by reference to the book value of the equity, as is universally conceded, and consequently it makes little sense to attach much meaning to the notion of assets divided by equity, at best a crude measure of leverage. That is assuming, of course, that the liabilities are shown at a meaningful value, an assumption it may be foolhardy to make.

Where does that leave us with the du Pont formula? In reality, the calculations are only as good as the published figures. The focal ratio is really that of ROE and the du Pont technique is intended to give users of published accounts a mechanism for pursuing the reason why the return on book equity, a key number for investors, may have changed with time. Any change must, quite truthfully, have to do with the 'margin' or the 'turnover' or the 'leverage' or some combination of the three, but one should not read more into these terms than the mathematical relationship between, respectively, income and sales, sales and assets and assets and equity. The formula tells us nothing about the reasons why any of these components has changed and the assumption should not be made that, as the terms are usually understood, the company's margin has improved or deteriorated, the efficiency of turnover has altered or the degree of leverage has gone up or down, unless these observations can be substantiated in some other way. It may well be that tax entries or accounting variations are disturbing the pattern and suggesting a totally false picture. When one compares performance over two successive years in the same company, provided that company has not undergone major structural alteration or unusual extraordinary items in the course of the year, the trend of the du Pont numbers may be illustrative of real trends. The further one goes from that scenario, by comparing performance over a longer period, by undertaking intercompany comparison or perhaps even international intercompany comparison, the less value the exercise will add.

Sustainable Growth Rate

Less well known than the du Pont formula, is the sustainable growth rate test used to establish the rate of sales growth a company can sustain without increasing its ratio of external liabilities to equity. Most companies aspire to grow because of the added profit growth is expected to bring, but experience shows that higher levels of sales dictate higher levels of assets and an inflated balance sheet inevitably poses a funding need. At zero or low rates of growth there is a tendency in profitable companies for the proportion of the balance sheet composed of external liabilities to fall as equity rises from retained profits and displaces the liabilities. At higher rates of growth, the increase in assets is greater than can be financed by retained profits and the dependency on external liabilities will rise.

Consider the following company:

$	
Sales	2 500 000
Net income	125 000
Dividend	50 000
To retained earnings	75 000
Assets	1 000 000
Liabilities	555 556
Equity	444 444
Liabilities/equity	1.25

The balance sheet is that at the year end after the income statement has been closed. What happens if we assume that the company now enjoys another year of identical trading and no growth in sales? Provided the ratio of assets/sales remains constant, equity will increase by $75 000 to $519 444 and the liabilities decrease by $75 000 to $480 556. The liabilities/equity ratio falls to 0.925.

A quite different picture emerges if, instead of maintaining its sales level, the company puts on a spurt and pushes sales up 30 per cent to $3 250 000. On the assumption that income and dividends and assets rise proportionately, retained earnings will expand by $97 500 but assets will leap by an alarming $300 000 and the difference will have to come from external liabilities. Liabilities/equity will shoot up to 1.399.

The mathematical formula:

$$g = \frac{p\,(1 - d)\,(1 + L)}{t - [p(1 - d)\,(1 + L)]}$$

where g = sustainable growth rate
   p = net income/sales
   d = dividends/net income
   L = liabilities/equity
   t = assets/sales

gives us the growth rate at which the rate of liabilities/equity remains constant, in this case about 20 per cent. The calculation runs as follows:

$$\frac{0.05 \times 0.6 \times 2.25}{0.4 - (0.05 \times 0.6 \times 2.25)} = \frac{0.068}{0.333} = 20.4\%$$

and its veracity can be easily demonstrated.

Growth Rate	0%	20%	30%
$			
Sales	2 500 000	3 000 000	3 250 000
Net income	125 000	150 000	162 500
Dividend	50 000	60 000	65 000
To retained earnings	75 000	90 000	97 000
Assets	1 000 000	1 200 000	1 300 000
Liabilities	480 000	665 556	758 056
Equity	519 444	534 444	541 944
Liabilities/equity	0.925	1.245	1.399

How valuable is this tool in real life? Can bankers really form some idea of whether a company will need to borrow just by looking at this proposed rate of growth and comparing that figure with the sustainable rate of growth? The answer is less than clear-cut.

The underlying dynamics that give rise to the formula are real enough. Rapidly growing companies do lean heavily on external suppliers of funds even when profitable; and profitable, stable companies do have a marked propensity to become cash-rich and under-borrowed. That said, there are certain assumptions built into the model which may or may not be appropriate. It is assumed in the calculation that the ratios of net income/sales, dividends/net income and assets/sales are fundamentally constant. In a stable business, this may be a reasonable assumption but few modern businesses, and certainly not multinationals, are that stable in the 1980s. If income rises faster than sales, as is highly likely in a company with any degree of operating or financial leverage, the company will be able to grow slightly faster than its sustainable growth rate while still keeping its liabilities/equity ratio intact, and the same will be true if assets rise more slowly than sales or dividends consume a smaller proportion of net income.

Conversely, growth at the sustainable growth rate will increase the liabilities/equity ratio if sales rise faster than income, dividends absorb a greater proportion of net income, or assets rise more quickly than sales. As all these ratios will inevitably vary to some extent there may be contradictory forces at play. This sensitivity to changing dynamics is interesting and can be observed in practice.

Below are some figures from Merck & Co. Inc.—a US pharmaceutical manufacturer:

$m	1981	1982	
Sales	2929.5	3063.0	+4.6%
Net income	398.3	415.2	
Dividend	196.8	207.1	
To retained earnings	201.5	208.1	
Assets	3310.0	3647.7	+10.2%

$m	1981	1982
Liabilities	1308.5	1443.7
Equity	2001.5	2204.0
p	0.136	0.136
t	1.130	1.191
L	0.654	0.655
d	0.494	0.499

$$1981 \quad \frac{0.136 \times 0.506 \times 1.654}{1.130 - (0.136 \times 0.506 \times 1.654)} = \frac{0.114}{1.016} = 11.2\%$$

$$1982 \quad \frac{0.136 \times 0.501 \times 1.655}{1.191 - (0.136 \times 0.501 \times 1.655)} = \frac{0.113}{1.078} = 10.5\%$$

At the end of 1981 the sustainable growth rate was 11.2 per cent and as it happened the company's sales grew rather less than this, by only 4.6 per cent. Liabilities/equity was virtually unchanged. According to the formula it should have fallen, but assets grew faster than sales, a development which raised the liabilities/equity ratio. The two effects cancelled out. For the next year, the higher asset base has depressed the sustainable growth rate slightly.

A glance at the formula shows that companies with high sustainable growth are those with low asset levels and high external profitability, both in relation to sales. Service and high tech companies would often be in this category. Companies with low sustainable growth are typically those with heavy asset stems and low retained profitability, e.g. those engaged in steel making and shipbuilding.

All in all, this is really quite a useful test, though it should be used with care. It depends entirely upon published accounting figures, and if these are unrealistic, as to some extent published figures always are, the results can be distorted. If a company grows by off balance sheet financing, its growth rate may well exceed sustainable growth rate without liabilities/equity reacting. To put it bluntly, the model assumes some simple linear relationships which are not in fact universal. As with cash flow analysis, acquisitions and demergers, foreign exchange translation and extraordinary items cloud up the picture.

Finally, the claim is sometimes made that the formula can be rearranged thus:

$$L = \frac{gt}{p(1 + g)} - 1$$

the object being to find an acceptable level of liabilities/equity and work back to the growth rate that produces it. It would be useful if we could do this, but unfortunately the formula as rearranged is only true of the sustainable growth rate and will not work for any arbitrary growth rate. The rearranged formula is in fact quite useless and the calculation impossible, as experiment with the example company given above will clearly prove.

Breakeven Point

In chapter 11, it will be shown how to calculate operating, financial and total leverage by building on the assumption that a company's costs can be divided into fixed and variable components. The same distinction is integral to the calculation of breakeven point, which can be defined as the level of sales at which a company makes neither a profit nor a loss. Take a very straightforward income statement:

	£
Sales	100
Variable costs	(55)
Fixed costs	(30)
Profit before tax	15

Using the formula

$$\frac{\text{fixed costs}}{1 - (\text{variable costs/sales})} = \text{breakeven}$$

we discover the breakeven of this company to be

$$\frac{£30}{0.45} = £67$$

a number that indicates the company can withstand a 33% drop in sales before profit disappears, a fact easy to check.

	£
Sales	67
Variable costs	
@ 55% of sales	(37)
Fixed costs	(30)
Profit before tax	0

The formula can be explained in terms of the 'contribution' to fixed costs made by the residue of sales less variable costs. The denominator of the fraction $1 - (\text{variable costs/sales})$ is the proportion of sales that is available to pay the fixed costs, and dividing the fixed costs by this proportion provides the sales level at which the contribution and the fixed costs are exactly equal, which is the breakeven point.

There are some properties to this model that are worth examining. A company with no fixed costs will inevitably make a profit, provided that the variable costs per unit sale do not exceed selling price, even if only one unit is sold. The risk attaching to that company is likely to be small. By contrast, a company whose only costs are fixed will lose money at sales levels below the point that revenue matches the fixed costs. Risk in this case will depend on how heavy the fixed costs are.

In reality, all companies fall somewhere in between these

two extremes. Retail, commodity and service companies will usually be low risk and have low breakeven points because fixed costs will be relatively insignificant. Companies involved in the manufacture of industrial equipment, mining, forestry, aviation and construction will tend to the other end of the spectrum owing to their heavy fixed costs. However, the calculation of breakeven point, as with leverage, depends upon an accurate identification of fixed and variable costs and is often tendentious.

Strictly speaking, it is theoretically doubtful whether a company manufacturing two separate products, one high margin and profitable, the other low margin and loss making, really has one breakeven point. Everything hangs on the relative proportions of the two products in the total turnover. We should more realistically be calculating separate breakeven points for each product.

In such cases, there is no linear relationship between overall sales and profit and the model breaks down. It will obviously be inappropriate to apply this tool indiscriminately to the consolidated accounts of complex companies.

That consideration apart, one can attempt to calculate breakeven point by reference to the results of successive periods in a business's life, though this will not work well if the two periods produced very similar performances or if the company is so profitable or loss making that breakeven is obviously far removed from current trading levels. Suppose, however, that sales in two successive quarters were £100 and £120 and that net income was £10 and £20 respectively. Analysis of these numbers either on a graph or algebraically suggests a breakeven point of £80:

$$\text{£100 (sales)} - \frac{(\text{£10 (income)} \times \text{£20 (change in sales)})}{(\text{£10 (change in income)})}$$

$$= \text{£80 (breakeven sales)}$$

The danger is that distortion may creep in if fundamental changes in the dynamics of the company have occurred over the two periods, or if either or both sets of figures are distorted by unusual entries or amounts. For all these caveats, breakeven, in origin a test for the extent to which sales could drop before losses start to occur, is a highly useful tool when employed correctly and it can reveal some insights about a company's workings that are not easily detected otherwise. One approach is to plot breakeven point over a series of reporting dates, either as an absolute number or as a percentage of sales. This may give some idea of increasing or decreasing risk as a company close to breakeven is likely to be riskier than one operating well above it.

A company that is insufficiently profitable has a number of options, thinking purely in terms of fixed and variable costs. The way to make money is to be selling well above breakeven point and profits are maximized when the gap between actual and breakeven sales is at its widest. There are two ways to achieve this result: by lowering breakeven point or by increasing sales revenue. From the basic formula, one can see that the former can be achieved by reduction in fixed costs or by an improvement in margin, which in turn can result from either a price hike or from reducing variable costs. The relative merits of each of these options will depend very much on the actual figures but many readers may be surprised at the extremely dramatic effects that can derive from altering the basic dynamics of a business even quite modestly.

Suppose that a product has a variable cost of £5 per unit and is sold for £10. Fixed costs are £200 p.a. Breakeven is calculated according to the formula at

$$\frac{£200}{1 - (£5/£10)} = £400 \text{ or } 40 \text{ units}$$

Let us vary this model in several different ways and examine the consequences. Assume that at present the company is selling £600 or 60 units and that breakeven is thus 66.7 per cent of sales.

(a) A 10 per cent reduction in fixed costs. From the formula one can see that breakeven point will fall likewise by 10 per cent to £360 or 36 units, which can be expressed as 60 per cent of sales. This is good but hardly startling.

(b) A 10 per cent reduction in variable costs as a proportion of sales. This has a fairly modest effect in this instance because variable costs are so low. The formula gives the result

$$\frac{£200}{1 - (£4.50/£10)} = £363.64 \text{ or } 36.4 \text{ units}$$

Breakeven point is now 60.6 per cent of sales.

(c) A 10 per cent price increase. This has a considerable impact on the company's results. Recalculating again, we find breakeven to be

$$\frac{£200}{1 - (£5/£11)} = £366.68 \text{ or } 33.3 \text{ units}$$

at the new price. If unit sales are unaffected by the price rise, monetary sales will rise to £660 and breakeven will be down to 55.6 per cent of sales.

Much depends on the sensitivity of sales to changing prices, but as a general rule increasing prices is a better way of improving profitability than reducing fixed costs. Whereas in our base example the company was selling 60 units and realizing a profit of £600 − £300 − £200 = £100, with a 10 per cent price increase and no diminution in sales, profit rose to £660 − £300 − £200 = £160, a jump of

60 per cent! Even if sales drop by 10 per cent in volume terms the company is still much better off and will be earning £594 − £270 − £200 = £124. This contrasts favourably with the effect of reducing fixed costs by 10 per cent. Profit would then be £600 − £300 − £180 = £120. The price rise has the added advantage that if unit sales drop, capacity may well be freed for other profitable work. Changing the cost structure has no such advantage and tends in practice to be painful and demoralizing to the workforce. It is no fun working for a company that is paring its costs to the bone, even if redundancy is avoided. We should reiterate, though, that if the loss of sales is too severe the implications of a price rise will be negative. It is no good driving all the customers away.

The consequences for large-scale business need little elaboration. Pricing products on a 'cost plus' basis prevents a company from making extravagant profits. That may be in the community's interest but it is not good for the company's managers who, if they wish to prosper, will price their product at whatever the market will bear and certainly to the point where some business (perhaps 10 per cent) is being lost through being too expensive. Demand for many products is not very price sensitive and price rises often do not deter business to the extent anticipated by timid management.

A peculiarly British failing has often been to seek market share by price cutting. This can work but it stacks the odds against one, as an example will show. A 10 per cent price reduction increases breakeven point to

$$\frac{£200}{1 - (£5/£9)} = £450 \text{ or } 50 \text{ units}$$

and if there is no change in units sold, profit falls to £540 − £300 − £200 = £40, a 60 per cent drop, and breakeven point will stand at 83.3 per cent of sales. Even if unit volume increases by 20 per cent, the company is still struggling and will generate a profit of only £648 − £360 − £200 = £88. The severity of the effect will depend entirely upon the relative importance of fixed and variable cost, the closeness to the breakeven point and the price elasticity of demand. This example should, though, be seen as a warning that price discounting to obtain growth through volume is a high-risk manoeuvre that may easily do more harm than good. Price increases, on the other hand, lower monetary breakeven point and, to a rather greater extent, unit breakeven point. No company is likely to succeed with breakeven point much in excess of 75 per cent of sales, since all the effort effectively goes into paying the fixed costs and there is so little room for error. Unless the drop in demand is very severe, price rises can be relied upon to increase the margin between breakeven and actual sales by acting on both elements of the equation.

Discounted Cash Flow

Imagine that a certain investment costs £100 now and is expected to produce cash flows, after tax, of £10, £20, £30, £40 and £50 at the end of each of the next 5 years. A constant interest rate of 10 per cent is expected over the whole period. Is the investment worthwhile?

Students of corporate finance will at once recognize this as a 'discounted cash flow' question. The essence of the concept is that a pound in the future is worth less than a pound today because a pound today can be invested to earn interest. A pound today is therefore more attractive and worth more than the promised future pound, even if there is no risk involved in the transaction. Provided that the interest payment is received at the end of the year and there is no tax to pay, £1.00 today, given an interest rate of 10 per cent, is worth £1.10 after a year and an investor will be indifferent as to which he would prefer to receive, £1.00 today or £1.10 in a year's time.

According to the same argument, £1.00 a year from now is worth 90.9p now, that being the sum which, invested now at 10 per cent, will be worth precisely £1.00 when one interest payment has been made. £1.00 two years from now is worth 82.6p and so on, the formula being

$$pv \text{ (present value)} = \frac{1}{(1 + x)^n}$$

where x = interest rate and n = number of periods.

The present value of the inflows in our example would be calculated as follows:

$$
\begin{array}{lr}
 & £ \\
10 \times 0.909 = & 9.09 \\
20 \times 0.826 = & 16.52 \\
30 \times 0.751 = & 22.53 \\
40 \times 0.683 = & 27.32 \\
50 \times 0.621 = & \underline{31.05} \\
\text{Total} \quad = & \underline{106.51}
\end{array}
$$

As the initial cost of the investment was £100.00 the investment is an intrinsically attractive one at an interest rate of 10 per cent. At higher rates, of course, the effect of discounting is more dramatic and the net present value of £6.51 will be reduced. It is possible to calculate the rate at which the net present value will be zero, in this case 12 per cent, and this rate is known as the 'internal rate of return'. For single payments or regular streams of payments, this rate may be derived from tables or a sophisticated pocket calculator. If payments are irregular it is more a question of trial and error or the use of an 'algorithm' as mathematicians prefer to call it!

In assessing the value of this technique, it will be well to see how standard accounting and cash budgeting formats would handle a transaction of this type and a suggestion is shown below:

Accounting

Year	0	1	2	3	4	5	*Total*
£							
Income		10	20	30	40	50	
Depreciation		(20)	(20)	(20)	(20)	(20)	
Interest		(10)	(10)	(9)	(6.9)	(3.6)	
Profit		(20)	(10)	1	13.1	26.4	10.5

Cash Flow

Years	0	1	2	3	4	5
£						
Opening balance	0	(100)	(100)	(90)	(69)	(35.9)
Inflow		10	20	30	40	50
Outflow	(100)					
Interest		(10)	(10)	(9)	(6.9)	(3.6)
Closing balance	(100)	(100)	(90)	(69)	(35.9)	10.5

Notice that the total profit is the same as the cash amount left in the bank at the end of the 5 years, and also that £10.5 discounted at 10 per cent from a distance of 5 years has a present value of £10.5 × 0.621 = £6.51, the same as the net present value of the whole payment sequence.

The most remarkable feature of this exercise is the profit figures produced by standard accounting. We have assumed straight line depreciation, but any other depreciation method would have yielded the same total profit after 5 years, and accelerated depreciation would only have heightened the losses in the early years and the profits in the later years. Readers may wish to check this for themselves.

Traditional double entry bookkeeping takes no account of the 'time value of money'. It is assumed that a pound today is worth the same as a pound in a year's time and most textbooks elevate this assumption to one of the cardinal principles of accountancy. The effect of this wholly unrealistic attitude is well illustrated in our example. If it is known from the outset what the cash inflow will be, it is an absurd portrayal that suggests that the investment is 'loss making' in the first 2 years and profitable thereafter. This bizarre effect arises from the device of writing off the investment over its lifespan by the process of depreciation. It is worth noting, too, that we need the cash flow to ascertain what the interest charges will be, there being no way to tell from the income statement how much is being borrowed at any point. Finally, the initial investment, being a capital item, will not affect the income statement but will be debited directly onto the balance sheet, a further point of possible confusion. The cash flow, by contrast, shows us exactly the pattern of inflow and outflow and could hardly be clearer. What it does not do, however, is indicate the attractiveness of the investment, for which we need to apply the technique of discounting.

The concept of discounted cash flow belongs to the twentieth century and is thus, by contrast with double entry bookkeeping, a relative innovation. It is significant that some attempts are being made to introduce discounting, on a limited scale, into the accounting standards, most notably in the area of lease accounting. The capitalization of leases meeting certain requirements, mandatory in the USA and strongly encouraged in the UK, is revolutionary in this respect and has led to calls for similar treatment of other liabilities expected to be paid out over future periods, particularly unfunded pension obligations.

Double entry bookkeeping is in origin driven by cash flows, with adjustments made for accruals. We have argued in this book that the accruals have assumed an exaggerated importance, to the point that the underlying cash flows are virtually obliterated. To create discounted liabilities on a balance sheet involves an extra step away from basic cash flow and one which does not sit easily with traditional accountants' notions of conservatism and historical cost. They object that for discounting to be valid in accountancy both future payments and future interest rates have to be known reasonably accurately, and that subjectivity cannot be eliminated from the calculation. This type of computation, it is claimed, belongs more in the realm of the actuary than of the accountant.

There is some justice in this. Discounting is a method of giving an economic value to a series of cash flows. It makes sense for determining trading values for bonds or fixed income investments. But it is not particularly effective for valuing future obligations when the cash-flow and interest rates are uncertain, and it is mainly for that type of situation that radical accountants and investor lobbies want to see it used. Historical cost is backward looking while discounting looks forward. The two do not naturally mix.

Discounting also has some unfortunate consequences when applied in the context of double entry. It is not possible under the double entry system merely to create a liability. For the books to balance there is an awkward debit needing a home, and the choice is the familiar and depressing one between the income statement (bad for profits), the equity section of the balance sheet (reduces capital and smacks of deviousness) and the asset side (creates an intangible item).

The principal disadvantage of discounting, the need to posit an interest rate, may be partly avoided in investment decisions by the use as a touchstone of the internal rate of return, but this has a number of theoretical weaknesses, chief among them the inability of that test to distinguish between large and small investments. It is impossible, without more data, to distinguish between an investment costing £100 now with an internal rate of return of 15 per cent and one costing £150 now with a 13 per cent rate of return, if the two are mutually exclusive. There are also some irregular patterns having multiple internal rates of return and others again that have no real internal rate of return at all. A further possibly unrealistic assumption in all discounting calculations is that the proceeds of the investment are reinvested at the discount rate.

The study of discounting is central to the teaching of the business schools and it has central importance today as one of the few tools of analysis that copes with the changing value of money. It is the primary technique for the valuation of bonds and, in many companies, for the making of investment decisions. Older methods such as pay-back are, however, still in use even in some sophisticated companies, not because their financial experts are unaware of the discounting concept, but because establishing cost of capital is so inexact a science, and cash flow more than a year or two into the future can be extremely difficult to predict. The same problem does not arise with bonds where the payment schedule is determined in advance.

Bierman and Smidt's classic book, *The Capital Budgeting Decision*, is essential and fascinating reading on the subject and all the possibilities are investigated at length with copious examples. Regrettably, much of the text is difficult in the latter part, and irredeemably theoretical. The allocation of probability factors to future cash flows is ingenious but a mathematical extravagance rarely if ever to be seen in real investment decisions.

Cost of Capital

Most costs in a business are readily identifiable and to some extent manageable. The managers will know how much they are paying for materials and salaries and premises. But before they can establish their selling prices they need to have some idea of their cost of capital, the expenses associated with funding the assets of the company. The idea is best illustrated with a small example. Suppose this is the liabilities side of the balance sheet:

	£
Bank debt @ 10%	75
Other current liabilities	100
Long-term debentures @ 12%	230
Deferred taxation	120
7% preferred stock	100
Common stock	25
Retained earnings	350
	1000

The company's 1000 shares are trading at 45p each and last year the company produced net income of £50 after suffering 40 per cent tax. What is the cost of capital? In problems like this the standard technique is one of weighted averaging with certain adjustments. The cost of the debt is easy to determine and the other current liabilities and the deferred taxation have no costs attaching to them. Seven per cent is being paid on the preferred stock but this is an after-tax charge and the true cost, grossed up for tax, is 7 per cent divided by $(1 - 0.4) = 11.7\%$. The cost of the equity is normally determined by reference to the market rather than the book value of the shares and the cost is the attributable profit, again pretax. One thousand shares @ 45p are worth £450 and the attributable profit is £50 divided by $(1 - 0.4) =$ £83.3. Tabulating all this, we calculate the 'weighted average cost of capital' as follows:

		£		£
Bank debt @ 10%		75 × 10%	=	7.5
Other current liabilities		100 × 0% *	=	0.0
Long-term debentures @ 12%		230 × 12%	=	27.6
Deferred taxation		120 × 0%	=	0.0
7% preferred stock		100 × 11.7%	=	11.7
Market value of equity		450 × 18.5%†	=	83.3
		£1075		£130.1

Weighted average cost of capital is $\dfrac{£130.1}{1075} = 12.1\%$

*Ignoring opportunity costs and possible discounting. †Derived.

How realistic and valid is this approach? As well as for pricing, managers use the cost of capital calculation for assessing potential investments. Any activity which involves assets on the balance sheet may be assumed to cost, in our example, 12.1 per cent on those assets each year, and if the activity does not earn that, pretax, before the capital costs are deducted, it is not paying its way. Actually, an investment will have to deliver considerably more than that to cover the element of 'dead capital' tied up in such non-productive assets as administration and central management office space. Against that, many capital type investments bring with them up-front tax advantages in the form of investment credits, and on a discounted cash flow basis these bolster up the return on assets employed.

Cost of capital is a real cost and one that cannot be ignored. A business failing to reckon that capital has a cost will suffer inevitable unexpected losses or at the very least will find its share price sliding, with negative implications for its ability to raise new money. The difficulty is that measuring the cost of capital with any accuracy is virtually impossible. There is, in our example, not much scope to disagree with the calculation for the first three items or for the preferred stock, but the cost of equity and to a lesser extent deferred taxation is another matter.

Our calculation implicitly suggests that the book value of equity is not a helpful number and that we should be looking at the market value. As explained in Chapter 10, the market value of each share multiplied by the number of shares outstanding is a poor guide to the real worth of the company and anyone attempting to buy control of the company would usually expect to pay a substantial premium. The day to day share price is a marginal trading price, not a valuation of the whole. The calculation also implies that £1075 is the value of all the company's assets, a seriously questionable assumption.

Secondly, deferred taxation is treated as a costless liability. This is not quite fair. In many cases, deferred tax is never likely to be paid and it is in reality largely a subdivision of equity. It is only legitimate to consider it a costless liability in so far as it represents an interest-free loan from the tax authorities. The tax authorities themselves certainly do not so regard companies' deferred tax provisions which are more realistically seen as a more or less meaningless product of accounting convention. The extent of provision for deferred tax varies enormously between countries, at the one end the USA demanding virtually full provision, in the middle the UK demanding limited provision and at the other end Japan making no provision. There is an argument for eliminating 'permanent' deferred tax provisions which are indistinguishable from equity.

Finally, the cost of equity is an imponderable. Instead of the earnings method used above, some practitioners employ the dividend yield (on market capitalization) plus the growth rate as the percentage cost of equity, an equally logical attitude to a virtually insoluble problem. What rankles is the implication that additional equity finance could be raised at the calculated cost of equity. If earnings and dividends are at all volatile, this must be nonsense, the presupposition that earnings per share, the dividend yield and the growth rate are the only determinants of the value and the cost of the equity not being entirely compelling. Once capital is invested in a business, it does not have to be repaid and dividend disbursements are not obligatory. The 'cost' of equity is a figure of speech meaning only 'that which the company is managing to provide for its present stockholders'.

According to corporate finance theory, it is an aim of management to minimize the cost of capital by balancing the relative quantities of debt and equity in the balance sheet. An inappropriate balance sheet structure is damaging because too much equity is invariably expensive and too much debt increases the cost of that debt as the company is perceived to be risky and reduces the share price which pushes up the cost of the equity. In broad outline, we agree with this perception. What we do not accept is that the managers or the investors in a large company, with perhaps two dozen different debt issues and several classes of equity, are capable of calculating the cost of equity with any precision. A US manufacturing company generally reckons that interest-bearing borrowings divided by equity should be in the order of 25–35 per cent. Above that figure, the debt ratings will fall and debt will become more expensive. In theory, the cost of capital is at a minimum when the borrowing level is within the stated bounds, but what that cost of capital is and how it is calculated is never stated. Annual Reports do not discuss the weighted average cost of capital and textbooks of corporate finance give only rudimentary examples like the one above.

The conclusion is that while it makes sense for a company to try to ascertain its weighted average cost of capital and for analysts to try to second guess it, the real world is too complicated for the calculation to be done with any precision. Our impression is that balance sheet structure is monitored by ratios and determined in part by what portions of equity or debt the market can be persuaded to swallow at the time that the company needs the money. If a company is heavily borrowed, and remember the world sees only the year-end, window-dressed balance sheet, comments in the press refer to this higher gearing or leverage, never to a high cost of capital. A low share price is a deterrent to equity issues because of the consequent dilution of earnings, but when the share price is high the effect of dilution is deemed of no consequence. It is a rule of thumb game, and there are no easy ways to determine optimum funding, even for the sophisticated corporate treasurer. For the analyst, reliant on Annual Reports and share movements, the analysis of a company via movements in its weighted average cost of capital is futile. The authors have, at any rate, never known such a calculation to influence a lending or investment decision.

Z Scores

Financial analysis always involves a lot of numbers, and the picture that emerges from an examination of the numerous conventional ratios may indicate that in some respects the company under consideration is becoming stronger while in other ways its condition is deteriorating. What, for instance, might one make of a company whose profitability is improving at the same time as its balance sheet is relying more heavily on short-term borrowings? Is such a company a safe borrowing customer for a bank?

Painfully aware that traditional ratio analysis does not always distinguish in a clear and consistent manner between the successful, likely-to-survive company and the deadbeat headed for reorganization or bankruptcy, analysts and researchers have sought for years for some method of spotting winners and losers well in advance, a method that is easy to use, effective and reliable. The technique of Z scoring, developed originally by Edward Altman, is one offering. It consists in reducing the financial data of a company to a single number, the sum of a series of ratios each multiplied by a coefficient, the idea being that the higher the total the less risky the company.

Altman's best-known formula runs thus:

$$Z = 1.2a + 1.4b + 3.3c + 0.6d + 0.99e$$

where a = working capital/total assets
      b = retained earnings/total assets
      c = earnings before interest and taxes/total assets
      d = market value of equity/book value of total
         liabilities
      e = sales/total assets

A score in excess of 3 is said to indicate a safe company, and one below 1.8 a likely candidate for bankruptcy.

To evaluate this formula as an analytical tool we need to

know something of how it was devised. It was not the product of anyone's particular opinion as to the importance of any given ratio in corporate analysis. What Altman did was to take a large population of companies, and put their accounts over several years into a computer. Some of the companies in the sample were 'goods', that is, companies which had gone on to obvious prosperity, the rest 'bads', entities which had subsequently filed for bankruptcy, or reorganization or negotiated major debt reschedulings with their bankers. The computer was programmed to calculate dozens of ratios for each company in the sample, and armed with this data Altman proceeded then to devise a statistical test that separated the 'goods' from the 'bads'.

His aim was to come up with a formula which would identify potential 'bads' at the earliest moment, if possible at least 2 or 3 years before the crisis occurred. The formula shown above was the fruit of these deliberations. As it appeared to work for the sample companies, it was tried out on others and shown to have an impressive power of prediction and to be a worthwhile method of picking companies that could eventually collapse.

Underlying this purely statistical approach was a belief that there are certain mathematical features commonly found in the accounts of 'bad' companies and the more extreme the incidence of these features in a set of accounts, the more likely the company is to fail. Care had to be taken in devising the Z score to ensure that each of the ratios measured something different and that no two of them were closely co-related, since there is no point in including two separate ratios that essentially measure the same phenomenon. This consideration in part explains the rather peculiar selection of ratios included in the formula.

In sum, Altman identified five independent ratios where a low score indicated a strong statistical likelihood of the company turning bad. Some of these were more significant statistically than others and, of course, the scale of the ratios also varied (ratio c almost always being a small number by comparison with ratios d and e), so different weightings were given to each ratio. An overall low scale meant that a company had to a significant extent characteristics associated with potential bankruptcy candidates and therefore stood a good chance of going bad itself. A score falling over time was a bad sign, a rising score an indication that the risk was improving.

Looking at the actual components of the formula, one is not surprised to see that low working capital, retained profits, current operating profits and asset turnover were all found to be crucial indicators (ratios a, b, c, e), and ratio d is curious only in that in measuring leverage Altman found that the market's evaluation of the equity of a company was a better number than the book value of equity. This is fully in line with what has been said in this book about company valuations, but it has been considered a weakness in the model because to apply the formula one needs information outside of that contained in an Annual Report.

There are two ways to evaluate the effectiveness of Altman's formula as a bankruptcy predictor. The first is to test it on companies and see how well it works: what one might call the 'proof of the pudding' approach. This is not the place for such a lengthy study, but it is our experience that for US manufacturing companies the model still works more than adequately and there is research evidence to back up this subjective impression. Supporters of the technique claim that potential bankruptcies can be spotted as far ahead as 5 years in some cases. As Altman's sample companies were all US manufacturers, one could hardly expect the formula to work accurately for companies outside that category, and this is also borne out by experience.

We have argued in this book that a company's financial statements owe a good deal in their structure and shape to the underlying nature of the business as well as to the accounting conventions prevalent in the country of domicile. It would be reasonable to expect that in the UK Altman's model would work after a fashion, but probably not as well as it does for US manufacturers, and this too is exactly what we find in practice. The model does not work at all for service or financial companies or indeed for any company where characteristics of a potentially bankrupt US manufacturer, as identified by Altman, are regular and normal features. High leverage, for example, is dangerous in a manufacturing company but absolutely essential (within reason) for a finance company or a bank.

The other critique of Altman's work is to ask whether it is conceptually sound even for the US manufacturing company. Our fundamental objection to the Z scoring technique is that it is almost entirely driven by historical financial data and that no weight at all is given to concepts of risk or market conditions. In other words, the implicit assumption that conventionally prepared accounts can be used to predict future failure is one that we could only accept in heavily qualified form. It seems to us that Altman's formula identifies companies with a high profile of financial risk, and such companies obviously do stand a higher than average chance of failure. They are more susceptible to a downturn in operating performance and have less resistance to adversity. It is quite reasonable to consider that a company with a low Altman Z score is a company at serious risk of failure.

What is unrealistic is to suppose that there is any degree of certainty about the prediction. Z scoring is akin to the technique of credit scoring practised by many leading institutions for deciding whether to lend smallish amounts to personal customers. Statistically it can be shown that a man who has steady employment, is married with two children, owns his own house, and goes to church on Sundays is unlikely to walk away from a personal loan, whereas a man who is periodically unemployed, is divorced, lives in rented accommodation and goes dog racing on Saturdays is an altogether poorer credit risk. However, every branch banker has met people in the first category who have defaulted and others in the second category who have not, and a credit scoring scheme can only identify higher-risk borrowers; it cannot predict in individual cases what the outcome will be.

So it is with Z scoring. Since Altman's celebrated model first appeared, other work (including significant refinements by him) has been done, much of it in the UK, to produce better predictive models and ones adapted to categories of company other than US manufacturers. It is not an easy project to devise a new Z scoring formula and to do the job properly requires perhaps three or four man-years of work. There is also a difficulty in finding sufficient 'bad' companies to make a worthwhile statistical sample. Remarkably few large companies actually fail and in some areas failure is virtually unknown. We really have no idea what the characteristics might be, say, of a potentially 'bad' Japanese bank or sogo shosha!

As a consequence, most other Z scores are commercial secrets. Their inventors own consultancies advising clients of scores and their interpretations but they do not reveal how the score is calculated.

One interesting refinement is to calculate the scores of a number of companies and then rank these companies in order. The advantage of this is that it compensates for the effects of general economic conditions. A score falling from, say, 2.6 to 2.4 on the Altman scale may be in part due to a depressed market, partly to factors internal to the company. Ranking this company with a hundred others, we might find that it had in fact risen from 24th to 18th and we would conclude that the drop in the Z score was wholly attributable to the economy and that the company's own situation was, in context, improving. These ratings are known as P scores and again they can be purchased from appropriate consultants.

Z scores are a byway of analysis and are unlikely ever to come centre stage. While credit scoring is extremely useful because of the huge number of applications made each year for personal loans, banks and investors are inevitably reluctant to make major lending or investment decisions based solely on the single number thrown out by a Z scoring technique. At best, the Z score will be a factor in a commercial decision, to be weighed along with other data, given due weight but not allowed to assume a disproportionate importance. It is hard to quarrel with that.

8

Putting it into practice—
Spotting the not so obvious

Confusion now hath made his masterpiece.
William Shakespeare,
Macbeth, Act 3, Scene 1

We have had many harsh things to say about the form and content of Annual Reports, and in this chapter we show three instances of how quite simple but important aspects of company structure and performance were hidden beneath excessively complicated and confusing figures. It is not suggested that there is in such instances any attempt to mislead or deceive, merely that devotion to well-tried formats and standard accounting practice tends to override any interest a company might have in laying the unalloyed fundamentals before readers of its Annual Report. We cannot overemphasize that pages of detailed footnotes complemented by countless numbers are unintelligible. The detail is so copious that the subtle trends this material is supposed to be illustrating are thoroughly obscured. Near total reliance on historical cost accounting contributes to the confusion. In modern business conditions it is a tool with severe limitations and few users of Annual Reports really understand its structural inadequacies.

The fourth example in this chapter, Unigate plc, demonstrates a rarely seen determination to make the figures more intelligible. Mr Daniel Hodson, the finance director and a well-known teacher and writer on corporate finance, has written a statement of source and application of funds that illustrates with unusual clarity the confusion that constantly abounds in this area and on which we have attempted to cast some slight illumination of our own.

Acme-Cleveland Corp.

Acme-Cleveland Corp., of Cleveland, Ohio, is a medium-sized producer and distributor of machine tools, supplying principally the Midwest motorcar industry. Between 1976 and 1981 it had been showing steady growth in sales from $194.1m to $400.7m, while net earnings had risen from $2.9m to a peak of $19.5m in 1979 before settling back to $10.9m in 1981. A steady, if unspectacular performer, Acme-Cleveland could be characterized as a capital-intensive, high fixed cost manufacturer, subject to cyclical trends in performance but in a fundamentally sound and stable industry.

The last recession hit the US machine tool manufacturer harder than anyone expected. In 1979, US business ordered $5.6bn of machine tools, a figure which dropped to a horrifying $1.5bn in 1982. At the same time, US producers were losing market share to imports, particularly from Japan, and to crown it all the Japanese manufacturers, who were generally part of much larger industrial groups, were gaining a lead over their American competitors in the introduction of computer controlled machines capable of greater flexibility and smaller batch production than more traditional models. In the USA, the industry was fragmented, with hundreds of companies employing fewer than a hundred people; even Acme-Cleveland, one of the largest operators in the field, never employed more than 6500 workers. The company's research and development expenditure was necessarily modest at $3–4m a year in the early 1980s, and was hardly enough to keep up with a technological revolution.

In 1983, sales plummeted to $327.0m and a year later to $172.7m, the lowest figure since 1974. It was as if 10 years of solid progress had been wiped out in the space of 2 years. Earnings held up in 1982 at $11.6m but turned negative the following year when the company recorded a net deficit of $32.0m. How did Acme-Cleveland respond?

Any company with high fixed costs is vulnerable to a fall in demand. The breakeven point of such companies is invariably high and a serious and prolonged reduction in sales below breakeven point threatens the very viability of the enterprise. In a time of fierce competition for busines when there are few buyers around, raising prices is out of the question and the only route to salvation lies in cutting fixed costs, by closing factories and laying off part of the workforce. Acme-Cleveland's response in 1982 was no different and the company made a point of telling its shareholders that management had reduced breakeven point from 'well over $300m' in early 1980 to about $240m at the beginning of 1983.

When a capital-intensive company suffers a severe loss of business, questions inevitably start to arise about its survival prospects and an analyst would want to test out the company's claim. An ideal method would be to plot the relationship between sales and net profit over a succession of quarters to see whether there was any evidence that the company was capable of breaking even at progressively lower levels of sales.

Exhibit 9, taken from Acme-Cleveland's Annual Report for the year to 30 September 1983, shows the company's presentation of its quarterly results over the previous 2 years. It is clear from a glance that this table was not prepared to help analysts do breakeven calculations. The emphasis is on the effect these quarterly results have had

Quarterly Data For Fiscal Years 1983 and 1982 (In thousands of dollars, except per share data)
(Unaudited)

1983	December 31	March 31	June 30	September 30
Sales	$ 40,797	$ 48,855	$ 44,424	$ 38,653
Gross profit[1]	6,455	8,408	10,825	7,313
Restructuring of operations.	-0-	3,867	-0-	17,799
Net (loss)[2]	(3,594)	(5,440)	(2,389)	(20,570)
(Loss) per Common Share[2]	(.84)	(1.26)	(.57)	(4.72)
Share prices (NYSE)				
High.	21-3/4	20-1/2	27-1/2	25-3/4
Low	16-3/4	17-1/4	19 1/8	21-3/8
Dividends per Common Share	.35	.35	.10	.10

1982	December 31	March 31	June 30	September 30
Sales	$101,922	$ 97,083	$ 77,419	$ 50,544
Gross profit[1]	25,071	27,175	23,589	17,981
Restructuring of operations.	1,688	225	410	7,304
Net earnings (loss)[3]	3,840	5,829	4,312	(2,381)
Earnings (loss) per Common Share[3]	.85	1.29	.95	(.53)
Share prices (NYSE)				
High.	23-1/8	24-3/4	22-1/2	20-3/4
Low	17-1/4	20-3/4	16-5/8	15-5/8
Dividends per Common Share	.35	.35	.35	.35

(1) Gross profit as used herein is defined as sales less cost of products sold including applicable portion of depreciation expense.
(2) Liquidation of LIFO inventory quantities decreased net loss by $1,253,000 in the first quarter ($.29 per Common Share), $596,000 in the second quarter ($.14 per Common Share), $1,582,000 in the third quarter ($.36 per Common Share), and $3,820,000 in the fourth quarter ($.87 per Common Share).

(3) Liquidation of LIFO inventory quantities increased net earnings by $409,000 in the first quarter ($.09 per Common Share), $630,000 in the second quarter ($.14 per Common Share), $2,215,000 in the third quarter ($.49 per Common Share), and $3,870,000 in the fourth quarter ($.85 per Common Share).

Exhibit 9

upon the share price, happily in this case not very much! The company can be forgiven for wanting to emphasize that the share price has suffered hardly at all from the fall-off in trade.

Further examination shows that breakeven analysis is not going to be easy; there appears to be little correlation between the sales and net earnings (loss) figures and part of the reason obviously lies in the restructuring costs charged to operations and in the liquidation of LIFO inventories described in the notes. Any attempt to relate net earnings (loss) to sales without adjustments is not going to work. Exhibit 10 shows unequivocally the erratic relationship.

However, we know that the concept of breakeven has its

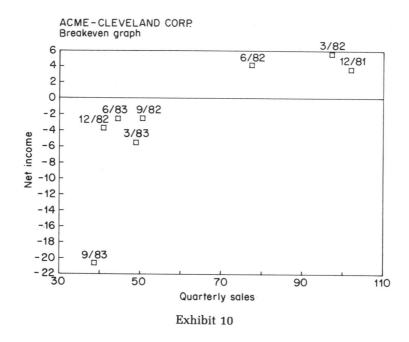

Exhibit 10

roots in the distinction between fixed and variable costs and neither restructuring costs nor LIFO liquidation profits fit easily into the mould. Restructuring costs are neither fixed nor variable but unusual. Likewise the paper profits arising when falling physical inventory levels cause costs incurred perhaps many years ago to pass through the income statement can only distort the calculation. We need to eliminate both these items from the net income figure to find an adjusted net earnings on which to base our break-even analysis. The results are tabulated below. Note that the restructuring charge shown on the table is pretax (though this is not obvious) and that the number must be multiplied by 1 − tax rate (say 40 per cent) to obtain the effect on net income at the earlier year. For the later year, the tax notes make clear that the restructuring costs were largely dis-allowed for tax purposes and that taxes were heavier overall because of loss of investment tax credit and foreign taxes. Accordingly, no adjustment has been made.

$m	12/81	3/82	6/82	9/82	12/82	3/83	6/83	9/83
Sales	101.9	97.1	77.4	50.5	40.8	48.9	44.4	38.7
Net earnings								
(loss)	3.84	5.83	4.31	(2.38)	(3.59)	(5.44)	(2.39)	(20.57)
Adjustments								
—restructuring	1.69	0.23	0.41	7.30	0.00	3.87	0.00	17.80
—tax adjusted	1.01	0.14	0.25	4.38	0.00	3.87	0.00	17.80
—LIFO	(1.25)	(0.60)	(1.58)	(3.82)	(0.41)	(0.63)	(2.22)	(3.87)
Adjusted net								
earnings (loss)	3.60	5.37	2.98	(1.82)	(4.00)	(2.70)	(4.61)	(6.64)

From the graph in Exhibit 11 a coherent picture now emerges. The last five points fall close to a straight line (line A) which passes through the x axis at quarterly sales of $55m indicating a breakeven point of $220m a year. The three earlier plottings are well to the right of this line, this

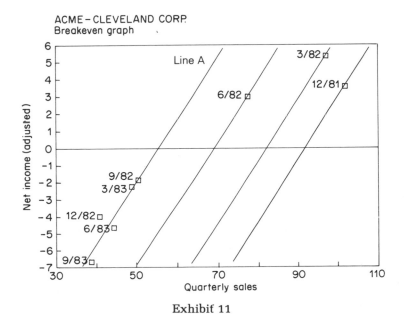

Exhibit 11

Quarterly Data For Fiscal Years 1984 and 1983 (In thousands of dollars, except per share data)
(Unaudited)

1984	December 31	March 31	June 30	September 30
Net Sales	$48,451	$51,321	$54,561	$58,510
Gross profit[1]	13,025	10,766	9,904	(616)[5]
Net (loss) earnings[2]				
Before extraordinary credit	234	(1,283)	(2,789)	(7,558)[6]
Extraordinary credit	325	(325)	–0–	–0–
	559	(1,608)	(2,789)	(7,558)
Net (loss) earnings per Common Share[2][4]				
Before extraordinary credit	.04	(.24)	(.47)	(1.25)
Extraordinary credit	.07	(.06)	–0–	–0–
	.11	(.30)	(.47)	(1.25)
Share prices (NYSE)				
High	26-3/4	27-1/4	22	17-3/8
Low	22	20	16-1/2	12-7/8
Dividends per Common Share	.10	.10	.10	.10

1983	December 31	March 31	June 30	September 30
Net Sales	$40,797	$48,855	$44,424	$38,653
Gross profit[1]	6,455	8,408	10,825	7,313
Restructuring of operations	–0–	3,867	–0–	17,799
Net (loss)[3]	(3,594)	(5,440)	(2,389)	(20,570)
Net (loss) per Common Share[3]	(.84)	(1.26)	(.57)	(4.72)
Share prices (NYSE)				
High	21-3/4	20-1/2	27-1/2	25-3/4
Low	16-3/4	17-1/4	19-1/8	21-3/8
Dividends per Common Share	.35	.35	.10	.10

[1] Gross profit as used herein is defined as sales less cost of products sold including applicable portion of depreciation expense.

[2] Liquidation of LIFO inventory quantities increased net earnings by $366,000 in the first quarter ($.08 per Common Share), and reduced the net loss by $1,129,000 in the second quarter ($.22 per Common Share), and $1,020,000 in the third quarter ($.17 per Common Share). In the fourth quarter increases in inventory levels caused a recovery of previously liquidated LIFO inventory quantities and increased the net loss by $802,000 ($.13 per Common Share).

[3] Liquidation of LIFO inventory quantities decreased net loss by $1,253,000 in the first quarter ($.29 per Common Share), $596,000 in the second quarter ($.14 per Common Share), $1,582,000 in the third quarter ($.36 per Common Share), and $3,820,000 in the fourth quarter ($.87 per Common Share).

[4] Due to the effect of the sale of 1,725,000 newly issued common shares in January, 1984, and the use of the weighted shares outstanding method of calculating earnings per share, the sum of the quarterly results per share amounts does not equal the results per share for the year.

[5] The fourth quarter includes adjustments which increased the net losses by $8,900,000 ($1.46 per Common Share) which were associated with certain inadequately priced contracts in the order backlog of the LaSalle Machine Tool subsidiary. No related tax benefit was provided because of the Corporation's net operating loss carryforward position.

[6] In the fourth quarter, changes in the effective tax rate caused tax benefits to increase by $1,949,000 ($.32 per Common Share) due to lower than anticipated results.

Exhibit 12

evidence indicating that breakeven point was falling as fixed costs were gradually eliminated, but that over the last four quarters little further progress was made. Lines parallel to line A have been drawn through the three earliest points to illustrate possible movements in the breakeven point.

Further complications ensued in 1984, as may be seen from Exhibit 12. There were no more restructuring costs, but in addition to the LIFO liquidation adjustment, there were unusual distortions in the final quarter attributable to 'inadequately priced contracts' and to 'changes in the effective tax rate'. Repeating the above exercise we have:

$m	12/83	3/84	6/84	9/84
Sales	48.5	51.3	54.6	58.5
Net earnings (loss)	0.23	(1.28)	(2.79)	(7.56)
Adjustments				
—LIFO	(0.37)	(1.13)	(1.02)	0.80
—contracts	0.00	0.00	0.00	8.90
—tax rate	0.00	0.00	0.00	(1.95)
Adjusted net earnings (loss)	(0.14)	(0.15)	(3.81)	0.19

Here the model seems to break down although none of these points is very far from line A (see Exhibit 13) and breakeven point does not appear to have shifted over the year. The size of the loss in the third quarter is particularly surprising. It is strange that gross profit declined over the first three quarters against a trend of rising sales and one suspects that the effect of inadequately priced contracts was also felt to a smaller extent earlier in the year. There is no way of telling without more information, perhaps from the quarterly reports or the 10-Q filings Acme-Cleveland will have made each quarter with the Securities and Exchange Commission. It would, in any case, be a mistake to attach too great a significance to any particular set of figures because of the inadequacy of the distinction between fixed and variable costs implicit in the model, and we have made no allowances for inflation as theoretically we should.

The point is that we have had to do some digging. As

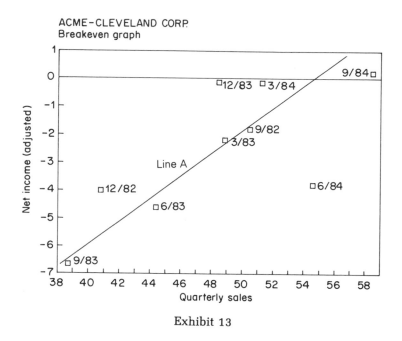

Exhibit 13

presented, with the emphasis on net income and the per share data, the numbers are hard to analyse and the trends unclear. Strip out some of the distortions caused by accountancy, and the underlying position starts to show its face. We lack the information to pursue the search much further, which is frustrating, and the frustration is needless since more helpful formatting, and rather less detail, would have illustrated clearly what any analyst should most like to know.

Finally, note that the parallel lines enable us to calculate total leverage. Acme-Cleveland is operating so close to breakeven that earnings are extremely sensitive to changes in sales. Provided, though (and it is a big 'provided'), that the cost structure does not alter, we know exactly what earnings will be for any suggested sales figure and from any given point on the line we can readily calculate the percentage effect on earnings for a 1 per cent change in sales.

Quarterly Data For Fiscal Years 1985 and 1984 (In thousands, except per share data)
(Unaudited)

1985[2][3]	December 31	March 31	June 30	September 30
Net Sales from Continuing Operations	$53,889	$54,755	$58,008	$54,281
Gross Profit from Continuing Operations [1]	15,133	17,628	18,114	19,491
Earnings from Continuing Operations [6]	48	1,573	1,722[11]	1,258[4][5]
(Loss) from Discontinued Operations	(642)	(555)	(5,465)	(9,432)[7]
Net (Loss) Earnings	(594)	1,018	(3,743)	(8,174)
(Loss) Earnings per Common Share[6][9]:				
Continuing Operations	-0-	.25	.26	.19
Discontinued Operations	(.11)	(.09)	(.87)	(1.50)
	(.11)	.16	(.61)	(1.31)
Share prices (NYSE)				
High	15-7/8	19-1/2	16-7/8	17-1/4
Low	12-1/2	13	13-1/2	12-1/4
Dividends per Common Share	.10	.10	.10	.10

1984[2][3]	December 31	March 31	June 30	September 30
Net Sales from Continuing Operations	$34,777	$37,637	$37,361	$41,260
Gross Profit from Continuing Operations [1]	10,650	10,014	10,203	8,312
Earnings (Loss) from Continuing Operations [8]				
Before Extraordinary Item	522	267	358	(1,195)
Extraordinary Item	325	(325)	-0-	-0-
	847	(58)	358	(1,195)
(Loss) from Discontinued Operations	(288)	(1,550)	(3,147)	(6,363)[10]
Net (Loss)	559	(1,608)	(2,789)	(7,558)
(Loss) Earnings per Common Share[8][9]:				
Continuing Operations:				
Before Extraordinary Item	.10	.03	.05	(.21)
Extraordinary Item	.08	(.05)	-0-	-0-
	.18	(.02)	.05	(.21)
Discontinued Operations	(.07)	(.28)	(.52)	(1.04)
	.11	(.30)	(.47)	(1.25)
Share prices (NYSE)				
High	26-3/4	27-1/4	22	17-3/8
Low	22	20	16-1/2	12-7/8
Dividends per Common Share	.10	.10	.10	.10

[1] Gross profit as used herein is defined as sales less cost of products sold including applicable portion of depreciation expense.

[2] The quarters have been restated to reflect the discontinuation of the LaSalle Machine Tool Group and the Systems Division (explained in Note C to the financial statements)

[3] On October 2, 1984, the Corporation purchased Communications Technology Corporation, whose operations are included from that date forward.

[4] The fourth quarter includes the effects of changes in inventory cost estimates which increased earnings from continuing operations by $1,488,000 ($.24 per Common Share).

[5] The restructuring of operations (explained in Note D to the financial statements) adversely affected earnings from continuing operations in the fourth quarter by $1,831,000 ($.29 per Common Share).

[6] In 1985, liquidation of LIFO inventory quantities increased earnings from continuing operations by $323,000 ($.05 per Common Share) in the first quarter, $761,000 ($.13 per Common Share) in the second quarter, $378,000 ($.06 per Common Share) in the third quarter, and $458,000 in the fourth quarter ($.07 per Common Share).

[7] The fourth quarter includes the effects of certain inventory costing adjustments made at the Systems Division which increased the loss from discontinued operations by $2,621,000 ($.42 per Common Share).

[8] In 1984, liquidation of LIFO inventory quantities increased earnings from continuing operations by $470,000 in the first quarter ($.11 per Common Share), decreased the loss from continuing operations by $372,000 in the second quarter ($.07 per Common Share), and increased earnings from continuing operations by $478,000 in the third quarter ($.08 per Common Share). In the fourth quarter, increases in inventory levels caused a recovery of previously liquidated LIFO inventory quantities and increased the loss from continuing operations by $516,000 ($.08 per Common Share).

[9] Due to the effect of the issuance of 168,981 common shares in April, 1985 for the acquisition of Industrial Innovations Special, Inc. and the sale of 1,725,000 newly issued shares in January, 1984, and the use of the weighted shares outstanding method of calculating earnings per share, the sum of the quarterly results per share amounts does not equal the results per share for the respective years.

[10] The fourth quarter includes adjustments caused by certain inadequately priced contracts in the order backlog of the LaSalle Machine Tool subsidiary, which increased the loss from discontinued operations by $4,806,000 ($.79 per Common Share).

[11] The third quarter was favorably impacted by a net adjustment of $1,064,000 ($.17 per Common Share) for reduced pension expense due to changes in certain actuarial assumptions used in valuing and funding various pension plans (explained in Note G to the financial statements).

Exhibit 14

Just to bring the story up to date, we have reproduced the equivalent page of the 1985 Annual Report (Exhibit 14) and performed the adjustments indicated by the footnotes. The outcome is given below:

	12/83	3/84	6/84	9/84	12/84	3/85	6/85	9/85
Sales	34.8	37.6	37.4	41.3	53.9	54.8	58.0	54.3
Earnings (loss) from continuing operations before extraordinary items	0.52	0.27	0.36	(1.20)	0.05	1.57	1.72	1.26
Adjustments								
—inventory cost estimates								(1.49)
—Restructuring								1.83
—LIFO	(0.47)	(0.37)	(0.48)	(0.52)	(0.32)	(0.76)	(0.38)	(0.46)
—Pensions							(1.06)	
Adjusted earnings (loss) from continuing operations	0.05	(0.10)	(0.12)	(1.72)	(0.27)	0.81	0.28	1.14

These points do not fall very close to a straight line (see Exhibit 15), but if we were to state that Acme-Cleveland's breakeven point was, during fiscal 1985, around $54m per quarter or $216m a year one would be hard put to disagree. Notice that in evey single quarter the adjusted results are worse than the recorded results and also how complicated the picture is becoming to follow. In October 1984, Acme-Cleveland purchased Communications Technology Corporation and thereafter its results were consolidated into those of Acme-Cleveland, this presumably being the reason for the jump in sales in the first quarter of fiscal 1985. What happened to the cost structure we can only guess.

Readers will also have noticed that the 1984 results have been restated to make a distinction between continuing and discontinued operations. It is hard to say that this is unreasonable as the company wants naturally to emphasize the viability of the core business it is retaining. Yet the

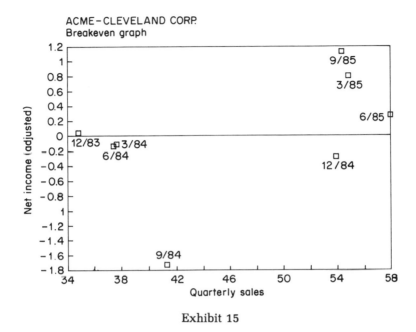

ACME-CLEVELAND CORP.
Breakeven graph

Exhibit 15

analyst's work is frustrated by this approach, as changes in accounting policy make it difficult to compare successive years. Management is, of course, trying to show that the losses are not structural but confined largely to areas of business destined to be sold. Given Acme-Cleveland's dropping share price and failure to show significant profits the change of emphasis is understandable.

Acme-Cleveland's Annual Reports are actually extremely frank and open and we do not in any way accuse its management of attempting any deception or distortion. All we would point out, in conclusion, is that for a company in Acme-Cleveland's position, success will depend upon generating sales. The management has probably handled the recession and the catastrophic fall in sales as well as was humanly possible. As an investor, we would want to know, first and foremost, what sales the company might be expected to deliver in coming years and how the breakeven point will move if extra capacity has now to be added. We do venture to suggest that straightforward answers to these questions would be more enlightening than the pages of highly detailed analysis of the past which in accordance with standard accounting practice the company has actually published for its shareholders' edification.

Revlon, Inc.

Revlon is a household word the world over and synonymous to millions with up-market cosmetics and glamorous advertising. Yet despite consistent sales of more than $2bn, from 1980 onwards the company's performance was definitely a lack-lustre one as net earnings fell from $192.4m to $111.1m in 1982 and $111.2m in 1983. It remained a very substantial and well-capitalized company throughout this period, but with a balance sheet that became gradually more reliant on interest-bearing debt and, interestingly, rather less liquid in terms of working capital and the current ratio.

The table below shows these trends:

$m (except ratios)	1980	1981	1982	1983
Sales	2203.3	2365.9	2351.0	2378.9
Net income	192.4	174.8	111.1	111.2
Total assets	2264.0	2316.6	2272.5	2215.3
Equity	950.9	938.7	950.7	903.1
Interest-bearing debt (including convertible debentures)	582.4	595.1	534.4	690.2
Current assets	1410.6	1403.7	1320.4	1292.7
Current liabilities	653.9	716.5	720.8	816.1
Debt/equity	61.2%	63.4%	56.2%	76.4%
Current ratio	2.2	2.0	1.8	1.6

In its 1983 Annual Report, Revlon published the 'Consolidated Statements of Changes in Financial Position' shown in Exhibit 16, and it is this document that we shall consider in detail. As a funds flow statement it is unusually detailed, although how a reader might benefit from that detail is hard to say. The apparent import of these statements can be summed up in a couple of lines. In each of the 3 years, uses of funds exceeded sources, causing a drop in

Consolidated Statements of Changes in Financial Position

Revlon, Inc. and Subsidiaries

Years ended December 31, 1983, 1982 and 1981

(thousands of dollars)	1983	1982	1981
Funds were provided by:			
Operations:			
Net earnings	$ 111,203	$111,140	$174,821
Depreciation and amortization, including amortization of intangibles	76,274	68,147	66,657
Deferred taxes on income	12,045	16,370	10,690
	199,522	195,657	252,168
Sale and retirement of property, plant and equipment	32,399*	10,427	9,669
Increase in long-term debt	127,122	11,795	5,665
Issuance of common stock, including treasury stock	10,659	29,633	15,640
Exchange of common stock for debt	—	32,550	—
	$ 369,702	$280,062	$283,142
Funds were used for:			
Dividends on common stock	65,478	63,805	66,079
Dividends on convertible preferred stock	8,490	22,298	22,298
Purchase of property, plant and equipment	80,520	129,047	151,774
Purchase of convertible preferred stock	240,640	—	—
Excess of the purchase price over book value of the convertible preferred stock on dates of purchase	47,203	—	—
Decrease in long-term debt from exchange of common stock	—	39,245	—
Other decreases in long-term debt	5,848	29,084	14,657
Decrease in long-term convertible debentures, principally conversions	—	24,676	3,831
Purchase of treasury stock	—	31,820	65,665
Increase in intangibles and other assets—net	22,050	15,086	13,367
Effect of foreign currency translation adjustments	22,460	12,582	14,921
	492,689	367,643	352,592
Decrease in working capital	$(122,987)	$ (87,581)	$ (69,450)
Changes in elements of working capital:			
Net increase (decrease) in current assets:			
Cash, time deposits and short-term investments	$ (11,940)	$ (43,810)	$ (11,185)
Receivables	6,180	(12,478)	(8,876)
Inventories	(32,205)	(20,311)	18,488
Other	10,294	(6,737)	(5,274)
	(27,671)	(83,336)	(6,847)
Net increase (decrease) in current liabilities:			
Notes payable and foreign bank borrowings	56,816	6,683	12,846
Accounts payable	(6,900)	11,120	(7,206)
Other	45,400	(13,558)	56,963
	95,316	4,245	62,603
Decrease in working capital	(122,987)	(87,581)	(69,450)
Working capital at beginning of period	599,613	687,194	756,644
Working capital at end of period	$ 476,626	$599,613	$687,194
Current ratio	1.6 to 1	1.8 to 1	2.0 to 1

*Includes net assets of subsidiary sold in 1983 of $20,477

Exhibit 16(a)   Reproduced by permission of Revlon, Inc.

Consolidated Statements of Earnings

Years ended December 31, 1983, 1982 and 1981

Revlon, Inc. and Subsidiaries

(thousands of dollars, except share figures)	1983	1982	1981
Net sales	$2,378,867	$2,350,988	$2,365,938
Cost of goods sold	988,184	988,942	944,157
Selling, administrative and general expenses	1,142,428	1,127,773	1,084,745
	2,130,612	2,116,715	2,028,902
Profit from operations	248,255	234,273	337,036
Other deductions (income):			
Interest expense	82,930	69,982	67,067
Interest income	(37,819)	(44,268)	(58,545)
Net interest expense	45,111	25,714	8,522
Miscellaneous, net	(3,864)	2,509	26,476
	41,247	28,223	34,998
Earnings before income taxes	207,008	206,050	302,038
Provision for taxes on income	95,805	94,910	127,217
Net earnings	$ 111,203	$ 111,140	$ 174,821
Net earnings per share of common stock:			
Primary	$ 2.81	$ 2.45	$ 4.10
Fully diluted	$ 2.80	$ 2.41	$ 4.02
Net earnings applicable to common stock:			
Primary	$ 100,205	$ 84,398	$ 148,160
Assuming full dilution	$ 100,606	$ 85,065	$ 149,200
Average common and common equivalent shares outstanding:			
Primary	35,625,000	34,477,000	36,103,000
Assuming full dilution	35,969,000	35,349,000	37,129,000

Exhibit 16(b)   Reproduced by permission of Revlon, Inc.

working capital. Principal sources were income and depreciation and in 1983 new long-term debt. This money was spent on dividends, capital expenditures and, particularly in 1983, the repurchase of Revlon's own securities.

That is about all that can be readily gleaned from this complex schedule. Yet, in fact, there is a wealth of information here of considerable interest which emerges by rearranging these numbers and introducing a few details from other parts of the Annual Report.

As we demonstrated in Chapters 5 and 6, the first task is to restore some mathematical discipline to the format of these numbers and to replace the net earnings line with its constituent numbers extracted from the income statement. We have added the figures for 1980 to obtain a clearer view of the trends, and to simplify the analysis we have shortened the titles and shown the numbers in round millions rather than thousands of dollars. Also, the earliest year is shown on the left in accordance with our preferred format.

Revlon, Inc.

$m	1980	1981	1982	1983
Sales	2203	2366	2351	2379
Cost of goods sold	(865)	(944)	(989)	(988)
SGA expense	(980)	(1085)	(1128)	(1143)
Interest expense	(48)	(67)	(70)	(83)
Interest income	35	58	44	38
Other income/expense	(8)	(26)	(3)	4
Tax	(145)	(127)	(95)	(96)
Net earnings	192	175	110*	111
Depreciation	53	67	68	76
Deferred tax	2	11	16	12
Sale of fixed assets	8	10	10	32
Increase in long-term debt	306	6	12	127
Issue of stock	18	16	30	11
Funding exchange	—	—	33	—
Issue of preferred stock	229	—	—	—
Sundry	1	—	—	—
Common dividends	(57)	(66)	(64)	(65)
Preferred dividends	(14)	(22)	(22)	(8)
Capital expenditure	(239)	(152)	(129)	(81)
Increase in intangibles	(117)	(18)	(2)	—
Purchase of preferred stock	—	—	—	(241)
Premium on purchase of p.s.	—	—	—	(47)
Funding exchange	—	—	(39)	—
Decrease in long-term debt	(58)	(15)	(29)	(6)
Decrease in convertible debentures	(7)	(4)	(25)	—
Purchase of treasury stock	(1)	(66)	(32)	—
Intangible/other assets	(60)	5	(13)	(22)
Foreign exchange translations	—	(15)	(12)	(22)
Cash/investments	(124)	11	44	12

Revlon, Inc (contd)

$m	1980	1981	1982	1983
Receivables	(146)	8	12	(6)
Inventories	(114)	(19)	20	32
Prepayments†	(28)	3	11	(14)
Other current assets†	(6)	2	(4)	4
Notes payable	66	13	7	57
Accounts payable	(3)	(7)	11	(7)
Employee benefits†	14	7	(4)	3
Taxes payable†	35	9	(13)	25
Current portion LTD†	—	13	13	(22)
Other current liabilities†	50	28	(9)	39
	0	0	0	0

*Rounding error.
†Individual figures broken out from balance sheets.

One irritating feature of Revlon's published statement is the size of the 'other' categories. US accounting standards are surprisingly relaxed about 'other assets' and 'other liabilities', 'other income' and 'other expense' and these meaningless phrases are deemed by some companies adequate explanation for entries running to tens of millions of dollars. Rarely if ever is any detailed breakdown provided in the notes or in the 10-K filing report and readers of the Annual Report who wonder why all the figures are given to the nearest $10 000 when it was permissible, in 1980, for cash flows of $98.435m to be classified as 'Net increase in current liabilities: Other' can only note the fact and register severe exasperation!

By looking at the balance sheets (see Exhibit 17) and noting the actual year to year changes in certain accounts we have been able to break out some detail of the actual changes lumped together as 'other'. Notice, however, that we have resorted to the balance sheet only to break down particular entries on the funds flow statement where there is reason to suppose some 'lumping together' has occurred. It is not permissible to introduce balance sheet changes in

Consolidated Balance Sheets

Revlon, Inc. and Subsidiaries

December 31, 1983 and 1982

(thousands of dollars)	1983	1982
Assets		
Current assets:		
Cash and time deposits	$ 254,150	$ 260,902
Short-term investments at cost, plus accrued interest, which approximates market	62,238	67,426
Accounts receivable—trade, less allowances of $20,391 and $21,678	429,979	423,799
Inventories	446,635	478,840
Prepayments	78,445	64,515
Other	21,272	24,908
Total current assets	1,292,719	1,320,390
Property, plant and equipment, at cost:		
Land and land improvements	46,554	47,701
Buildings and leasehold improvements	387,092	373,106
Machinery and equipment	384,419	388,704
Construction in progress	18,348	36,294
	836,413	845,805
Less accumulated depreciation and amortization	226,125	203,232
Total property, plant and equipment	610,288	642,573
Other assets:		
Excess of cost over net assets acquired, less accumulated amortization of $39,041 and $34,466	192,421	209,803
Patents, less amortization	10,241	12,906
Other	109,661	86,834
Total assets	$2,215,330	$2,272,506
Liabilities and Stockholders' Equity		
Current liabilities:		
Notes payable and foreign bank borrowings	$ 244,901	$ 188,085
Accounts payable	132,254	139,154
Employee compensation and benefits	115,740	113,232
Taxes on income	97,029	69,405
Other taxes	38,153	40,235
Current installments on long-term debt	4,259	26,496
Other	183,757	144,170
Total current liabilities	816,093	720,777
Long-term debt	427,399	306,125
Convertible debentures	13,644	13,644
Deferred taxes on income	52,883	40,838
Convertible preferred stock (Series A adjustable rate, redeemable at $2,791)	2,242	240,374
Stockholders' equity:		
Common stock of $1 par value a share. Authorized 75,000,000 shares; issued 37,791,582 shares in 1983 and 37,463,424 shares in 1982	37,792	37,463
Additional paid-in capital	202,436	193,204
Retained earnings	854,325	866,801
Equity adjustment from foreign currency translation	(129,010)	(83,148)
	965,543	1,014,320
Less common stock in treasury, at cost; 2,073,809 shares in 1983 and 2,096,370 shares in 1982	(62,474)	(63,572)
Total stockholders' equity	903,069	950,748
Total liabilities and stockholders' equity	$2,215,330	$2,272,506

Exhibit 17   Reproduced by permission of Revlon, Inc.

an undisciplined fashion into the cash flow or the resulting
series of numbers will not cast to zero.

The schedule we have produced is a complicated one
and in order that we may generate a cash flow in our chosen
format some simplification is necessary. It is a matter for
the analyst's discretion which items he chooses to amalga-
mate, but the following is probably not unreasonable:

	1980	1981	1982	1983
1.				
Cost of goods sold	(865)	(944)	(989)	(988)
Depreciation	53	67	68	76
Net cost of goods sold	(812)	(877)	(921)	(912)
2.				
SGA expense	(980)	(1085)	(1128)	(1143)
Employee benefits	14	7	(4)	3
Net SGA expense	(966)	(1078)	(1132)	(1140)
3.				
Tax	(145)	(127)	(95)	(96)
Deferred tax	2	11	16	12
Taxes payable	35	9	(13)	25
Cash taxes paid	(108)	(107)	(92)	(59)
4.				
Interest income	35	58	44	38
Other income/expense	(8)	(26)	(3)	4
Funding exchange	—	—	33	—
Sundry	1	—	—	—
Funding exchange	—	—	(39)	—
Other assets	(60)	5	(13)	(22)
Foreign exchange translations	—	(15)	(12)	(22)
Other current assets	(6)	2	(4)	4
Other current liabilities	50	28	(9)	39
Other cash income	12	52	(3)	41

	1980	1981	1982	1983
5.				
Common dividends	(57)	(66)	(64)	(65)
Preferred dividends	(14)	(22)	(22)	(8)
Dividends	(71)	(88)	(86)	(73)
6.				
Decrease in long-term debt	(58)	(15)	(29)	(6)
Decrease in convertible debentures	(7)	(4)	(25)	—
Current portion LTD	—	13	13	(22)
Debt repayment	(65)	(6)	(41)	(28)
7.				
Issue of stock	18	16	30	11
Issue of preferred stock	229	—	—	—
Purchase of preferred stock	—	—	—	(241)
Premium on purchase of p.s.	—	—	—	(47)
Purchase of treasury stock	(1)	(66)	(32)	—
Equity	246	(50)	(2)	(277)

And we can now construct a full cash flow statement.

	1980	1981	1982	1983
Sales	2203	2366	2351	2379
Receivables	(146)	8	12	(6)
Net cost of goods sold	(812)	(877)	(921)	(912)
Inventory	(114)	(19)	20	32
Accounts payable	(3)	(7)	11	(7)
Net SGA expense	(966)	(1078)	(1132)	(1140)
Prepayments	(28)	3	11	(14)

	1980	1981	1982	1983
Cash after operating items	134	396	352	332
Other cash income	12	52	(3)	41
Cash taxes paid	(108)	(107)	(92)	(59)
Cash after quasi-operational items	38	341	257	314
Interest expense	(48)	(67)	(70)	(83)
Dividends	(71)	(88)	(86)	(73)
Debt repayment	(65)	(6)	(41)	(28)
Cash after financing costs	(146)	180	60	130
Capital expenditure	(239)	(152)	(129)	(81)
Increase in intangibles	(117)	(18)	(2)	—
Sale of fixed assets	8	10	10	32
Cash after discretionary items	(494)	20	(61)	81
Notes payable	66	13	7	57
Increase in long-term debt	306	6	12	127
Equity	246	(50)	(2)	(277)
Cash	124	(11)	(44)	(12)

We can see at once that 1980 was a year in which cash generation from the asset conversion cycle fell short of that needed to meet the quasi-operational items, the financing costs and the debt repayment. Cash generation in subsequent years seems to have been more than adequate and would give no cause for concern.

From an analyst's point of view, we are already deep in what would normally be considered uncharted waters and one could rest here on one's laurels and content oneself with a discussion of the pattern of the numbers above. Such a discussion would, in fact, be virtually futile because the funds flow statement as published fails almost entirely to acknowledge the effect of purchases and sales of subsidiary companies; apart from the footnote to the funds flow statement and the striking number of increases in intangibles, there would be no way to discern that these were important.

Happily, the notes are more enlightening and a couple of extracts are reproduced in Exhibit 18. There are some very substantial numbers in these transactions and it will come as no surprise to find that the purchases and sales in question were for amounts that do not appear on the published funds flow. The reason, as usual, is that reconciling the balance sheet was a higher priority for the company than demonstrating the true cash flows, and given that it is impossible to do both, the components of the sales and purchases relating to fixed assets, working capital, etc., have been split up and allocated to those sections within the published funds flow.

From the last paragraph in the 1982 extract (Exhibit 18a), we learn that major corporate purchases in 1980 affected the balance sheet as follows:

$m
148   working capital
 82   fixed assets
 62   other assets
less (88) long-term debt
──────
204
──────

In addition, we know that the increase in intangibles was $117m suggesting a total purchase price of $321m. That corresponds quite well with the company's own breakdown given in the notes.

$m
228.7 preferred stock
  1.4 common stock
 59.0 cash
 29.3 cash
──────
318.4
──────

Acquisitions

During 1982 and 1981, Revlon acquired companies in purchase transactions for aggregate cash consideration approximating $4,800,000 and $5,500,000, respectively.

In August 1980, Revlon acquired Continuous Curve Contact Lenses, Inc. ("Continuous Curve"), a manufacturer and supplier of various types of contact lenses and accessory care products, for approximately 2,184,000 shares of common stock, of which approximately 51,000 shares were returned from escrow in 1982. Such acquisition was accounted for as a pooling of interests, and its operations are included in the consolidated financial statements for the full year 1980.

In May 1980, Revlon acquired Technicon Corporation ("Technicon") in a purchase transaction. The purchase price consisted of 11,435,040 shares of a newly-created series of Revlon preferred stock (value $228.7 million); approximately 38,000 shares of Revlon common stock (value $1.4 million); and approximately $59 million in cash. Technicon is primarily engaged in the development and manufacture of automated clinical diagnostic equipment. The results of Technicon's operations are included in the consolidated financial statements from May 2, 1980.

Pro-forma consolidated results of operations for 1980 (unaudited) as though Technicon had been acquired as of January 1, 1980 follow:

	1980
Net sales (in thousands)	$2,302,000
Net earnings (in thousands)	$194,000
Earnings per share of common stock:	
Primary	$4.67
Fully diluted	$4.56

During 1980 Revlon also acquired, in purchase transactions, four companies for an aggregate cash consideration of approximately $29,300,000.

Principal assets acquired and liabilities assumed in all 1980 purchases approximated: working capital, $148,000,000; property, plant and equipment, $82,000,000; other assets, $62,000,000; and long-term debt, $88,000,000.

Taxes on Income

Revlon's earnings before taxes and the applicable provisions for income taxes are as follows (in thousands of dollars):

Earnings before taxes	1982	1981	1980
Domestic	$124,581	$215,096	$242,255
Foreign	81,469	86,942	95,141
	$206,050	$302,038	$337,396

Provision for taxes			
Federal	$ 45,704	$ 82,044	$ 96,795
Foreign	40,112	30,340	30,998
State and local	9,094	14,833	17,196
	$ 94,910	$127,217	$144,989
Current	$ 87,866	$117,422	$150,712
Deferred	7,044	9,795	(5,723)
	$ 94,910	$127,217	$144,989

The effective rate of taxes on earnings before income taxes for each of the three years ended December 31, 1982 is reconciled to the statutory Federal income tax rate as follows:

	1982	1981	1980
Statutory Federal income tax rate	46.0%	46.0%	46.0%
Change in normally expected income tax rate resulting from:			
State and local income taxes, net of Federal income tax benefit	2.2	2.6	2.7
Operations outside the U.S. and its possessions	5.9	2.3	(1.2)
Tax incentive exemptions	(9.5)	(7.3)	(6.2)
Other	1.5	(1.5)	1.7
Effective tax rate	46.1%	42.1%	43.0%

In the above reconciliation, "Other" includes such items as income subject to tax at capital gains rate; the investment tax credit; non-deductible amortization of intangible assets; the non-taxable gain in 1982 arising from the exchange of common stock for outstanding debt securities; and foreign exchange items that do not give rise to tax effects, none of which, if listed individually, would significantly affect the normally expected income tax rate.

Appropriate United States and foreign income taxes have been accrued on foreign earnings that have been or are expected to be remitted in the near future. Unremitted earnings of foreign subsidiaries which have been, or are currently intended to be, permanently reinvested in the future growth of the business aggregated approximately

Exhibit 18(a) Reproduced by permission of Revlon, Inc.

The acquisition of Continuous Curve was treated as a pooling of interests and no entries of substance seem to have been passed to the 1980 funds flow statements to accommodate it. 2.148m shares should have been worth in the order of $80m but no such entry is to be found on the funds statement and one suspects that the surprisingly large 'other' entries in this year have to do with this transaction. There is no way of proceeding further with this.

Revlon, Inc. and Subsidiaries

Acquisitions and Disposition

In June 1983, Revlon disposed of all the capital stock of Alford Industries, Inc. ("Alford"), a wholly-owned domestic subsidiary which manufactured product packaging for Revlon and other consumer product companies in various fields. The disposition, for cash of approximately $60,000,000, was made to a company in which Alford's former management participates, and resulted in a pre-tax gain of approximately $27,000,000. Sales and assets of Alford for periods prior to its sale were not significant to the sales and assets of Revlon. The pre-tax gain has been substantially offset by a provision relating to the revaluation of certain assets located in Latin America. Both the gain and the provision are included in "Other deductions (income)."

During 1982 and 1981, Revlon acquired companies in purchase transactions for aggregate cash consideration approximating $4,800,000 and $5,500,000, respectively.

Taxes on Income

Revlon's earnings before income taxes and the applicable provisions for taxes on income are as follows (in thousands of dollars):

Earnings before income taxes	1983	1982	1981
Domestic	$134,644	$124,581	$215,096
Foreign	72,364	81,469	86,942
	$207,008	$206,050	$302,038

Provision for taxes on income			
Federal	$ 48,271	$ 45,704	$ 82,044
Foreign	36,306	40,112	30,340
State and local	11,228	9,094	14,833
	$ 95,805	$ 94,910	$127,217
Current	$ 89,179	$ 87,866	$117,422
Deferred	6,626	7,044	9,795
	$ 95,805	$ 94,910	$127,217

The effective rate of taxes on earnings before income taxes for each of the years in the three-year period ended December 31, 1983 is reconciled to the statutory Federal income tax rate as follows:

	1983	1982	1981
Statutory Federal income tax rate	46.0%	46.0%	46.0%
Change in normally expected income tax rate resulting from:			
State and local income taxes, net of Federal income tax benefit	2.9	2.2	2.6
Operations outside the U.S. and its possessions	7.3	5.9	2.3
Tax incentive exemptions	(11.3)	(9.5)	(7.3)
Other	1.4	1.5	(1.5)
Effective tax rate	46.3%	46.1%	42.1%

In the above reconciliation, "Other" includes such items as non-deductible amortization expense; certain foreign currency items that do not give rise to tax effects; the non-taxable gain in 1982 arising from the exchange of common stock for outstanding debt securities; income subject to tax at capital gains rates; and the investment and other tax credits, none of which, if listed individually, are significant.

Appropriate United States and foreign income taxes have been accrued on foreign earnings that have been or are expected to be remitted in the near future. Unremitted earnings of foreign subsidiaries which have been, or are currently intended to be, permanently reinvested in the future growth of the business aggregated approximately $360,000,000 at December 31, 1983, including certain preacquisition earnings of acquired companies, and excluding those amounts which, if remitted in the near future, would not result in significant additional taxes under tax statutes currently in effect.

Deferred taxes relate principally to depreciation methods and leasing activities, and also include the effect of certain income and expenses which are reported for tax purposes in different periods than for financial statement purposes.

Foreign Operations

Net assets of foreign subsidiaries and branches located outside the United States were $503,000,000 and $532,000,000 at December 31, 1983 and 1982, respectively. The net assets do not reflect the $125,000,000 11% Eurodollar notes due 1990 which were issued by wholly-owned overseas finance subsidiaries in July 1983.

The amount of retained earnings of all foreign subsidiaries included in consolidated retained earnings amounted to approximately $322,000,000 and $302,000,000 at December 31, 1983 and 1982, respectively. At the present time, substantially all the retained earnings from Revlon's foreign operations are remittable to Revlon in United States dollars, in accordance with foreign laws and regulations.

Net transaction losses (net of tax) approximated $400,000 ($.01 per share) in 1983; net transaction gains (net of tax) approximated $5,800,000 ($.16 per share) in 1982; net transaction losses (net of tax) approximated $8,300,000 ($.22 per share) in 1981.

Inventories

Inventories consist of the following (in thousands of dollars):

	December 31	
	1983	1982
Finished goods	$221,947	$244,627
Work-in-process	89,375	83,506
Raw materials and supplies	135,313	150,707
	$446,635	$478,840

Exhibit 18(b)   Reproduced by permission of Revlon, Inc.

The purchases in 1981 and 1982 were relatively small and need not detain us, though we are put on notice that there are more pieces of the jigsaw around than we are able to pick up and reassemble. In our cash flow below we have substituted the correct figures from the obviously non-cash increase in intangibles and rebalanced the statement by making appropriate adjustments to the quasi-operational items section. We can, however, do something more interesting with the sale of Alford Industries in 1983 (Exhibit 18b). The arithmetic would appear to be that the subsidiary was sold for $60m at a profit of $27m. There is a curious little note on the face of the funds flow stating that net fixed assets of $20.477m were disposed of in the sale of a subsidiary and it follows that the $13m or so unaccounted for is probably, though not necessarily, included in the reported changes in the working capital accounts.

	1980	1981	1982	1983
Cash after operating items	134	396	352	332
Adjustment	148	—	—	(13)
Adjusted cash after operating items	282	396	352	319
Other cash income	12	52	(3)	41
Cash taxes paid	(108)	(107)	(92)	(59)
Adjustment	62	(12)	3	(27)
Adjusted cash after quasi-operational items	248	329	260	274
Financing costs/debt repayment	(184)	(161)	(197)	(184)
Adjusted cash after financing costs	64	168	63	90
Capital expenditure	(157)	(152)	(129)	(81)
Purchase of subsidiaries	(321)	(6)	(5)	—
Sale of fixed assets	8	10	10	12
Sale of subsidiaries	—	—	—	60
Adjusted cash after discretionary items	(406)	20	(61)	81
Notes payable	66	13	7	57
Increase in long-term debt	218	6	12	127
Equity	246	(50)	(2)	(277)
Cash	124	(11)	(44)	(12)

	1980	1981	1982	1983
Cash flow from NTI:				
Receivables	(146)	8	12	(6)
Inventory	(114)	(19)	20	32
Payables	(3)	(7)	11	(7)
Accrued expenses (employees)	14	7	(4)	3
Adjustments	148	—	—	(13)
Total	(101)	(11)	39	9

From these figures an altogether new and different view emerges. The company's most profitable year ever was 1980, and in 1981 the downturn began. In 1980, in addition to the substantial corporate acquisitions funded by a mixture of debt, equity and to a lesser extent cash, Revlon invested in NTI to the tune of $100m. In 1981, with profits tailing off, the additional investment was much smaller. Both in 1980 and in 1981 the rises in NTI were more or less in line with the increases in sales. A year later, with profitability starting to sag badly on broadly unchanged sales, the company started to reduce investment in NTI and even so its cash flow was much reduced by the declining margins it obtained on its sales. Consequently, adjusted cash after financing costs was only half the figure for capital expenditure. The year 1983 was broadly similar to 1982 and the reduction in NTI continued. Capital expenditure was cut back severely and $60m in cash was raised from the sale of Alford Industries. This money plus the new long- and short-term debt was applied to the repurchase of preferred stock, a move designed to replace the non-tax deductible dividend with a tax deductible interest charge.

We are starting, just starting, to shed some light on Revlon's cash flow. It has been a laborious process to get us this far and there is abundant evidence that there are a lot more adjustments that could be made if we had more of the right information. One such obvious instance is contained in the extract from the 'Management's Discussion and

Management's Discussion and Analysis of
Results of Operations and Financial Condition

Revlon, Inc. and Subsidiaries

Results of Operations

Health Products and Services sales of $1,262.7 million in 1983 reflected a 6.0% increase over 1982 sales, which had increased 7.1% over 1981. The sales growth in 1983 was principally in vision care (an increase of 20.7% in 1983 as compared with a 15.3% increase in 1982) and in the diagnostic business (7.3% growth in 1983 and 4.8% from 1981 to 1982). Worldwide ethical pharmaceuticals showed a 1.6% decrease in sales in 1983 after a 1.1% increase from 1981 to 1982.

Beauty Products sales were $1,116.1 million in 1983, a decrease of 3.8% from $1,159.6 million, which had decreased 7.5% from 1981. Sales of beauty products in 1983 in the United States, Canada and Puerto Rico were approximately the same as in 1982 after a 3.6% decrease from 1981 to 1982. International sales of $325.5 million in 1983 decreased 11.6% from 1982 after a 14.8% decrease from 1981. While international sales increased in local currencies in 1983, the continuing strength of the dollar reduced reported dollar sales, particularly in Latin America.

Cost of goods sold, as a percentage of net sales, was 41.5% in 1983, 42.1% in 1982 and 39.9% in 1981. Worldwide increases in costs of materials and increased labor rates have been partially offset by manufacturing efficiencies achieved through continual improvement in operating procedures, capital investments, and price increases. The decrease in 1983 reflects savings which resulted from actions taken to consolidate manufacturing facilities and to control labor and overhead spending.

Selling, administrative and general expenses, as a percentage of net sales, were 44.0% in 1983 and 1982, and 45.8% in 1981. The 1983 amount reflects a significant increase in marketing expenditures from 1982, offset by savings which resulted from certain cost reductions in general overhead categories. The increase in 1982 was due principally to significantly higher expenditures for marketing and for research and development. Revlon's investment in research and development was $113.7 million in 1983, $114.7 million in 1982 and $91.3 million in 1981.

Interest costs incurred, after capitalization of interest as part of property, plant and equipment, increased to $82.9 million in 1983 from $70.0 million in 1982 and $67.1 million in 1981; capitalized interest approximated $4.1 million, $29.1 million and $32.5 million in 1983, 1982 and 1981, respectively. The increase in 1983 resulted from increased borrowings, including the 11% Eurodollar notes and domestic borrowings relating to the purchase in 1983 of the Series A Convertible Preferred Stock ("Series A Stock"). The increase has been offset in part by lower amounts of foreign short-term borrowings in certain countries having high interest rates, and generally reduced rates in other foreign countries.

Interest expense in 1982, approximately the same as that in 1981, resulted from an increase in short-term borrowings, partially offset by the effect of the exchange of 1.2 million shares of common stock for $40 million principal amount of the 10⅜% Sinking fund debentures and the conversion of $21 million of convertible debentures into common stock during 1982.

Interest income was $37.8 million in 1983, $44.3 million in 1982 and $58.5 million in 1981. The decline in 1983 resulted principally from lower interest rates and a reduction in invested funds which were used to purchase the Series A Stock in 1983. The decline in interest income in 1982 resulted from a reduction of invested funds which were principally used to acquire shares of common stock.

The total net additional interest costs which resulted from the purchase of the Series A Stock and which are reflected in the 1983 statement of earnings approximated $15 million; the purchase also had the effect of reducing the amount of preferred dividends and amortization of the excess of redemption value of the Series A Stock over its fair value, which are deducted from net earnings to compute earnings applicable to common

stock. The net benefit arising from the purchase approximated 23 cents per share.

During the second quarter of 1983, the Company realized a pre-tax gain of approximately $27 million resulting from the disposition of Alford Industries, Inc. ("Alford"), a wholly-owned domestic subsidiary which manufactured product packaging for the Company and other consumer product companies in various fields. The disposition, for cash of approximately $60 million, was made to a company in which Alford's former management participates. Sales and assets of Alford for periods prior to its sale were not significant to the sales and assets of the Company. The gain has been substantially offset by a second quarter provision relating to the revaluation of certain assets located in Latin America. Both the gain and the provision are included in "Other deductions (income)." Net earnings in 1983 include a benefit (net of tax) of approximately $2.2 million resulting from the fourth quarter sale of certain common stock investments. In 1982, net earnings were adversely affected by a charge of 19 cents per share as a result of the first quarter settlement of litigation. Earnings were also affected by a non-taxable gain of 19 cents per share in the second quarter resulting from the exchange of common stock for debt. Net earnings in 1981 were reduced by the effect of non-recurring costs associated with the restructuring of certain overseas operations.

Net transaction losses (net of tax) in 1983 approximated $.4 million; net transaction gains (net of tax) in 1982 approximated $5.8 million; net transaction losses (net of tax) in 1981 approximated $8.3 million.

The provision for taxes on income was 46.3% of earnings before taxes in 1983, compared with 46.1% in 1982 and 42.1% in 1981. In 1983, increased earnings by companies which have been granted tax incentive exemptions and income subject to tax at capital gains rates were offset by losses in certain foreign operations which did not generate tax benefits. Significant factors affecting the increase in the effective tax rate in 1982 as compared with 1981 were foreign losses in 1982 which did not generate tax benefits, and favorable tax effects realized in 1981 attributable to certain reorganizations; these factors were offset in part by the non-taxable gain relating to the exchange of stock for debt in 1982, non-taxable currency gains in 1982 and currency losses in 1981 which did not generate tax benefits.

Earnings per share in the fourth quarter increased from $.42 in 1982 to $1.03 in 1983. The principal reasons for this increase were: increased net earnings resulting from slightly higher sales and from reductions in operating expenses; a reduction in the effective tax rate from 1982 to 1983; the benefit resulting from the purchase of the Series A Stock in 1983, as discussed above; and the gain on sale of common stock investments in the fourth quarter of 1983.

The high inflation rates which have been experienced worldwide in recent years have had an economic impact upon the Company's reported earnings and other financial information that is being presented as supplemental information to the historical financial statements. Revlon's results have been restated for the impact of current costs (specific price changes) as required by Statement of Financial Accounting Standards No. 33, as amended. The restated information is provided elsewhere in this report.

Financial Condition

Revlon's capital expenditures amounted to $80.5 million in 1983, $128.1 million in 1982 and $151.7 million in 1981. The higher capital spending in these years resulted from modernizing and constructing manufacturing and research facilities. It is expected that the Company will maintain a

Exhibit 19   Reproduced by permission of Revlon, Inc.

Analysis' reproduced as Exhibit 19. In plain English, this says that the $27m gain on the sale of Alford Industries is not shown separately in the accounts because, first, it has been largely offset by the write-off of certain Latin American assets, and secondly, both entries have been added into 'Other deductions (income)'.

We are not suggesting that any laws or accounting conventions are being broken in this treatment, but Alford Industries had nothing to do with Latin America that we know of, and it is hard to avoid the impression that the company seized the opportunity of a windfall profit to reduce the carrying value of certain assets without affecting net income to any noticeable extent.

To Revlon's credit, if it were not for the very full supplemental data (very full, that is, by the prevailing standards) there would be no way to penetrate at all behind the numbers given in the funds flow which would simply confuse the reader, as they probably do anyway. The irony is that Revlon provides pages of numbers and analysis in tiny print, apparently in an attempt to be helpful. Yet from our manipulation of the figures, partial and imperfect as it may be, it is clear that much of the detail is so confusing that the broad picture underneath eludes all but the most skilful and persistent. There is no reason why this should be so except the obduracy of accountants and producers of accounts in refusing to get the standards changed so that accruals can be banished forever from the funds flow statement to allow an unadulterated, meaningful cash flow to arise like a phoenix from the ashes.

Espley Trust plc

It is not often that the publication of an Annual Report of a profitable company provokes that company's immediate and terminal decline, but it happened in the summer of 1984 when Espley Trust's handsomely produced report hit

Espley Trust plc

Group profit and loss account and movement on reserves
for the 15 months ended 31st December, 1983

	NOTE	1983* £'000	1982 £'000
Profit on ordinary activities before taxation (including the results both of activities being retained and being sold)	2 & 3	1,712	2,765
Taxation	5	(1,154)	(581)
Profit on ordinary activities after taxation		558	2,184
Minority interests		—	(357)
Extraordinary items including goodwill written-off	6	(411)	(873)
Profit attributable to shareholders		147	954
Dividends	7	(1,258)	(569)
Transfer to/(from) reserves	18	(1,111)	385
Other reserve movements during the period			
Revaluation of investments and properties	18	4,157	127
Other	18	274	(35)
Increase in reserves		3,320	477
Opening reserves		2,585	2,108
Closing reserves	18	5,905	2,585
Earnings per share — basic	8	2.31p	15.10p
Earnings per share — fully diluted	8	2.50p	—

Exhibit 20

Espley Trust plc

Company balance sheet
31st December, 1983

ASSETS EMPLOYED	NOTE	1983 £'000	1982 £'000
Fixed assets			
Tangible assets	9	185	72
Investments:			
Shares in group companies	10	15,897	6,325
Investments other than loans	10	1,965	1,350
		18,047	7,747
Current assets			
Work in progress	11	3,100	—
Debtors	12	27,717	10,333
Proceeds of rights issue		—	5,028
Cash at bank and in hand	21	4,110	—
		34,927	15,361
Creditors: amounts falling due within one year	13	(5,636)	(3,019)
Net current assets		29,291	12,342
Total assets less current liabilities		47,338	20,089
Creditors: amounts falling due after more than one year	14	(24,816)	(4,000)
		22,522	16,089
FINANCED BY			
Capital and reserves			
Called up share capital	16	6,719	3,448
Share capital to be issued	16	556	1,552
		7,275	5,000
Share premium account:			
Arising from called up share capital	17	12,737	5,804
Arising from share capital to be issued	17	1,222	3,269
Profit and loss account	18	1,288	2,016
		22,522	16,089

R.A. SHUCK
P.F.B. COOPER   Directors
3rd August, 1984

Exhibit 21

the desks of its shareholders. The group accounts themselves were not overtly depressing as can be seen from
Exhibits 20 and 21. In the 15 months to 31 December 1983
this property company showed a profit of £147 000 on
turnover of £1 712 000 and the balance sheet did not seem
badly structured. Admittedly, this result was poor by comparison with that for the year to 30 September 1982 and the
dividend shown was way beyond what the company had
earned, but there had been considerable reorganization in
the interim and, in the words of Mr Ron Shuck, the chairman, 'In September 1982 we were a property and
construction company. In August 1984 we are an
investment holding company with interests in property,
construction, homebuilding and engineering.'

Mr Shuck was clearly hoping for the indulgence of the
shareholders. He would probably have got it but for the
rather less optimistic words of Coopers & Lybrand reproduced in Exhibit 22. To the uninitiated, the qualification
contained in the audit report might seem innocuous enough.
Nothing critical or hostile is said about the group or its
management and the second paragraph ostensibly refers
only to normal business activity; if there were plans to dispose of the UK assets, as was conceded by the company,
obviously their bankers would be involved. The City knew
a lot better and understood precisely what these words were
driving at, and it was not good. The auditors were really
saying that Espley Trust had run out of money and that their
survival depended upon the willingness of their lending
bankers to prop them up!

Conventional ratio analysis of the balance sheet and
income statement does not shed much light on Espley
Trust's problems. The 1982 figures describe, as Ron Shuck
indicated, a different animal and comparison is therefore of
limited value. Yet it is possible to see what was evolving by
examining the 'Group statement of source and application
of funds' (see Exhibit 23) together with the most interesting

Espley Trust plc

Auditors' report

To the members of Espley Trust plc

We have audited the accounts set out on pages xii to xxix in accordance with approved Auditing Standards. The accounts have been prepared under the historical cost convention as modified by the revaluation of certain assets.

As explained in the directors' report, the Group is negotiating for the disposal of a substantial part of its United Kingdom property interests and is, therefore, in continuing discussions with one of its principal bankers concerning the structure of finance required during the planned period of disposal. These accounts have been prepared on the assumption that these negotiations and discussions will be concluded satisfactorily and that the Group will have adequate working capital for its needs.

Subject to this uncertainty, in our opinion the accounts give a true and fair view of the state of the Company and the Group at 31st December, 1983 and of the results and source and application of funds of the Group for the period then ended and comply with the Companies Acts 1948 to 1981.

The accounts do not contain the current cost accounts required by Statement of Standard Accounting Practice No. 16.

COOPERS & LYBRAND
Birmingham
3rd August, 1984

Exhibit 22

part of the income statement, which happens to be contained in Notes 2 and 3 (see Exhibit 24).

The way the notes are laid out makes it hard to see the total scenario in its full glory and we need to condense these figures into something we can work with. Below is a fair summary:

£000s	1982	1983
Sales/revenue	50 814	89 612
Operating costs	(64 049)	(88 831)
Depreciation	(399)	(750)
Interest expense	(2464)	(5237)
Other income/expense	365	(185)
Capitalization of costs	16 464	3389
Capitalization of interest	2034	3714
Net profit before tax	2765	1712

Espley Trust plc

Group statement of source and application of funds

for the 15 months ended 31st December, 1983

SOURCE OF FUNDS	1983 £'000	1982 £'000
Profit on ordinary activities before tax and extraordinary items	1,712	2,765
Extraordinary items before tax	(411)	(976)
Items not involving the movement of funds	293	257
Funds generated from operations	1,594	2,046
Funds from other sources		
Ordinary shares, net of expenses	4,821	1,834
Long-term loans	1,819	4,219
Proceeds from sale of fixed assets	12,459	—
	19,099	6,053
	20,693	8,099

APPLICATION OF FUNDS		
Cost of shares and expenses on acquisition of subsidiary	(1,514)	—
Goodwill on acquisition of subsidiaries	—	(1,154)
Acquisition of minority interests	—	(1,060)
Long-term loans repaid	(331)	(3,883)
Purchase of investments net of sales	(605)	(2,463)
Purchase of fixed assets	(659)	(1,739)
Development properties transferred to investment properties (net)	(4,000)	—
Taxation paid	(249)	(366)
Dividends paid	(976)	(465)
	(8,334)	(11,130)
Net source/(application) of funds	12,359	(3,031)
Less: increase in working capital (see below)	(17,644)	(10,625)
Movement in net liquid funds	(5,285)	(13,656)

Analysis of increase in working capital		
Work in progress	(3,435)	(12,395)
Debtors	(16,575)	(3,053)
Creditors	2,366	4,823
	(17,644)	(10,625)

Note: The above statement excludes the effect of ordinary shares and Convertible Unsecured Loan Stock issued since 31st December, 1983.

Exhibit 23

The profits look immediately unusual because of the sizeable amounts of operating costs and interest capitalised. While it is legitimate for a building company to put these charges onto the balance sheet valuation of work in progress in certain circumstances, where capitalisation amounts are substantial the profit can become suspect. Whether a cost should be capitalised or expensed is a matter for judgement and since the auditors have not made any comment on this occasion we may assume that accounting principles have been complied with.

Let us look now at the funds flow. As usual we shall first lay out the numbers as a list casting to zero with simplified captions.

£000s	1982	1983
Sales/revenues	50 814	89 612
Operating costs	(64 049)	(88 831)
Depreciation	(399)	(750)
Interest expense	(2464)	(5237)
Other income/expense	365	(185)
Capitalization of costs	16 464	3389
Capitalization of interest	2034	3714
Extraordinary items	(976)	(411)
Non-cash items	257	293
Share issue	1834	4821
Long-term loans	4219	1819
Sale of fixed assets	—	12 459
Acquisition of subsidiary	—	(1514)
Goodwill	(1154)	—
Acquisition of minority interest	(1060)	—
Debt repayment	(3883)	(331)
Investments	(2463)	(605)
Capital expenditure	(1739)	(659)
Development properties reclassified	—	(4000)
Tax	(366)	(249)
Dividends	(465)	(976)

Espley Trust plc

Notes forming part of
the financial statements

1. Period of accounting and prior year adjustment

The year end date of the Company and its subsidiaries has been changed from 30th September to
31st December. As a result these financial statements cover the fifteen month period to 31st December, 1983,
whereas the comparative amounts relate to the year ended 30th September, 1982.

An adjustment has been made to the prior year's results (see note 6).

2. Turnover and profit on ordinary activities before taxation	1983	1982
	£'000	£'000
Turnover		
Activities being retained:		
United Kingdom construction and housebuilding	64,150	45,711
Overseas property development and housebuilding	4,703	1,765
Engineering and other	6,405	–
	75,258	47,476
Howard Tenens Services Limited	7,973	–
	83,231	47,476
Activities being sold:		
United Kingdom property development and rentals (see below)	6,381	3,338
	89,612	50,814
United Kingdom	83,527	49,049
Overseas	6,085	1,765
	89,612	50,814
Profit on ordinary activities before taxation		
Activities being retained:		
United Kingdom construction and housebuilding	567	1,530
Overseas property development and housebuilding	223	201
Related companies and overseas partnerships	(305)	35
Engineering and other	604	–
Listed securities	(128)	47
	961	1,813
Trading results and surplus on realisation of the assets of Howard Tenens Services Limited	2,052	–
	3,013	1,813
Activities being sold:		
United Kingdom property development and net rentals (see below)	(1,301)	952
	1,712	2,765
United Kingdom	1,717	2,564
Overseas	(5)	201
	1,712	2,765

Exhibit 24(a)

Espley Trust plc

3. Profit on ordinary activities before taxation	1983	1982
	£'000	£'000
Profit is stated after charging or crediting:		
(a) Net trading expenses:		
Change in work in progress and own work capitalised	(3,389)	(16,464)
Realised foreign exchange gain	(413)	—
Other operating income	(2,397)	—
Raw materials and consumables	31,718	21,474
Other external charges	41,318	32,663
Staff costs:		
Wages and salaries	11,716	5,702
Social security costs	1,176	657
Other pension costs	435	179
Depreciation and other amounts written off tangible assets	750	399
Leasing and hire charges	1,709	1,467
Auditors remuneration	191	129
Other operating charges	3,878	1,778
	86,192	47,984

	1983	1982
	£'000	£'000
(b) Share of profits less (losses) before tax of related companies and overseas partnerships:		
Unlisted	(305)	35

	1983	1982
	£'000	£'000
(c) Income and profits less (losses) from fixed asset investments other than related companies and overseas partnerships:		
Listed on a recognised stock exchange	(128)	47

	1983	1982
	£'000	£'000
(d) Interest receivable and similar income:		
Bank interest	18	130
Other	230	153
	248	283

	1983	1982
	£'000	£'000
(e) Interest payable and similar charges:		
Interest payable on sums:		
Wholly repayable within five years	3,954	2,302
All other loans	1,283	162
	5,237	2,464
Less: Charged to work in progress	(3,714)	(2,034)
	1,523	430

Exhibit 24(b)

£000s	1982	1983
Work in progress	(12 395)	(3435)
Debtors	(3053)	(16 575)
Creditors	4823	2366
Cash	13 656	5285
	0	0

Depreciation, non-cash items and other income/expense can be added together and called 'other cash income'. Acquisition of subsidiary, goodwill, acquisition or minority interest and investments can be combined into a single line for investments. We know that work in progress has possibly been the subject of some manipulation and with it, in the asset conversion cycle part of the cash flow, should go all the apparent cash flows that would seem to have anything to do with that manipulation. This includes the two capitalization entries and the curious 'development properties reclassified'. No real cash moved as a result of the reclassification of some development properties (i.e. work in progress) as investments, and the £4.0m really represents an increase in work in progress and a cash outflow as part of the asset conversion cycle.

Rearranging, therefore, in our preferred format we have:

	1982	1983
Asset conversion cycle:		
Sales/revenues	50 814	89 612
Debtors	(3053)	(16 575)
Operating costs	(64 049)	(88 831)
Work in progress	(12 395)	(3435)
Capitalizations	18 498	7103
Development properties reclassified	—	(4000)
Creditors	4823	2366
Cash from asset conversion cycle	(5362)	(13 760)

	1982	1983
Quasi-operational items:		
Other income/expense	223	(642)
Tax	(366)	(249)
Extraordinary items	(976)	(411)
Cash after quasi-operational items	(6481)	(15 062)
Financing costs:		
Interest	(2464)	(5237)
Dividends	(465)	(976)
Debt repayment	(3883)	(331)
Cash after financing costs	(13 293)	(21 606)
Discretionary flows:		
Capital expenditure	(1739)	(659)
Investments	(4677)	(2119)
Cash after discretionary flows	(19 709)	(24 384)
Funding flows:		
Long-term debt	4219	1819
Share issue	1834	4821
Sale of fixed assets	—	12 459
Change in cash	(13 656)	(5285)

When the numbers are arranged like this one can see immediately why Espley Trust got into such trouble. Its asset conversion cycle was absorbing cash at a devastating rate; there was no money to settle the quasi-operational items, the funding costs and the debt repayment and the company had a funding need of £19.7m in 1982 and £24.4m in 1983. It met this funding partly from new borrowing and equity injections, but in the main by reductions in the cash balance and from asset sales.

If Espley Trust's bankers did not realize after the 1982 figures appeared that the asset conversion cycle was consuming money on this scale, they certainly should have done and taken that fact into full consideration before lending it any more. As over £6.6m of outside money was put into the company in the 15 months to 31 December 1983, there is a suspicion, first, that some people did not know about the cash-draining qualities of this company, and secondly, that they paid the penalty.

The end of the story, in brief, is that Mr. Shuck was replaced by a 'company doctor' who was appointed to push through the asset sales. In the end the assets could not be sold for enough money sufficiently rapidly to satisfy the lenders and receivers were called in to liquidate the company in April 1985.

Unigate plc

The morning pint of milk deposited fresh on the doorstep is a national institution in Britain, as is the cheery Unigate milkman who delivers it with his quaint, brightly painted, electric float. Unigate is one of the country's best-known companies. Apart from this, its most conspicuous activity, Unigate has interests in meat packing and restaurants as well as owning a number of apparently quite unrelated businesses principally in the areas of transport, garages and engineering, and in exhibitions and freight services. Lorries bearing the marques of Wincanton and Giltspur are often seen on the roads but few people know that these have any connection with the dairy product company. However, milk is the main product and it is on the fortunes of that industry that Unigate's performance mainly depends.

While over the last 5 years Unigate has shown a steadily rising trend in turnover, profit before taxation dipped in 1981 and did not surpass the 1980 level of £51.4m until 1984 (see Exhibit 25). This unexciting performance has depressed the stock price and the market has been looking to see a lesser dependence upon milk, an area perceived as having little growth potential. Not only is milk drinking

Group profit and loss account *for the year ended 31 March*

	Notes	1985 £m	1984 £m
Turnover	2	**1,932.2**	1,766.2
Cost of sales		(1,516.7)	(1,375.1)
Gross profit		**415.5**	391.1
Distribution costs		(229.5)	(230.7)
Administrative expenses		(112.1)	(92.4)
Other operating income		3.1	3.9
Operating profit	3	**77.0**	71.9
Income from related companies		2.7	2.0
Interest payable, net, and other finance charges	4	(16.1)	(16.8)
Profit on ordinary activities before taxation	2	**63.6**	57.1
Taxation on profit on ordinary activities	5	(22.6)	(16.0)
Profit on ordinary activities after taxation		**41.0**	41.1
Minority interests		(0.5)	(0.3)
Profit attributable to shareholders before extraordinary items		**40.5**	40.8
Extraordinary items after taxation	6	(9.2)	(26.7)
Transfers from reserves		–	5.0
Profit attributable to shareholders		**31.3**	19.1
Dividends	7	(18.2)	(16.6)
Retained profit transferred to reserves	21	**13.1**	2.5
Earnings per ordinary share	8	**18.3p**	18.5p

Exhibit 25   Reproduced by permission of Unigate

now less fashionable than it has been, but the milk market is controlled through governmental intervention and the offices of the EEC. Alas, the Brussels bureaucracy is no friend to Unigate. Attempts have been made to discourage

Group source and application of funds

	Notes	Total 1985 £m	Total 1984 £m
Inflow from trading operations:			
Profit on ordinary activities before taxation		63.6	57.1
Depreciation		43.6	40.3
		107.2	**97.4**
Other operating inflows/(outflows):			
Fixed asset purchases		(74.6)	(73.4)
Fixed asset disposals		28.8	24.4
Net (increase)/decrease in working capital	15	(9.4)	(6.5)
Taxation		(19.7)	(6.0)
Dividends	7	(16.6)	(15.0)
Minority interests		(1.1)	0.4
		(92.6)	**(76.1)**
Net flows from operations		**14.6**	**21.3**
Non-operating inflows/(outflows):			
Extraordinary items before taxation		(10.4)	(22.5)
(Increase)/decrease in investments, net		7.6	(7.1)
Shares issued, including premium		–	1.6
Property revaluations		0.7	0.2
Goodwill		–	–
Provisions		2.3	0.3
Non-cash movements in reserves		3.1	(3.4)
Deferred taxation		(2.2)	12.5
(Increase)/decrease in net borrowings:			
Year ended 31 March 1985		**15.7**	
Year ended 31 March 1984			**2.9**
Represented by balance sheet movements in:			
Cash at bank and in hand		13.8	4.6
Loans falling due within one year		17.0	(18.5)
Loans falling due after more than one year		(18.0)	25.0
Obligations under fixed rate finance leases		2.9	(8.2)
		15.7	**2.9**

Exhibit 26(a)   Reproduced by permission of Unigate

| Analysis of 1985 movements | | | | | |
| Cash flow | | | Non-cash movements | | Total |
Operations £m	Business acquisitions & disposals £m	Total £m	Currency translation £m	Other £m	£m
63.6	–	63.6	–	–	63.6
43.6	–	43.6	–	–	43.6
107.2	–	107.2	–	–	107.2
(58.6)	(9.7)	(68.3)	(6.3)	–	(74.6)
19.7	9.1	28.8	–	–	28.8
3.9	(11.8)	(7.9)	(1.5)	–	(9.4)
(19.8)	–	(19.8)	0.1	–	(19.7)
(16.6)	–	(16.6)	–	–	(16.6)
(0.1)	(1.2)	(1.3)	0.2	–	(1.1)
(71.5)	(13.6)	(85.1)	(7.5)	–	(92.6)
35.7	(13.6)	22.1	(7.5)	–	14.6
(3.0)	(7.4)	(10.4)	–	–	(10.4)
7.6	–	7.6	–	–	7.6
–	–	–	–	–	–
–	–	–	–	0.7	0.7
–	3.4	3.4	–	(3.4)	–
1.6	0.7	2.3	–	–	2.3
–	–	–	0.4	2.7	3.1
(2.9)	0.7	(2.2)	–	–	(2.2)
39.0	(16.2)	22.8	(7.1)	–	15.7
22.4	(18.3)	4.1	(1.2)	–	
					13.8
					17.0
					(18.0)
					2.9
					15.7

Exhibit 26(b)   Reproduced by permission of Unigate

the delivering of milk to homes in the UK and the removal of import restrictions on UHT milk in 1983 brought
additional unwelcome competition.

It is not our purpose here to examine Unigate's performance, but rather to call attention to its unusually informative funds flow statement (see Exhibit 26). The left-hand
side, showing the totals, is unremarkable. Much more
interesting is the breakdown of the figures on the right-
hand side to show the separate components of the cash and
non-cash movements. According to Unigate's analysis, its
final funds flow statement is the sum of the four separate
columns: Operations, Business acquisitions and disposals,
Currency translation and Other non-cash movements.

We have argued that in analysing a company's cash flow,
our prime interest lies in the operations of the business and
that so far as is possible we should strip out any apparent
flows that we know to be related either to purchases or sales
of subsidiary companies or to non-cash items. That is
exactly what Unigate has done with its funds flow statement. If we wished to recast this statement into our cash
flow format we would first take the numbers only from the
left column since these are the numbers that illustrate the
cash-generating properties of the asset conversion cycle. In
addition, in order to make the final statement balance we
need the totals of the other three columns. The published
funds flow balances at the level of change in net borrowings
and it follows that the non-cash movements must be
reflected in one or more of the elements making up that
number.

Non-cash movements cannot by definition affect cash. As
the sum of the non-cash movements is not zero, that sum
has to be included in the cash flow even though we know
that it is an error. The compensating error can only be in the
cash change itself or, as in this case, in one of the four lines
shown as tantamount to changes in cash. A moment's
thought will show that a loan or a cash deposit in a foreign
currency can fluctuate in value owing to changes in

13. Debtors

	Group 1985 £m	Group 1984 £m	Company 1985 £m	Company 1984 £m
Trade debtors	153.2	138.6	–	–
Amounts owed by Group companies	–	–	49.5	64.7
Amounts owed by related companies	–	0.5	–	–
Finance lease debtors due within one year	6.8	7.0	–	–
Other debtors	14.3	15.6	0.9	0.8
Prepayments and accrued income	9.2	7.7	0.2	0.1
	183.5	169.4	50.6	65.6

Included in amounts owed by Group companies are finance lease debtors of £11.2m (1984: £8.7m).

14. Other creditors

	Group 1985 £m	Group 1984 £m	Company 1985 £m	Company 1984 £m
Payments received on account	4.7	2.4	–	–
Dividends payable	18.1	16.5	18.1	16.5
Trade creditors	144.7	135.4	0.2	0.1
Bills of exchange payable	10.7	9.3	9.0	9.0
Amounts owed to Group companies	–	–	36.7	35.7
Amounts owed to related companies	3.1	–	–	–
Current corporation tax	16.5	15.7	10.2	4.0
Other creditors including social security	55.4	61.4	0.8	0.9
Accruals and deferred income	34.4	22.8	4.3	2.9
	287.6	263.5	79.3	69.1

15. Net (increase)/decrease in working capital

	Group Stocks £m	Debtors £m	Creditors £m	Total £m
Movements affecting cash flow:				
Operations	(8.8)	(8.9)	21.6	3.9
Business acquisitions/disposals	(7.8)	(4.1)	0.1	(11.8)
	(16.6)	(13.0)	21.7	(7.9)
Non-cash movements:				
Currency translation	(0.4)	(1.1)	–	(1.5)
1985 Total movements	(17.0)	(14.1)	21.7	(9.4)
1984 Total movements	(6.6)	(8.5)	8.6	(6.5)

16. Contingent liabilities

	Group 1985 £m	Group 1984 £m	Company 1985 £m	Company 1984 £m
Guarantees relating to overseas borrowings:				
US commercial paper and related credit facilities	–	–	23.3	11.5
Other	0.6	0.4	0.1	2.1
	0.6	0.4	23.4	13.6

Unquantified contingencies exist in respect of proceedings by the Italian fiscal authorities relating to payments made by a former subsidiary. The directors have been advised that appropriate defences can be prepared. Other guarantees and contingencies exist in the ordinary course of business.

Exhibit 27   Reproduced by permission of Unigate

exchange rates, and it is therefore quite within reason that the balance of cash or loans may change without there being any actual cash flow.

The breakdown of the changes in working capital can be extracted from note 15 (see Exhibit 27) and again it is the operational changes that we seek, not those attributable to acquisition, disposals or non-cash movements. Putting all this together with the income statement, our balancing series of cash flow numbers might read as follows:

£m	1985
Sales	1932.2
Cost of sales	(1516.7)
Distribution/administration expense	(341.6)
Other operating income	3.1
Income from related companies	2.7
Interest expense	(22.1)
Interest income	6.0
Depreciation	43.6
Capital expenditure	(58.6)
Disposals of fixed assets	19.7
Receivables	(8.9)
Inventory	(8.8)
Creditors	21.6
Tax	(19.8)
Dividends	(16.6)
Minority interests	(0.1)
Extraordinary items	(3.0)
Decrease in investments	7.6
Provisions	1.6
Deferred taxation	(2.9)
Acquisitions/disposals	(16.2)
Foreign exchange translations	(7.1)
Cash	(13.8)
Short-term debt	(17.0)
Long-term debt	18.0
Finance leases	(2.9)
	0.0

and it is no great labour to rearrange and simplify these numbers into our standard cash flow format:

£m	
Sales	1932.2
Receivables	(8.9)
Cost of sales	(1473.1)
Inventory	(8.8)
Creditors	21.6
Distrib./admin. expense	(341.6)
Cash from asset conversion cycle	121.4
Other operating income	3.1
Income from related companies	2.7
Interest income	6.0
Extraordinary items	(3.0)
Tax	(22.7)
Provisions	1.6
Cash after quasi-operational items	109.1
Interest expense	(22.1)
Dividends	(16.6)
Minority interest	(0.1)
Reduction in finance leases	(2.9)
Cash after financing costs	67.4
Capital expenditure	(58.6)
Disposal of fixed assets	19.7
Acquisitions/disposals	(16.2)
Decrease in investments	7.6
Cash after discretionary flows	19.9
Short-term debt	(17.0)
Long-term debt	18.0
Foreign exchange translations	(7.1)
Increase in cash	13.8

A healthy cash flow indeed! Unigate did not provide excessive amounts of detail, but the company did give us the information we wanted to enable us to construct a reasonable cash flow statement. Had we ignored this information, or been deprived of it, we should have been misled as the

full funds flow suggests a quite different scenario. Allowing Unigate's classification of 'fixed asset purchases' as an
operating item, which is unconventional to say the least,
the funds flow statement says the 'net (cash) flows from
operations' were £14.6m in 1985 whereas the true figure
was the rather better £35.7m. This is indisputable as this is
the figure given in the 'operations' column!

Note finally that even in the left-hand operations column
there is no escaping the accrual concept at the top. The
column begins, as does the full funds flow, with 'profit on
ordinary activities before taxation' and there is an add-back
of depreciation. Depreciation, as we know, is neither a cash
flow nor an operating item but is added back because it has
already been deducted in the profit figures above. Of
course, in writing the full funds flow, Unigate was constrained by the dictates of SSAP 10, the UK accounting
standard governing funds flow statements, and the company was not at liberty to begin the statement otherwise.

Unigate's presentation is a fascinating glimpse of how
the presentation of cash flow data might develop in the
future. We do not delude ourselves that other companies
will rush to follow suit either in the UK or abroad, but if
there is to be any value in published funds statements
it is absolutely imperative that the operational cash flows
can be extracted relatively unadulterated by acquisition
and disposal flows and non-cash movements. Without this,
the value of the funds flow is severely restricted and will,
more often than not, serve only to confuse the reader.

9
Structure, substance, risk and reward

My dear friend clear your mind of cant. . . . You may talk in this manner; it is a mode of talking in society: but don't think foolishly.
Dr Samuel Johnson,
from Boswell's *Life of Johnson*

Whether you are looking at a company with a view to lending or investing, it should by now be abundantly clear that, more often than not, what you see is not necessarily what you are going to get. We have given particular emphasis to our thesis that the financial statements of companies are not valuation statements and, perhaps more important, that the conventions of accountancy are simply too primitive to capture or render with much validity or accuracy the intangible realities and subtle vagaries that drive the dynamics of the modern corporation.

To surmount these hurdles lenders and investors have to adopt almost contradictory approaches in tandem. First comes the need to analyse the financial structure of a company, the minimalist approach as it were, by the use of all the sophisticated techniques at one's command. The glossy, neatly packaged bundles of arcane financial data must be taken apart, strand by strand, and recombined to yield coherent financial information which actually informs.

The second or maximalist approach addresses the primary substantive issues of what the business is all about. The task is to develop a lucid comprehension of the asset conversion cycle, the life mechanism of any business without which it can have no existence. To achieve this requires an effective grasp of the dimensions of the business and a thorough insight into the dynamics of the industry or industries in which the company is operating. Finally, comes the job of placing the entire analysis within the context of the relevant economic environments. Only then has one brought to fruition the perspectives and perceptions which the analytical process has to yield.

To do all of this with precision and brevity, the analyst must be fluent in the language of all business, accounting; must recognize that the life blood of all business is cash; must accept that the very core of corporate viability is strategic business risk; and that the guts of every business lie in transactional business risk.

Just as an analyst needs to start from sound basic premises, so he should have a methodology. In practice, this means that a written analysis should have a clearly defined and logical structure within which the analyst can work. Obviously, different structures are possible and formality should not become an end in itself, but we have developed the style and structure described below specifically for use in a lending environment where getting the most value added out of analysts' time and effort is a high priority. Our approach is based on seven steps and we have found it exceptionally efficacious in providing a route towards an informed risk decision. The seven steps run as follows:

(1) Proposal,
(2) Recommendation,
(3) Summary,
(4) Economic and Competitive Environment,
(5) Management Assessment,

(6) Financial Analysis and, finally,

(7) Sources of Repayment

One might well look askance at this staging sequence when 'Recommendation' is placed second. Quite clearly it is not there because an analyst is expected to decide first and analyse afterwards! It is placed immediately after 'Proposal' to highlight the 'business driven' purpose of the analytical effort. A similar comment would apply to 'Summary' which should encapsulate in two to three tight paragraphs the essence of the risk to the lender and to the borrower. We only *appear* to be defying logic; really we have in this sequencing pattern a highly logical structure.

First, we want to understand the proposal; second, we want to know what has been recommended; third, we want to comprehend the level of risk this action implies for both the lender and borrower and, finally, since this work will be read by busy decision makers who are intolerant of long reports we want it all within a readable span of no more than one page.

The 'Proposal' must define concisely and accurately the purpose and terms of the loan. It embodies the degree and nature of the risk to be evaluated and upon its complexity or ordinariness will depend the scope of analysis. Though, as we have observed, many corporations offer the phrase 'for general corporate purposes' as their reason for borrowing, this should be the exception rather than the rule. The widespread prevalence of ill-defined and undisciplined lines of credit and loans is little recognized, and even less appreciated is the hazard they represent to lending institutions and borrowers alike.

When reviewing the purpose of the loan, the analyst must frame it within the business context of the borrower. Bankers generally recognize four types of lending and need to determine within which category or categories it should be placed. This is not as simple as it may sound, nor indeed is it at all a mechanical exercise for the serious lender.

The four types of lending may be categorized as *seasonal lending*, *cash flow lending*, *asset-based lending* and *project lending*. Each type of lending addresses a given functional or corporate business need. Some banks call the seasonal loan category 'asset conversion' loans. Nothing wrong or untoward about this except that in this book we have insisted upon a critical definition of the asset conversion cycle of the corporation as a key tool to unlock the business and financial risks that a company represents both to its owners and to its lenders, and we prefer to keep that phraseology distinct.

We have already touched upon the theme of seasonal lending as it originated in ancient agricultural times and it has continued essentially unchanged to this day. Such loans are made to businesses that require supplemental capital to meet their peak needs of short duration, usually arising from build-ups in the inventory and receivables accounts. As these slope off, cash re-enters the business and the bank loan is extinguished. Seasonal loans are not riskless, of course, but they are attractive to lenders in that they have a short-term horizon with the underlying transactional base usually not of a complex nature. It is wrong to think of such loans as simply financing trading operations; many do, but just as many support manufacturing functions. This naturally affects the risk contour of a seasonal loan since the heavier the asset base of a company, the greater the level of risk which is associated with it and its products.

Cash flow lending represents longer-term loans, usually to industrial entities to finance the purchase of plant and equipment or to support rising levels of permanent net trading investment. Such loans have to be repaid from the anticipated streams of cash generated by a business over the life of the loan. For the banker, this type of business represents both an extended financial and business risk, as the lender is now looking to the continued financial liquidity and solvency of the firm over a prolonged period of time. But he is also looking to the prudent and successful management of the business risk of the corporation by its owners or managers to realize the required earnings.

To sketch a quick distinction at this point between seasonal and cash flow loans, we would say that in seasonal loans we are looking at short-term horizons where earnings are not critical. What is required is the recovery of cash costs through the successful completion of the transactional cycle in order to repay the loan, whereas the cash flow loan requires the continued generation of earnings over a longer period. The extended exposure and the requirement for earnings immediately serve to expand the risks inherent in such lending. If cash generation is insufficient, the banker will be forced either to reschedule or to find another financing or equity source to take him out. In the midst of such unsmiling circumstances, new lenders or equity infusions are hard to come by. For this reason it is absolutely essential with such loans to identify clearly sources of repayment prior to committing bank funds.

Asset-based lending in its purest form is where short-term finance is provided on a virtually permanent basis to support high levels of essentially liquid assets. Typically, finance companies, car dealers and commodity traders are asset-based borrowers. The reason lending is kept on a short tether is primarily to assure control. But the borrower's need is fundamentally a continuing one since such businesses depend upon maintaining a revolving and often rising level of trading assets.

Within the ambit of asset-based lending are the half-breeds, for mortgage loans are essentially asset-based as are leasing, shipping and industrial loans against plant and equipment. These, of course, are longer-term transactions and the lender looks partly towards the assets, partly to the earnings stream.

Asset-based loans are often secured, reflecting a conceptual bias towards the belief that the underlying assets carry a resident, residual value which the market will have to transform into cash to pay the lender in the event of financial distress. Furthermore, the nature of true asset-based lending is such that a lender is only repaid either by liquidation of the assets (perhaps involving the liquidation of the business itself in the process) or by being taken out by a third party. Since equity is characteristically narrow in such borrowers, equity injection is not usually a realistic alternative.

The risk here tends to be correspondingly higher than in other types of lending. With the more elaborate administration required in such loans, this type of loan can be an expensive proposition to have on the ledgers. Ultimately in asset-based lending, the banker has to be fairly certain that he has unchallenged access to enough sufficiently liquid assets to avoid a loss. It is for this reason that when security is taken, the lender must ensure the seniority of his claim, that there is both physical and fiscal protection of the assets and that control of those assets is never lost.

A good case can be made for the inclusion of leveraged buyouts in asset-based lending, for these loans are very highly reliant on asset values. These operations have, of course, given rise to the advent of the 'junk bond', hardly a respectful designation for an instrument of high finance! But one should understand that the underlying justification for leveraged buyouts has little to do with this instrument at all. Such buyouts are constructed on two fairly rational bases which may in the end become speculative because they have been extended to the extreme. The first centres on the buyer's perception of higher resident values in the assets and the belief that these values can be extracted more profitably by the new owners or disposed of for sums higher than their stated values. Alternatively, the new

buyers may well have identified material earning opportunities which have not been exploited by the current
owners or management.

Project lending is cited elsewhere in the book, but we
may emphasize here that such lending combines features of
both asset-based and cash flow loans. Oil operations might
be a case in point. In the industrial world, the construction
of a factory would not be considered a project loan, but in
lesser developed countries the financial magnitude and the
cumbersome complications of construction could easily
classify it as one. Certainly, a very strong case can be made
for considering the funding of nuclear power plant construction as project lending. Despite their proliferation, the
problems and disasters associated with such constructions
and operations surely place them in a specialized category.

It may appear that we have taken a major detour from
where we were in our discussion of structure. This was
quite by intent. When the analyst is framing his or her
proposal, that is the time when a thorough understanding
of the borrower must be most evident. Misreading a company's business and establishing short-term facilities when
a cash flow loan is called for invites danger both to the
borrower and the bank. Confusing a cash flow loan with an
asset-based loan can be equally perilous. These seemingly
mechanical differentiations are vital.

Though we have spoken of four classifications of lending, one should be very much aware that often they do not
occur in isolation. Combinations are not only possible, they
may be desirable and reflect correct discernment on the
part of lender and borrower alike. Many seasonal and cash
flow loans incorporate asset-based elements. However, to
lose sight of the real nature of the business in a surfeit of
marketing zeal is to court disaster.

The 'Economic and Competitive Environment' stage in an
analysis is crucial and helps us to understand the strategic
business risks faced by the firm. Upon these and their

resolution depend prospects for continued healthy existence. By strategic business risk we mean the viability of a firm within its industry and indeed the viability of that industry within the economy. Thus, this section of the analysis should lay bare the external factors which affect the borrower and indicate the borrower's relative position within its industry and economic setting. The analysis must concentrate sharply on the current and anticipated condition of the industry and how such conditions will impinge upon the present and future competitive structure and profitability of the constituent companies. How are such factors in turn going to be affected by the macro-economic and microeconomic environments within which both the company and the industry operate? Is the company in a mature and stable or old and decaying industry? Is it in a new and vibrant industry? What are the real and perceived dangers in each of these sectors?

The company's performance must be reviewed to determine what it is doing well or poorly. What must the company continue to do well in order to prosper? What are the constraints which it faces? Marketing, distribution, production, demand, financial base?

Lastly, one must look at where the company ranks in its industry. Is it a minor player, a leader or a laggard? What are the exit barriers for a company in that industry and, equally pertinent, what are the entry hurdles? How does the company compare on its breakeven point, on its operating and financial leverages, on its discriminant analysis score, on its return on assets and investment? On equity? On its cost structure and expense curve? On its debt profile?

Companies within the same industry can have significantly different results because they may be using dissimilar accounting conventions and business practices. Patterns of trade, production cycles, vulnerability to economic recessions and own industry cyclicality must be considered.

Financing needs which are the logical manifestations of a given industry configuration must be identified and examined with particular attention given to asset, cost, liability and equity profiles. Only at this point does one begin to understand that a firm's pattern and quality of corporate existence are heavily influenced by external dynamics that are central to its future ability to survive.

The next step in our structural approach is 'Management Assessment'. Quite apart from those books on how to make a million dollars starting with something less than ten, literature on 'management' is voluminous and often heavy reading.

It remains, nevertheless, the bounden duty of a lender to assess the quality of management in a borrowing company. Certain aspects of management capability are easily readable. The track record of most companies is in plain view to the market place, and the better a company has performed, particularly in difficult times, the greater must be the respect for that company's management ability. Depth of management is important as are age levels, areas of demonstrated proficiency, previous assignments and the percentage of equity in management's hands. Last but never least must be the issue of integrity.

Even the bluest of blue chip companies may sometimes use legitimate, prescribed and permitted accounting conventions which can befuddle lenders and investors. This is an accepted part of modern corporate behaviour and certainly not illegal, but when the facts can be made to speak lucidly for the benefit of the financial community the application of accepted principles which can obscure those facts is in our view undesirable. We are not seeking out the virtuous, the noble or the charismatic and the sublime in conducting our assessment of management. We only want to know that they have exhibited a consistent level of competent performance and that the business results are not contrived.

We now arrive at 'Financial Analysis', the stage where
the analyst can, in a manner of speaking, go to town. It
is senseless to probe a company from all sides at once.
Of course, the accrued coats of accounting rust must be
stripped away to develop meaningful insights into the
financial statements. But, fundamentally, you are looking at
the business and the risks which surround the survival of
that business. As already noted, there are numerous computerized formats that will grind out statements, ratios,
cash flows, regression analysis, sensitivity analysis, sustainable rates of growth, operating and financial leverages
and a host of other techniques of analysis which are the
tools of the trade. In the most intricate instances, you may
have to use all of them.

It is disheartening but generally true that most exercises
in financial analysis are undertaken as a matter of necessary
routine. Indeed, the preponderance of such work reflects a
shallow, cursory overview of a company's financial performance with little evidence of any attempt at seriously
understanding either the asset or cost base of the business.
Yet these two areas are central to any meaningful examination of a business as they provide vital clues to identifying
key risks and suggest the optimal capital and liability
profiles of the borrower.

Both the mass and composition of the assets of a company provide conduits to the rationale underpinning a
company's capital and liability stems. Any number of business studies and consequent theories will postulate that
the evolution of debt and capital in the firm is a random
event. While we do not dispute this piece of scholarship, it
simply has no relevance in the context of our argument that
the asset base and cost structure should, and invariably do,
interact to mould debt and capital structures.

The analyst's concern with present and future viability of
a business should always be paramount. This ties in very

comfortably with modern business theory's definition of the value of the firm as being represented by the totality of its discounted cash flow streams. One cannot escape the stark linkage between the asset and cost configurations of the firm and resultant cash inflows and outflows.

Concentrating on the capital and liability structure without an immediate reference to asset and cost configurations is a waste of the analyst's time. Dwelling on asset and cost configurations without plotting them against the cash-generating capabilities of the firm is equally futile. We have said enough about the shortcomings of financial statements but these failings must remain in the forefront of any analytical presentation because the analyst works, in the main, with passive indicators.

It is perhaps somewhat artificial to designate certain indicators passive, others active and still others dynamic. Ultimately, they are all passive to the extent that they reflect upon 'gone events'. However, despite this artificiality, it does make some sense, particularly when analysts start confusing static expressions of past performance with realities. We would suggest that in the passive indicator column belong such ratios as total debt to net worth; current assets to total debt or liabilities; fixed assets to net worth; reliance on inventory and indeed the current and quick ratios which purport to reflect liquidity values (and which do not).

Indeed, liquidity, as defined in statement and financial analysis, is often illiquid both in the layman's and the economists' understanding of liquidity. Liquidity, except for the cash caption, is largely ore. It is solvency, or a company's ability to pay off its obligations with cash, that we seek to determine in analysis and on which the value and viability of a firm obviously depend. The relationship between liquidity and solvency cannot be denied; related they are or may be, but identical they are not.

Active indicators are to be found in cash flow ratios as they relate to contributions to capital and as they reflect the level of lubricated movement in the asset base. The ultimate dynamic indicator in financial analysis is revealed in the asset conversion cycle of cash flow which directly attacks the business risk, hence the firm's present and future viability mirrored in its financial risk profile. Our chapter on cash flow centres on this issue fully and highlights the overriding need to determine a firm's ability to subdue its costs with cash and to generate that cash through the visible and timely mobilization of the firm's assets.

As already stressed, much more critical is the analyst's understanding of that company's asset conversion cycle and one should be at pains to establish whether there is a sensible and safe fit between the company's needs and a bank's lending ambitions. Once the business risks and the asset conversion cycles have been analysed, the analyst must examine the financial risk inherent in the company's liquidity and solvency profiles.

Regardless of the type of loan under consideration, the analysis must be geared to determining the true corporate debt capacity of the firm. Debt capacity depends entirely on debt-servicing ability and that is demonstrated only through projections showing sufficient streams of cash income or intrinsic values in the assets being financed. This area of analysis should weigh with great care the *quality of earnings* that have been and are being reported. A change in accounting rules can bring about material distortions in both the quality and dimension of reported earnings. At the end of 1985, the Financial Accounting Standards Board pulled off another blinkering device by changing two pension accounting rules (SFAS 87 and 88). Both a construction company and a bank availed themselves liberally of these rulings by tapping into their pension surpluses to boost reported earnings. As usual, all interested parties had to read minuscule print in the footnotes to figure out what happened.

Thus the analyst must ask: What caused the increase or decrease? Is it real? Is it a one-off situation? Is it sustainable if an increase? Is it damaging if a decrease? Implications for the business—the balance sheet and operating statement? Two elements which often spell 'danger ahead' are rapid growth and change of direction in a company. Probe the first clinically and assess the latter with something less than the company's uncontainable enthusiasm. Most changes, mergers and acquisitions have a sorry record.

One of the major pitfalls lenders are prone to is the curious belief that working capital and net worth are fluid creatures against which the banker proceeds in the event of trouble. Working capital is not a limpid pool of cash. No one ever draws a cheque on working capital. The only cash reserves on a balance sheet are those designated by the caption 'cash', to which may be added only the most marketable of marketable securities. The other misconception surrounding working capital is that it is determined by events above the current assets and liabilities lines. The working capital level is only impacted by an increase or decrease in non-current assets, non-current liabilities, or an increase or decrease in net worth or profits.

Another and more accurate view of working capital is that it is the difference between non-current liabilities plus net worth and non-current assets. This at least steers the analyst away from believing at first sight that a positive working capital implies a liquid company. The error lies in the careless use of the word 'liquidity'.

This is also true, and more powerfully so, of net worth. Net worth is an even drier well of liquidity for it is mostly embedded in plant and equipment. To speak of working capital as the little cushion and net worth as the large cushion for creditors may be to find oneself in a surprisingly arid oasis.

Two other major deadly sins in analysis merit iteration. The first is a sin of omission where the analyst does not choose to examine whether the loan is in fact a capital infusion into the firm. Capital is rarely distributed out of the firm. Loans may indeed be, generically, a form of capital. They are supplemental to capital, and the key modifier is the word *supplemental*. The other is a sin of commission where the analyst equates profitability with cash. Net profit, very much like working capital and net worth, is not a cash figure. 'Profitable' companies can be cash broke while unprofitable companies may contain rich cash lodes.

The cash flow which we have designed and used in this book is, in our judgement, the most sensible method of tracking a company's life blood against the pulse of its business rhythm. It is based on an appreciation of the asset conversion cycle by which cash flow is driven. In looking at a company, one should construct and review a minimum of three years of historical flows. Five is much to be preferred. Cash flow projections should also be undertaken covering the period of any proposed loan, and the sensitivities of these should be fathomed.

Beware of balance sheets in general, especially the asset side. The Romans called anything on the left-hand side 'sinister' and that is precisely where, at least in the USA, the assets are listed. Asset values are, broadly speaking, costs rather than current valuations, and overstatement in the balance sheet points directly to hidden financial and business risks. Do not put more faith in a balance sheet than it deserves.

Having completed the 'Financial Analysis' section, the analyst now has a sound grasp of the financial risks, the business risks, the strategic risks and the efficacy of a company's asset conversion cycle. Now he moves to the last stage which is 'Sources of Repayment'. The analysis should have established a clear pattern and source of repayment that can be identified and demonstrated.

The analyst can now revert to the proposal and, if the business under review falls within the zones of safety on all scores, complete the second section, the 'Recommendation'. The Recommendation is a statement calling for action. It must be concise, with no qualifying remarks. Terms such as 'reluctantly' and 'unreservedly' are emotive and do not help anyone to form a judgement. Having completed the 'Recommendation', the analyst should devote a couple of paragraphs to distilling the analysis and pointing out the risks to the borrower and the lender, and this is placed under 'Summary'.

In preparing a financial analysis, it is important to adopt a selective approach, not to clutter the work, and to develop a focus quickly. One should concentrate on the substance of risks which are in the business, financial and strategic areas. The writing should reflect the thinking process and a dynamic rather than descriptive style is much more likely to produce worthwhile results. Nothing is worse than the analysis that blandly states 'this ratio went up, but that ratio declined'. Such description is a redundant gloss on the figures and profoundly unilluminating.

A diagrammatic summary of our approach to risk analysis is shown below. We have designated it the Fatigue/Risk Model and it centres on five key areas, all of which directly impact the value of the firm. Any inefficiency or 'fatigue' at any of the five points acts to detract from the value of the firm and any strength will move to contribute to the value of the firm. Critically located and crossed by the other four main risks which a firm faces, is the *risk of metal fatigue in management*. The ultimate source of the failing firm is embedded here and is exhibited by an internalising process that largely ignores the external realities which the firm was born to cope with. We have suggested a cluster of telltale signs in this area which should alert both lender and investor that a wary attitude is indicated. The *Business Risk*, the *Financial Risk*, the *Asset Value Risk* and the *Cost Base Risk* and, indeed, the *Management Risk* are usually camouflaged in good times and in periods of inflationary pressures. A firm, however, must be viewed in terms of its ability to withstand, periodically, economic recessionary forces and own industry cyclical downturns. Many expert signal readers will decode poor profit performance as a cause. We read it primarily as a symptom traceable to a number of causes. Those who possess the right blend of analytical skills can fathom these causes that have induced the poor profit symptom(s) and will surely profit by avoiding loss.

A valuable aid in any analysis is the grading given to corporations by such prominent rating agencies as Standard & Poor's, Moody's, Fitch, Duff & Phelps, McCarthy, Crisanti and Maffei and, for insurance companies, Best. Standard & Poor's bond rating methodology covers such important areas as: industry risk; market status; operating efficiency; management; accounting quality; earnings protection; cash flow sufficiency and financial strength. A series of ten key ratios is also examined.

Our approach has not been much different. Perhaps the single most striking qualitative difference between a rating agency's analysis and any other analysis lies in the depth and level of accessibility to the management, business investment programme and confidential contingency plans of the firm.

An almost palpable aura of mystique, wisdom and authority instantly cloaks the banker who utters the words 'risk and reward'. Why this should be so surely defies any understanding. Apart from the fact that risk and reward are incommensurable, they are also a tiresome pair of incongruous words; each carries a separate idea that neither in substance nor in direction equates to the other. Indeed, the empirical evidence strongly suggests that risk is bereft of reward. Contrary to popular belief, professional gamblers and market speculators know this in spades.

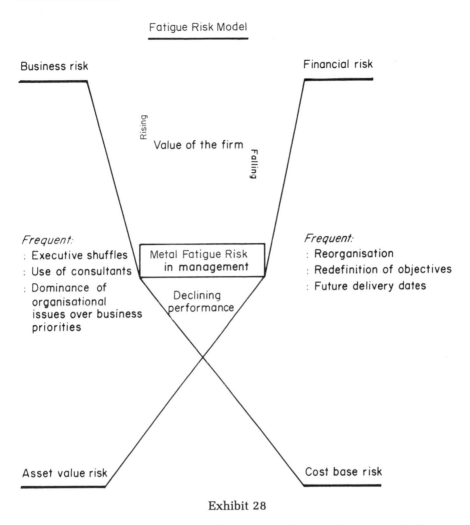

Exhibit 28

Still, for as long as bankers are about, the use of these words will not cease and it is futile to offer that the words have no link, and trying to tease a spliced recombinant meaning out of them yields mis-shapen thought and a derelict result.

But when bankers persist in parroting this phrase, you have a more serious case on your hands. In the first instance, it reflects a grave misapprehension of the nature of banking. It also promotes the loitering idea that banks manage by slogans and catchy phrases. More dangerous, however, is the implication that by tinkering with the reward side of this disconnected equation, the risk can be, or worse, has been ameliorated. This can be febrile folly, and the percentage of loans which bankers neutrally style as non-performing assets attests to it. Winners concentrate on understanding and mastering the dynamics of risk. Losers toy with reward and construct rationales for suppressing untoward realities.

The loan portion of a bank's assets is usually termed 'risk assets'. However clever one wants to be about the matter, the ultimate definition of risk must centre on the concept of uncertainty. It follows that when banks designate loans as risk assets, they are in fact saying that these loans represent an uncertain value. This uncertainty is only extinguished when the risk asset has been repaid. For enduring this uncertainty of repayment of principal, the 'reward' is highly ironic as it is often seen in the fractions of a single percentage point! Even pious orders who have taken a vow of poverty could chastely reap such a reward without violating the sanctity of their oath.

But if the reward is so puny as to pass the most stringent poverty line test, why call it reward and in the process further addle a confused thought process? The answer is not readily to hand because the philosophy of commercial bank lending is not truly oriented either to evaluate risk, to master it or, least of all, to absorb it or to reap rewards. While bankers do grasp this reality of their business, in practice it does not translate well. One must ask: Why?

There are many central and peripheral risks to evaluate when a loan is being considered, and earlier in the chapter we outlined a methodology to ferret out risks. But if we had to reduce the bundle of risks to two core issues which should dominate the entire process, these would be:

(1) the risk that the borrower will not have cash or readily realizable assets with which to repay the obligation and

(2) the risk that the borrower is in the wrong business/
    industry.

At this stage of the process, there should be no concern
whatever with 'reward' since one is in the act of isolating
and evaluating risk. The first risk, the risk of non-payment,
we will designate as the specific risk and the second we
will call a portfolio risk. When these risks ignite in tandem,
they are a deadly brace. Yet very few banks have their act
right when it comes to comprehending these two risks in
combination. Despite many ill-conceived actions with most
uncomfortable results, American banks are far ahead of
their British and European counterparts in attempting to
reach these risks by placing their best and brightest in the
management of the risk apparatus. The British and European tendency runs heavily biased to the transactional or
specific risk area where individuals dominate. These cultures are also more oriented towards respect for hierar-
chical authority. Risk, on the other hand, has no such
hang-ups. The art of mastering risk requires a disciplined
intellect that ignores personalities. One of the authors inter-
viewed the executive vice-president of the international
department of a large bank who had recently appointed
his top credit officer. The interviewer was anxious to find
out the qualities such a sage executive sought in his First
Risk Lord. The answer was stunning: the man had charisma
and an air of authority!

The demands of strategic portfolio risk management are
much more strenuous. The intellectual, managerial and
business acumen necessary to blend the right balance into
grasping the variety of strains and intensities of risks is in
rare supply. In the long run, the commitment of US banks
to provide this dimension to their disciplined evaluation of
risk will ensure that they will stay ahead of their international peers. There is no sustained, serious work evident
in Europe or Britain today which would indicate that risk
assessment, which is the core element in any bank, is receiv-

ing anything but intermittent attention and direction. And the ongoing fascination with the specific risk continues to overwhelm any serious concern with strategic, portfolio risk management.

The evidence of the inability of banks to evaluate correctly commercial or sovereign risk is littered all over their balance sheets. The historicity of this fact is not in dispute. Nor is the oft-cited counterpoint proffered in apologia that good lending far exceeds bad lending. More on this later. What is quite remarkable, however, is the capacity of banks to take fresh, healthy and expensive liabilities and to turn them into scrofulous assets with a fair degree of regularity. The critical fact to bear in mind is that it takes a small proportion of bad lending decisions to destroy or seriously impair the dynamics and viability of a bank. And this point returns us to the logic of banking which structurally demands that a bank must tolerate nothing but minimal, if any, risk.

The logic of the banking industry dictates that it requires a fair measure of leverage to operate at all gainfully. How high should that leverage be? Most banks would find it economically inefficient to operate with a leverage of less than 10. Many banks operate in the $15\times$ to $20\times$ range and some Japanese, Italian, French and Canadian banks soar to $40\times$ or $50\times$. Banks are not notably profitable institutions, and even with a narrow equity base and high leveraging the results are not significantly enhanced. This usually means that the capital base expands at an arithmetic rate while the asset base moves on a geometric scale. This further element of logic of the business relentlessly demands that bankers as a breed should develop genetic characteristics that reduce any propensity to boldness in them.

When Continental Illinois announced to the world that it could no longer continue in business without a couple of billion of Federal and other support it was one of the best capitalised banks in the USA with equity to assets standing at some 7 per cent. This is not the measure of a bank's strength. A bank's financial stamina and solidity are gauged by the resident liquidity in its risk assets. When the perception develops that this resident liquidity is congealing, a bank's capital cannot save it. Indeed, it is perfectly tolerable on a conceptual plane to eliminate capital from a bank by substituting long-term contractual debt. Both in the USA and the UK debt instruments are already being given the divinity of equity. What ultimately matters is that the risk assets of a bank command the confidence of the market place. The greater the strength of these assets, the less need there is for equity.

When regulatory authorities demand higher equity of a bank that is experiencing liquidity problems in the risk asset base, they are helping further to cripple such a bank. The generous provisions of FASB 15 that permit banks to forgive portions of troubled loans and extend repayment schedules on altered terms with a minimum of disclosure, only add to the problem and allow banks to keep their depositors and investors in the dark. The cost of capital is high and fewer risk assets fail to generate the necessary servicing capacity. But the concern of these authorities to include the ocean of icebergs that appear nowhere on a bank's main balance sheet is a sensible step in alerting bankers, investors and depositors that concealed risks are not absent risks. We use the term 'icebergs' to cover a host of products that range from ordinary letters of credit, bank guarantees or performance bonds or the back-up lines for note issuance facilities, revolving underwriting facilities, to the exploding phenomena of Treasury-generated products such as interest rate swaps, options and countless more. The 15 largest US banks have over a trillion dollars of these invisibles. At least in the USA they are beginning to have to declare these risk products whereas in Europe, including the UK, and elsewhere the need to inform the investing, lending and depositing public is, at best, a tepid concern.

It also creates another imperative: the need for an acute

and fundamental understanding and ability to size up risk. Bankers could not pour loans into Latin America fast enough in the late 1970s and early 1980s. They called these loans sovereign risks and one of the mightiest bankers in America blandly declared: countries don't go bust! Countries do not have to go bust to injure the health of your loan and your bank. As sovereign entities, these countries deal with lesser mortals such as commercial banks with something less than total obeisance. Indeed, despite their plight and threat of no further pocket money in the future, they deal from a position of power. But the 'rewards' were terrific, running as high as 2 per cent over LIBOR or prime lending levels. Was this grand spread to compensate for the risk? Was it a sensible or acceptable 'reward' for the risk taken? Absolutely not! Once this sort of lending got underway, it became speculative and should have commanded speculative 'rewards'. Rates of 20 or 30 per cent would have been more reasonably aligned to the risk. The concern of banks should not be with marginally better rates. The sole concern ought to be with watertight risks. In no manner whatever does a rate spread of 1, 2, 3 or even 25 per cent 'reward' a bank for a fool's risk. A $100m loan will require 50 years at 2 per cent to recover principal alone— without considering inflation or opportunity costs.

Sovereign loans also constitute the most economically unproductive use of funds. Usually they go into the infrastructure of the borrowing country which rarely yields a nickel in hard currency; or, as balance of payments loans, they go to right basically maladjusted economies which further exacerbates the availability of hard currency for future servicing. In fact, the US$300 odd billion of loans to Latin America are serviced by a continuum of additional lending to pay interest in order to keep these loans from being classified delinquent, which means setting aside hard-earned chunks of money to get ready to write the loans off.

But these loans have received enough publicity and we

only cite them as the most blatant example of the 'risk and reward' mentality. There were also billions in loans made to commercial borrowers, industrial borrowers, traders, real estate operators, oil companies and so on, where lenders took risks that were clearly not in their mandate and, more important, their capacity to absorb. The point to keep at the fore of every loan proposal is simply this: a banker is not in business to take the risk of losing the principal of the loan regardless of the 'reward'.

'Reward', as it is, seems to be the wrong word to use in the first place. Money, as the layman understands it, is wealth. In economic terms, it is defined as a medium of exchange—not much different. What is different, however, is that money is simply a commodity and banks have known this since the hapless but necessary institution of banking began.

The implication deriving from the use of the term 'commodity' is that it is a trading and tradable item. And so it is. The commodity of money is traded at a price. International and domestic prices differ vastly for the different quality versions of this commodity. The lower the intrinsic value of the commodity, the higher the price will be in its domestic setting. Loans in Brazilian cruzeiros have gone for a price of 100 per cent which is not enough when inflation is careering at 101 per cent, let alone 200 per cent. No one outside of Mexico, Turkey or Italy would hold Italian and Turkish lire as an expression of wealth any more than they would the Mexican peso.

But returning to the focal issue, we have to view a loan as a temporary transfer of a commodity at a slight price differential which is a rental fee for the use and return of the original transfer at its original face value. Once lenders grasp this major distinction between price and reward, the issue of why concentration on risk is absolutely paramount becomes obvious. We are not trying to impress ourselves or the reader with a fine semantic subtlety.

Repeatedly in bank jargon and at loan committee meetings, the presenter focuses on the 'reward'. 'Reward' also falsely suggests a certain uniqueness. No single bank controls the price for the commodity, hence the reward is the ordinary prevailing price for the denominated period of transfer. Nothing unique or extraordinary about this. Just a common price for a common commodity. Again, the price is minimal, the commodity very valuable. Thus again, one returns to the concept of value when it comes to risk. One should never risk present true value for a forfeiture of that value on the basis of a marginal price differential in the future.

Earlier we remarked that the logic of a bank's structure demanded that only virtually riskless assets be taken on the books. We also said that a bank's measure is often taken by the percentage of non-performing assets to the total portfolio of risk assets, i.e. loans. When a bank is leveraged at 20 to 1 and has 5 per cent in non-performing loans, its equity has already been wiped out. We have also said that leveraging of 20x is not uncommon. Nor is that 5 per cent in non-performing loans. A more genteel idiom has crept into the language: equity is not wiped out, it is frozen. You pay your money and you take your choice.

At many banks these rising levels of troubled loans have given Problem and Workout Loan Committees a new prominence. Serious banks staffed such units with seasoned lending and credit personnel who, apart from engaging in recoveries, set about to develop significant concepts of risk portfolio management, concentrating on *loss avoidance* and elaborate loan gradations for continuous tracking. Other banks simply co-opted the generic classifications of satisfactory, watchlist, substandard, doubtful and loss.

Usually, a triage of the dead and dying was entered into their computerized mortuaries. The entire process fell to bright, inexperienced but profuse memo writers who aspired to cull cosmic principles of lending for future generations.

We did not set out to prove a theory in geometry nor indeed to design an unbreakable case for our contention about the banal use of the term 'risk and reward'. We do say, however, that it is wrong nomenclature which deceptively leads lenders to believe that they are risk takers in the first place, which they should not be, and that they are rewarded for such risks which they surely are not. Lending to a risk-laden company which 'makes it' simply returns the transferred commodity with the agreed price for its use. No other riches follow as they might well have done to the owners of that business. Strangely, when a banker is finally given the privilege of reaping the rewards that accrue to an owner, it is because the business has succumbed and has no further rewards to offer.

10

For investors—What price value?

A cynic is . . . a man who knows the price of everything and the value of nothing.

Oscar Wilde, *Lady Windermere's Fan*, Act 3

Dr Beecham, so the story goes, once invented a patent medicine and devised a method of producing it at a cost of one halfpenny a dose (an old halfpenny that is). A friend of his suggested to the good doctor that if he could sell it for a penny a time he could make his fortune and retire a rich man. 'I am doing much better than that,' replied Dr Beecham, 'I am selling it for half a crown a time and on the packet is written "Worth a Guinea!". People are queueing up to buy it!'

A trivial story, perhaps, but the philosophical question it raises is worth examining. What were Dr Beecham's pills worth—a halfpenny, half a crown or a guinea? What indeed do we mean when we say that something is 'worth' a given sum of money?

According to the standard texts, it is one of the functions of money to act as a measure of value. Without money, trade continues in the form of barter (or countertrade as it is more politely known nowadays), but it is difficult to express the value of any object that is not being traded except in primitive agricultural terms—the equivalent of so many sheep or so many days of a man's labour. The invention of coinage and, much later, paper money allowed rather more sophisticated transactions to be made, and more particularly established a bench-mark against which any object or commodity could be measured. If an object could be sold for $5 it was said to be 'worth' $5 and it was intrinsically more desirable than an object worth $4 and less desirable than one worth $6. Of course, opinions might vary as to the price an object should fetch in the market, particularly if the object were not actually for sale. A smart trader would try to buy for $4 what he perceived to be 'worth' $5, perhaps trying at the same time to convince others that it was worth $6, in the hope that he could sell the same object for $5 or more. In this way, it becomes possible for an article to have two quite distinct values, the one its current market value, at which it changes hands today, the other an intrinsic value, that may exist only in the mind of one individual, representing the potential market value for which it is supposed the article could be sold at some future date.

Central to both definitions of value is the existence of a market which permits the easy exchange of articles for money, what economists would call a deep and liquid market. It makes sense to talk about a house having a certain value since houses are being sold all the time, and if the identical house down the road goes for £50 000 it is no fiction to say that your house is worth a like amount, all other things being equal. It does not make sense to put a value on the Tower of London, the World Cup or the girl nextdoor because none of these ever changes hands for money, and without a market the very concept of value is meaningless. Even where it is possible to attach a monetary equivalent to an object, a valuation is usually only approximate and will very often fluctuate widely over short periods of time. We live in inflationary times and have become used to finding that last week's price has been superseded by a higher one, and in the commodities markets, where the forces of supply and demand move prices quickly, market rates fluctuate by the moment.

A further complication is that money itself has a price and can be traded as a commodity, the existence of different currencies in almost every country in the world permitting one country's currency to be valued by reference to another's. Constant changes in interest rates, trading conditions, speculative traders and political developments all combine to keep the world's system of value in constant flux.

Money is itself rather an intangible thing. The great debates in England and the USA in the nineteenth century about the propriety of issuing paper money are now long behind us—and we no longer care that the proud promises on our banknotes about 'paying the bearer on demand' are empty bombast. A pound note or a dollar bill are worth a pound or a dollar in that a bank will give exactly that amount of credit for those documents, but the note itself no longer represents a claim on anything tangible. In fact, although one naturally thinks of money in terms of pieces of paper the vast bulk of money in the financial systems of any country consists of bank deposits, nothing more than entries in a bank's books, recording the bank's obligation to its customer. We have now what is known as fiduciary money, money based solely upon trust.

A banknote is acceptable in exchange for goods and services because it is acknowledged and accepted even by the most sceptical in the community that, at least in the immediate future, a banknote can be spent and will be acceptable to other parties with whom the bearer may wish to trade. Banknotes, and deposits in banks, retain value only because their supply is limited by a government with a monopoly on the printing of money and which limits the creation of credit by the banking system. If the government abuses its position of trust and prints money in unreasonable quantity, as the Germans did in the early 1920s when the Weimar Republic tried to print its way out of the war reparations imposed at Versailles, the value of money itself will plummet. Wealth cannot be created out of thin air by the use of a printing press and the creation of money and credit in excess of that demanded by the level of trade and volume of goods and services available, leads inexorably to inflation, the debasing of the national tender.

The temptation for those controlling the currency to try to print themselves into wealth is usually irresistible and for centuries the traditional hedge against inflation and monetary collapse has been the hoarding of precious metals, especially gold. Gold has the inestimable advantage that its supply is extremely limited by nature and to allow individuals the right to convert their paper money into gold is a cast-iron method of restraining monetary growth. Of course, monetary growth is in those circumstances limited by the supply of gold rather than the needs of the economy, a less than ideal situation, but there is certainly no way the government can allow the currency to lose its purchasing power or it will see its own gold reserves depleted with great rapidity.

With one accord the nations of the world abandoned the 'gold standard' some years ago in the belief that laxer monetary policy would encourage growth and trade. But not everyone was convinced, and to this day gold continues to attract investors who wish to diversify their portfolios. Lord Keynes predicted that the price of gold would fall, once it was demonetized, from the $35 per ounce at which the Bretton Woods Conference had fixed it after the war, to a few cents an ounce, the price that dentists were prepared to pay for the raw material of fillings for their patients' teeth. Dentistry apart, gold is used only for jewellery, for gilding and to a very limited extent in the pharmaceutical and chemical industries. A gold ingot is utterly useless except as a doorstop (an acquaintance of ours is known to use a silver ingot for this purpose!) and all one can do is hoard it. The unavailability of interest on gold deposits and the heavy costs of secure storage render this activity none too attractive.

Gold today stands at over $300 per ounce, and that price has nothing whatever to do with the demand for gold fillings or gilded leather book bindings; gold is still perceived as a store of value despite the lack of any government-guaranteed convertibility into currency. At times of international tension and crisis in the financial markets the price of gold still shoots up as wary investors take cover in what they see as a safe investment.

Why was Lord Keynes wrong? In part, he underestimated the age-old attraction of gold with its association of wealth, power and royalty. But principally, he failed to perceive that so long as men continued to believe in the value of gold, gold would actually retain and increase its value. As with other commodities, the price of gold is dictated by supply and demand. Demand for gold did not dry up, irrational reasons continued to encourage investors to buy it and so its value increased. It was a self-fulfilling prophecy and a tautology: gold was valuable because people wanted it, people wanted it because it was valuable and a store of value!

There is little cash flow to be derived from holding gold. It can be lent in large quantities at 2–3 per cent per year but against that are the heavy storage, insurance and transport costs. That, however, is not the point. Gold, for all its erratic fluctuations on the gold markets, is believed to be a store of value immune to whatever becomes of the world's international monetary system and investors buy it secure in the knowledge that there will always be another investor willing to take it off their hands for a reasonable and not insubstantial consideration.

Gold is an extreme case of an investment which has a market value greatly in excess of what might be considered rational, but it illustrates that 'intrinsic' value may be a chimera, backed by nothing at all except the whims of individuals.

Gold is not unique in this respect. Curiously similar considerations dictate the value of other, more 'normal' investments, even though members of the relative markets would not tend to analyse their own activities in these kinds of terms.

Take the equity markets, and let us consider why people buy the shares of public companies. A small shareholder in, say, J. Sainsbury, the largest British supermarket chain, owns a minute proportion of the equity in the assets of Sainsbury's. He has no claim to the actual assets of the company and he has no claim to any particular piece of equipment, leg of lamb or can of beans that belongs to the company. If he shows up at a store intending to realize his shareholding in kind, he will be shown off by the security guard. The assets of the company belong to the company, not to the shareholders. For the price of his shares, the investor receives a flow of information, Annual Reports, letters, invitations to shareholders' meetings and the like and, if the directors of the company see fit, a dividend. The dividend will generally be a modest proportion, probably a good deal less than half, of the declared profit of the company and the shareholder will receive in proportion to the ratio of his shareholding to the total shareholdings outstanding.

The dividend is the return on the shareholder's investment and in ordinary circumstances it is all the money he ever receives from his company. Successful private companies occasionally go into voluntary liquidation because the owners no longer wish to continue in business and prefer to divest the company of its assets, pay off the debts and return the residue to themselves. But this is rare, and usually there is more money to be gained by selling the business as a 'going concern' to other entrepreneurs. Shareholders will also get their investment back if their company is taken over by a predator in a takeover battle or if a private company goes public. If the company collapses or liquidates involuntarily, the shareholder may receive something back for his shares, but shareholders in compulsory liquidation can generally reckon to receive virtually nothing after all the debts are paid.

None of these possibilities is in the mind of the small investor in Sainsbury's. It is most unlikely that Sainsbury's will be either taken over or liquidated in the foreseeable future and consequently there is no way in which he is going to get his money back from the company. If he wants his money out, he will have to find a buyer, someone else willing to take on his shares in Sainsbury's at an acceptable price. Of course, this is not an insuperable difficulty because there is a ready market for Sainsbury's shares and any bank or stockbroker will be able to handle the transaction.

The conundrum is why there should always be people willing to hold the shares of Sainsbury's. What makes this company an attractive investment? The first thing to notice is that it is not the assets of Sainsbury's because the shareholders have no access to them. What the investor receives, and all he can reasonably expect to receive, is a dividend and the yield on Sainsbury's shares, currently around 2 per cent, does not make the shares an exciting investment compared with Government securities which are not only risk-free when held to redemption, which Sainsbury's shares are not, but offer a guaranteed return of around 10–11 per cent. It should be added that Sainsbury's is an extremely successful company with first-class management.

The conventional answer is that Sainsbury's is a growth stock and investors in Sainsbury's are looking to see capital gains from a constantly rising share price in addition to their dividends. Shareholders, in other words, are content to receive only modest dividends because the remainder of the profits, which are substantial, are reinvested in the business thereby increasing its value. As a result, up go the shares on the Stock Exchange. The market accepts that reinvestment of profits back into the business is an attractive way to deploy the wealth created and investors are willing, therefore, to accept a rising share price in lieu of full dividend payout. The popular mind perceives the process as 'investment in industry', an activity that leads to higher profits for the shareholders, as well as creating employment and, more broadly, adding vitality to the economy.

On one level there is no disputing any of this. Annual Reports of growth companies and comment by stock exchange analysts strongly encourage precisely this interpretation when they urge readers to purchase the shares of enterprises like Sainsbury's. It is certainly hard to conceive of any other reason for holding an investment yielding 2 per cent. Doubt only creeps in when one asks why it is that investors are willing to tolerate a yield of 2 per cent virtually *indefinitely*. If the bulk of Sainsbury's profits are reinvested this year, is not the same likely to be true next year and the year after? Sainsbury's is not likely to be liquidated or taken over, so far as can be seen, and those possibilities would not seem to enter into the calculations investors perform. Sainsbury's can get away with being a growth stock more or less for ever and only by selling his shares will an investor realize the growth in his bank account. Such realization involves finding a purchaser willing to invest his money at 2 per cent on the new higher price and he in turn will want eventually to sell, and so on *ad infinitum*. It is not clear that at any stage does the total amount of money invested in Sainsbury's ever get returned.

The figure of 2 per cent will not apply strictly to a long-term investor in Sainsbury's. Although an initial investment of £1000 will produce only £20 of dividends in the first year, in subsequent years the dividend will increase. While the published yield may stay at 2 per cent, to the investor of the £1000 the dividend yield on his original investment will rise and there is academic support for the idea that the dividends will, in the long term, amount to an adequate return regardless of the capital appreciation.

Considerable special pleading is necessary to demonstrate this for Sainsbury's. Assuming 10 per cent compound growth on the share price and the dividend, dividends over the next 5 years will be £22.0, £24.2, £26.6, £29.3 and £32.2, all of which we should be discounting in calculating economic yields. It is quite clear that some quantum leap must be introduced into the dividend pattern if the dividends alone are ever to become realistic compensation in themselves. Investors do not in practice make this kind of calculation. They do note the dividend yield and the capital appreciation taking place and decide whether they believe the combination sufficient to justify an investment.

There is a paradox to be resolved: a dividend yield of 2 per cent is not, in isolation, attractive. To render the yield attractive there must also be continuous capital appreciation. Capital appreciation not only increases the value of the shares, it increases the total amount of wealth tied up at 2 per cent and the investors at large never receive this money back. It is a permanent investment, and if capital appreciation ceases, investors are immediately starting to get a raw deal.

The resolution to this paradox lies in the willingness of the investing public to hold equity shares in companies like Sainsbury's as a store of value, while believing that the market will continue to exist, and will be disposed to hold ever increasing amounts of wealth in the form of Sainsbury's shares as the company grows. If for any reason the market collectively decided that these conditions no longer obtained, the price of Sainsbury's shares would undoubtedly fall, either to a level at which the dividend yield was appropriate to the degree of risk perceived by investors, or to the point where the totality of the shares were worth roughly what could be obtained from the physical assets of Sainsbury's if the company were dismembered, whichever was the higher. Both of these levels would be very much lower than the currently prevailing share price. What keeps the share price up is the willingness of investors to maintain wealth in the form of Sainsbury's shares. As that willingness increases, the share price tends to rise; as it declines so does the market valuation.

Financial newspapers often quote a figure for market capitalization that is the total value of the entire issued share capital, with the implication that this figure is the 'value' of the whole company. Sainsbury's market capitalization is currently around £2.3bn. Arithmetically correct, there is little meaning that can really be attached to this number and it most decidedly is not the 'value' of Sainsbury's or the price at which one could buy the whole company, even assuming it were for sale. Anyone attempting such a coup would certainly have to reckon on a much higher price for the whole company and even a bid to buy partial control or complete control would elevate the share price and hence the market capitalization steeply. The quoted share price approximates to the price at which jobbers are prepared to make a market in relatively small numbers of the company's shares; it is, in effect, a marginal price and it fluctuates not directly in line with the company's fortunes, but in response to supply and demand pressures, one constituent of which (among others) is the actual performance of Sainsbury's.

At any one time only a tiny fraction of the issued shares of Sainsbury's is being traded, the bulk being held as long-term investments by institutions, pension funds, insurance companies and the like. Provided that these institutions do not wish to sell, day to day fluctuations make absolutely no difference to them as their aim is to achieve long-term growth in accordance with the aims and needs of their beneficiaries. To say, as newspapers tend to, that on a day when confidence is shaken either by some discouraging news from Sainsbury's or perhaps a gloomy prognosis on the state of the British or world economy, that hundreds of millions of pounds were wiped off the share valuation is a meaningless exaggeration. The share price has merely responded to a rush of selling (which lowers the price of anything) which may or may not represent a permanent or semipermanent revision by the market of its willingness to hold wealth and resources in Sainsbury's shares.

A number of independent factors influence the market and help to establish the magical share price quoted in the newspapers, but fundamental is a willingness on the part of the market to see a particular share issue as a suitable medium for the storing of wealth.

Where this willingness is absent the shares will be worth virtually nothing. An interesting example is the case of Reuters, the international news agency. In the 1920s Reuters had set up a quite extraordinary shareholding arrangement designed for the sole purpose of maintaining the ownership in hands that would keep Reuters' impartiality as a reporter of news unbesmirched. The British interests which had founded Reuters were anxious above all that no one should ever use it as a propaganda vehicle, and normal commercial considerations were of minimal import as the company made little money. Under the new arrangement shares were to be held in a kind of trust by various publishing concerns and worthy organizations and individuals. No dividends were ever paid.

From the 1920s onwards Reuters continued to grow, first as a news agency but latterly as a supplier of financial information services. Highly sophisticated Reuters equipment came to grace banks and brokers' offices around the world and supplied them with up-to-the-second data on markets and prices. This side of Reuters' business came to dominate financially the old news gathering arm and in June 1984 the decision was taken to revise the shareholding situation. Until then the shares had not attracted significant attention for many years. A few had changed hands for money, but not at prices remotely resembling the economic value of the underlying assets and some uncertainty existed as to who the precise owners were of certain shares. Ownership of shares in Reuters conferred only the right to a voice in the directing of the company, a right that could not really be used for personal advantage.

On the analogy of Sainsbury's, this was very odd. If growth could sustain the Sainsbury's share price way above the level suggested by the dividends, Reuters' shares should have been worth something—as Reuters' had exhibited the most phenomenal growth. The trouble was that Reuters' shares never produced any cash at all. No dividends were paid and there was no likelihood of any liquidation. The whole purpose of the exotic shareholding arrangements was to prevent a takeover. Logically, and in fact, the shares were worth precisely nothing, however prosperous Reuters became.

Once it was suggested that Reuters should pay dividends, and its shares be traded, the shares shot up in value from nothing to several thousand pounds each. Some of the owners became millionaires overnight. Nothing, of course, had really happened to Reuters but its shares had unexpectedly been reassessed as an acceptable store of wealth and its 'value' had responded accordingly.

Not to pay a dividend at all is unacceptable practice and failure to pay a dividend, or indeed to reduce dividends, is seen on the Stock Exchange in a poor light unless the company is very persuasive about its reasons for conserving cash. Growth on its own is insufficient reward and even the most unabashed growth company has to pay some dividend, even if only a penny or two, to keep its shareholders well disposed. It is not easy to discern the rationality behind this attitude, but a measure of cash flow is evidently required from an investment if it is to retain a claim to serious attention as a long-term store of value. It is as though the market is prepared to accept a reasonable mixture of dividends and capital growth for its return on an equity, but it does not expect all profits to be paid back in dividends and it will not tolerate capital growth in isolation. In 1961, two American scholars, Modigliani and Miller, proposed a theory of 'dividend indifference' by which they claimed that the dividend policy of a company had no impact on its share price since every dollar of dividend forgone was another dollar added to the equity of the company. At first glance, this does not look convincing. With tax taken into the reckoning, the picture becomes positively bizarre; dividends will be taxed in the hands of the shareholders, often at high rates of income tax, whereas the equivalent growth in the share equity will suffer only capital gains tax and that only when the shares are realized. The argument suggests that logically companies should minimize their dividends if their management's aim is actually to maximize the wealth of the shareholders.

The logic is impeccable, but the conclusion is so obviously at odds with the market's own view of dividend reductions that something must be wrong with the premises on which the argument is founded. Actually, there are more factors at play here than Modigliani and Miller were prepared to acknowledge, not least that the paying of dividends is perceived by investors as a statement of confidence in the future on the part of the company's managers and that, as often, money speaks louder than mere words.

The other point to remember is that every investor needs some cash income to pay expenses. Capital growth will not pay the rent. A man might own a house in London whose value is rising by £20 000 a year. He might make it rise even faster by working full time to improve the house—putting a new roof on and decorating, perhaps. Unless he has other cash income he will soon, however, have to liquidate his property to pay his mounting debts; alternatively he can sell his labour for cash by going out to work, and he will then have to sacrifice some of his capital appreciation for a stream of cash payments. This may well be the optimum solution. Fund managers and investors (and for that matter bankers) are in a similar position and prefer to have some cash coming in without the constant need to liquidate holdings. It is partly for this reason that bankers are notoriously reluctant to finance customers' interest payments.

A line of thought much in vogue with the US business schools is that every investment is priced at the present value of expected future cash flows, discounted at appropriate rates of interest. On the principle that $1 today is worth exactly $1.10 in a year's time, if one assumes an interest rate of 10 per cent per annum, and that an investor is indifferent between $1 now and $1.10 in a year's time provided there is no risk, it is possible to take a stream of cash flow running into the future and calculate a present value or price at which that stream of payments may be bought or sold. The share price, it is claimed, is the discounted value of expected future profits attributable to a single share.

It is undoubtedly true that the markets do value some investments in this way, notably bonds and government securities. A bond normally has a redemption date on which the holder will receive back from the borrower or insurer of the bond the capital sum invested. Interest payments are similarly predictable because a bond invariably carries a coupon rate, this rate determining the interest payments precisely because it relates to the capital sum invested rather than the market value of the bond. Thus, a 10 per cent bond for £1000 redeemable in 10 years' time will pay £100 p.a. in interest and will be redeemed at £1000 10 years from now. If interest rates in the market rise, the price of the bond will fall since the unaffected cash flow from the bond will no longer be attractive to an investor with £1000 to invest. The cash flow from the bond discounted at 10 per cent will give a present value of exactly £1000; but at, say, 11 per cent the present value will fall below £1000 so that anyone purchasing the bond for the new lower price will effectively earn a return of 11 per cent, which is what he expects.

If interest rates fall, the price of the bonds will rise. Again, the cash flows from the bond are unaffected, but if an investor expects only 9 per cent for his money he will be prepared to pay more for the bond and the price will in fact rise to a level at which the investor's money earns the required rate of 9 per cent only. It is all a question of the price today of a stream of cash payments of £100 p.a., plus a final payment of £1000 after 10 years, and what determines the price of such a cash stream is the price of money, an abstraction known more familiarly as the interest rate.

Bonds and similar debt securities trade in open markets and prices obviously fluctuate in response to supply and demand. If a government tries to issue too much debt at any one time the price will be depressed. Shortage of paper or an unusually lively demand for an issue will push the price up. Perceptions of risk are also important in that the debt of governments and very powerful companies is more attractive than that of inferior or weaker entities. As a second-tier company borrower is seen by the market to be moving into the first tier, the price of its bonds will tend to move upward, effectively narrowing the rate of return, this even when market rates are stable. Ultimately, the value of a bond is determined not by what it is 'worth' in some abstract sense, but by what people are willing to pay for it. In this respect, bonds and equities behave in exactly the same way. Bonds, however, have predictable cash flows and it is most unlikely that the price will fluctuate far outside the area dictated by interest rates and risk perception. That is because there is a lively band of money managers, speculators and arbitrageurs around the world who will spot the opportunity for making a quick profit and who, by buying or selling the security, will push the price back into line to where the market as a whole supposes it ought to be.

It is possible to value equities in the same way by predicting future profits and discounting them at an appropriate rate of interest. There are certainly those who would argue that that is precisely what the market does and they produce formidable arrays of statistics in support of their contention. The argument embodies a certain logic since it is quite true that shares can only be valuable for the wealth accruing to the shareholders, though there is no direct access to the underlying assets of the company. These belong to the company, not to the shareholders.

Proponents of this theory claim that the stock market, as an efficient market, absorbs all the relevant knowledge publicly available relating to each and every traded company and the players within the market use that knowledge, acting individually, together or in competition with each other, to establish a price at which supply and demand are balanced. This price is effectively the market's collective opinion on the present value of the profits coming from the equity shares discounted at what the market assumes are appropriate rates of interest. All this is highly logical and difficult to dispute from the purely intellectual point of view.

The crunch comes when we look to see the use to which this theory is put. Few observers are really interested purely for sociological or philososphical purposes in the

way the markets value shares. The object of most stock
market analysis is to form a better understanding of the way
in which markets move so that investors armed with the
right information may predict these movements with a
view to more profitable investment. As in most walks of
life, knowledge is power.

The direct consequence of the 'discounted cash flow'
approach to equity valuation is what has become known as
the Random Walk Theory. If the market's price for a share is
the result of an efficient market digesting and feeding into
that price all the information known to that market, information not only about the company whose shares are being
traded, but about the industry and the macroeconomy and
about interest rates, it follows that the next piece of information to emerge may cause the price to move up or to
move down and it is a fifty–fifty chance which it will be.
The market will have factored various expectations into the
price and as these are confirmed, confounded or surpassed
the share price will respond. However, from any given
point new pieces of information which increase optimism
and those which encourage pessimism can be expected
statistically to occur with equal frequency.

Suppose that next year X Inc. is expected to make a profit
of $1.0m and that is the expectation reflected in the share
price. There will be some in the market expecting $900 000,
some $1 100 000 and others anything in between or around
these numbers. Subsequently information comes to light
that shows that the profit will in fact be nearer $1 100 000
than $1.0m. The share price rises. Had the new information
suggested less than $1.0m profit next year the price would
have fallen. What the Random Walk Theory says is that,
given this scenario, it is just as likely that either of these
eventualities will occur. This is a good argument which, if
you think about it, holds a good deal of force.

Taking it one stage further, one has to acknowledge that
over time the movement of the share price must be random.

There will be some new information coming to the market that raises the price and other data tending to depress it. There will be no pattern to these information flows and consequently the share price plotted against time on a graph will move in a 'random walk'. Any pattern which might appear will be an illusion unless information is being used which is not known to the whole market, a phenomenon known as *insider trading*. The ultimate consequence is that any attempt to predict which shares will go up and which down on the stock exchange is nothing more than futile guesswork. The Random Walk Theory says that there are no patterns and that the effective prediction of stock movements is impossible. Unless you can act on information before the market absorbs it, and it is universally acknowledged that share prices respond almost instantaneously (not always correctly!) to important news, it is a waste of time trying to outguess the market.

That is a pretty gloomy conclusion and not one to gladden the hearts of stockbrokers, investors or analysts. Not only gloomy, the Random Walk Theory is downright dangerous and poses a direct threat to the livelihood of some extremely well-paid people, who have not been slow to offer quite different interpretations of how the market works, interpretations (of course) which show their own activities in a more favourable light. As in the discussion of cash flow, vested interests have mobilized against revolutionary beliefs. And always will.

The principal objection to The Random Walk Theory is that the starting premise, that shares are valued by reference to expected future cash flows and profits, is wrong. Opponents of the theory would point out that, whatever the theoretician might say, no one active in the market appears to make this calculation and even a casual glance at the output of stockbrokers' reports would show that the market uses quite other criteria to evaluate shares. It is doubtful even whether the calculation is feasible since no one can with any confidence predict interest rates over the next 6 months, let alone over several years, and the value of company dividends and inflation is similarly impenetrable in the medium to long term. Any attempt to evaluate a share on the basis of the profit flows to be expected would have to make so many unprovable assumptions that the resulting figures could have no credibility, as being founded on guesswork and surmise.

Cato the Elder, a renowned judge in Republican Rome, acquired an undying reputation for his wisdom in often asking the question 'Cui bono?', 'Who stood to gain?' when he was investigating some nefarious action and trying to identify the culprits. Similarly, before arbitrating on the clash of ideas just outlined, we need to understand something of the motivation of traditional stock market analysts, few of whom have any sympathy whatever with the Random Walk Theory.

Stockbrokers work for commission, and the more trading they do on behalf of clients, the more money they make. Unless they trade on their own account it makes little difference to a stockbroker whether the prices move up or down. Jobbers, who take positions in stocks, are exposed but they are not pure speculators since they generally attempt to limit their risk by matching their sales and purchases. The exposed party on the stock exchange is the investor, and he is the source of the livelihood of all who work out there.

It is possible for an investor to use a stockbroker purely to execute transactions and stockbrokers are not generally averse to being used in this way. In New York 'discount brokers', as they are known, have grown tremendously in recent years, offering precisely this service at bargain basement prices. But stockbrokers also presume to give advice. Many investors have a great deal of money, but little time or expertise to analyse markets, trends or company information and these people are often willing to pay for a professional to guide them in their investment deci-sions. In order to provide that advice, stockbroking firms employ teams of analysts to write reports and put out circulars to clients, recommending shares usually as 'buys' or 'holds', just occasionally as 'sells'. 'Holds' are unattrac-tive to the broker because he only makes money if his client buys or sells!

Such advice may be exactly what the client wants, but in giving it stock market analysts and their employers are tacitly assuming that it is possible to make predictions with some confidence about the way the market and individual shares will move. No one who sincerely believed the Ran-dom Walk Theory could in all honesty recommend a share as a 'buy' or a 'sell' since according to that theory all move-ments are random. A share perceived in the market as over or under valued is sold or bought by arbitrageurs whose action drives the share to a new equilibrium price. It is believed that this process happens within a space of minutes and that there is accordingly no opportunity for anyone outside the immediate market to benefit by being ahead of the game. It is not surprising that supporters of the Random Walk Theory are mainly to be found in banks and business schools and opponents are usually in the markets. This is not necessarily to imply any intellectual dishonesty on the part of either group, but it should serve as a warning that there are vested interests at play.

Of those rejecting the Random Walk Theory, many fall under the blanket term 'chartists'. They believe that by plotting share movements on a graph it is possible to disclose distinctive patterns emerging over time. As these patterns tend to recur, it is feasible to buy at a low point in a given configuration and sell out at the high point. The best-known of these configurations is the 'head and shoul-ders' pattern whereby a share is supposed to stay on a plateau for a period on either side of a peak in the price. Watch for the plateaux, so the theory runs, and sell on the peaks. Numerous highly sophisticated and ingenious mathematical models have been devised to perfect this approach and help an investor beat the market.

It is, by the nature of these things, hard to disprove such theories, and it certainly cannot be done without entering into the deep water of calculus and algebra, into which we shall not venture here. However, from what we do know of market behaviour one struggles to see how any of these methods can be valid. Investors buy and sell in accordance with their willingness to hold the shares in a particular company. Buying and selling of large volumes of shares moves the price. Jobbers, who fix the prices according to their own books, respond to the flow of information and the need to keep purchases and sales roughly in balance. None of the parties involved is likely to have much regard for historical movements in the share price. There is, in other words, no conscious desire to move the price in accordance with any preordained pattern and there is little reason why any of the parties should care.

Undoubtedly there are some technical reasons, the results of the rules of the market, which may cause recurrent patterns; the London Stock Exchange works on a system of two week 'accounts' on trading periods, and settlement for all transactions undertaken during an account takes place 10 days after the account ends. If the market has been rising over the account and many speculators have bought shares which have risen in value by the end of the account there will inevitably be quite heavy selling on the final day as long positions are closed. This ensures the speculators their profit, while saving them from having to pay out the cost price of their shares. There are certain times when large amounts of money flow into and out of the financial system and if these flows occur regularly it might create a recurring pattern in stock market prices. There is no evidence, though, that the effects of such phenomena are very profound or long lasting, and as they are identified, arbitrage operations will tend to compensate for them.

In short, 'chartism' has apparent elements in common with astrology in that however impressive the results might be, establishing either a consistent pattern of success or any causal link between the prediction and the eventuality is extremely difficult. If the prediction comes true, it may only be chance in either case, but if we wish to be convinced, the evidence somehow will look a lot stronger. No rigorous justification of chartism has ever appeared, yet it continues to attract investors as a theory, possibly as a consequence of wishful thinking, in the total absence of any explanation of why it should work at all.

It is not that modern theories of the workings of the stock market are wrong, it is more that they are unable to comprehend the whole, a large component of which is the fundamental irrationality implicit in the attitudes of players in the stock market. Academic studies of stock market behaviour tend to use sophisticated statistical analysis to clarify the market's response to various types of event. 'How does the market react to cuts in dividends?' 'What effect does a change in FIFO to LIFO have on a company's share price?' 'Is debt/equity a good measure of likely success or failure?' A standard technique is to identify a statistical sample of instances where certain events occurred and then qualify the market's behaviour subsequently. Identified responses are then rationalized in accordance with current notices about the efficiency of the market and theories of investor preference.

What such studies rarely seem to do is to ask investors how they make their decisions. There is abundant evidence that the sophistication of participants in the markets ranges all the way from the most naïve to the highly professional, the former dominant in number, the latter in the amount of money they control. The market does respond intelligently to new information emerging about a company, but it has a long memory, it has its favourites and it responds unpredictably. Most shareholders are not buying and selling from one day to the next and prices are determined by the forces of supply and demand among those who are trading, principally professional money managers of one sort or another. Underpinning the whole market is a willingness of investors to hold their wealth in the form of company equities and the belief that this communal willingness will continue to exist into the future. Capital growth is expected and is the main inducement attracting investors to these shares, the majority, whose dividend yields are inferior to the returns obtainable risk-free on government debt securities.

When market confidence increases because the economy is perceived to be advantageous to business, money comes into the stock market, and more money pursuing the same number of shares available for purchase pushes the prices up. Conversely, depressing news about the economic climate discourages investment in equities and prices fall. The totality of prices is, in sum, a function of the willingness of the investing community to own shares and the supply of shares available.

Financial newspapers, analysts' reports and discussions with investors tell a rather different story from that propagated by the academic community, and those with a practical interest in how the market works cannot ignore the beliefs of the market about the ways in which prices are determined. The crucial question is how the market values shares and what considerations contribute towards establishing the trading range within which the share price will move under normal trading conditions. If we know that, we will know a good deal about how to make money on equities and, indeed, how to avoid losing it.

Contrary to academic theory, investors do not do discounted cash flow calculations on equities, nor do they worry much about cash flow at all. They worry about profits, in particular last year's profits and next year's profits. This is not the only aspect of an investment considered by investors and in extreme and unusual cases profit may not even figure at all, but the overwhelming factor in most share relations is the 'return', equated usually to accounting profit, which the company can 'earn' on the money the owners have invested in it.

The specific tool most used in stock market analysis of share prices is the price/earnings ratio, the price of one share divided by the earnings or profit, usually in the UK calculated on a fully taxed basis, that is, the pretax profit minus the amount of corporation tax the company would have paid had it suffered the full rate with no allowances. Thus Sainsbury's is, at the time of writing, trading at 330p per share or 21.7 times the 'fully taxed' earnings per share. Another way of perceiving this is to assume that by buying one share of Sainsbury's one is purchasing 21.7 years of earnings. This number tells us that Sainsbury's is a growth stock. We have seen already that dividend yield is nothing exciting and, as most shares trade on much lower price earnings ratios, the market is clearly pinning its hopes on much greater returns in the future. To buy 21.7 years of earnings at the present level would be expensive and the investors in Sainsbury's are looking for higher and growing profits in the next few years.

Turn the equation the other way around and the market is saying that for a company like Sainsbury's a higher price/earnings ratio than the norm is expected, say between 18 and 23. Such a belief would define the market range between 275p and 350p and the shares would move within that band in response to supply and demand without any major news emerging about Sainsbury's prospects. Of course, in deciding whether to buy or sell, investors will have regard to all the other information that is known about Sainsbury's from past Annual Reports, press releases and comments by influential people on Sainsbury's itself, the supermarket industry and the wider economy. The market undoubtedly is efficient in that it does absorb all this information and feed it into the share price, and there is no reason to dispute that arbitrage pressures keep the share price in line with overall market expectations. All that is known and perceived about the risks, business and financial, which Sainsbury's faces will be fed into the share price, and as perceptions change, the price will move accordingly. Dividend yield will also not be forgotten.

However, the trading range is effectively determined by reference to the price/earnings ratio. Published price/earnings ratios reflect last year's results, but cunning investors and their advisers will have an eye too on the price/earnings ratio calculated on the present year's or next year's expected earnings, and it may be that those figures will be quite different and suggest a higher or lower trading range. It is not sensible to be dogmatic but, as a basic rule, share prices will not normally move to where their price/earnings ratio, however calculated, is no longer perceived to be reasonable.

Analysts use all their skill and judgement to refine the current figure for earnings. Obvious accounting peculiarities will be stripped out of the figures and other adjustments will be made so as to give as clear an earnings result as possible. The market is unlikely to be deceived by unusual treatment of goodwill, depreciation and non-cash items generally, and will consider warily how extraordinary and unusual items so described really are. The practice among British analysts of applying full corporation tax to earnings is dying out as it has become increasingly unrealistic in recent years, and many companies use leasing and capital allowances to shelter their income from tax more or less indefinitely. Few British companies ever pay the full rate. US analysts have always considered it important to get the tax rate right and in the many other countries where taxes are imposed on published profits there is obviously no problem.

This framework of pricing seems, from pure disinterested observation, to be the way the market fundamentally thinks and it would not offend the majority of investors, either professional or amateur. It is precisely the scenario that the securities industry itself encourages investors to envisage, even though the academic schools would consider it un- scientific, which indeed it is.

The fun really starts when we consider how the market, first, changes its perception of a share's value and, secondly, copes with loss-making companies and circum- stances which the price/earnings mechanism is incapable of addressing. Where it is obvious that the device is inappro- priate, other considerations take over.

It was suggested as a hypothesis that Sainsbury's shares might be trading between 18 and 23 times last year's earnings. What would it take to push the price outside of that range? How might the model break down?

The first thing that could happen is that the market effectively changes the figure for earnings in the ratio. Historical earnings are usually beyond meddling with but future earnings are a matter of keen interest and specu- lation. Day to day experience shows that share prices will make quantum leaps in response to profit reports, interim or final, and to newly published estimates from established brokers and analysts of what future profits will be. If Sainsbury's publishes interim figures for the first half of the year suggesting that the whole year's profits would be significantly higher, provided that the 18–23 band for the price/earnings ratio is still deemed in order, the price will rise to ensure that the prospective price/earnings ratio remains within that band. The rise in price may not be sudden unless the news is unexpected because operators in the market may have pushed the price up in anticipation of the news, and even if the news is as good as expected the price may in fact fall as those speculators who pushed up the price cash in their profit and sell. The net result, however, should be that the price ends up still within the market's idea of the current range for the price/earnings ratio, historical or prospective.

Profit announcements and forecasts have a keen following among investors and it is no exaggeration to state that the announcement of the year's results usually affects the market more than the publication of the full report unless something very significant appears there that was not known to the market before. Profits, however calculated and whatever their cash content, are the meat and drink of investors!

As a direct consequence, any news that might impact on future profits tends to affect the price. The announcement of a major new order, the building of a new factory, the appointment of a dynamic new company chairman or the decision to sell some assets, will all affect investor behaviour. Curiously, even when the profits from such changes may not be seen for several years and indeed the short-term effect may be to reduce earnings, perhaps by higher depreciation charges or greater research and development or advertising costs, the market tends to react favourably so long as the announcement is seen as on balance good for the company. There is no real contradiction here, and this phenomenon does not negate what has been said about the market's near obsession with short-term results. Enough investors are willing to take a longer view that the price moves up rather than down. Really this is to say little more than that if 'prospects' for the company are seen to be improving, that is perceived as good news and feeds into the price accordingly. Investors are human individuals capable of responding to mixed stimuli in diverse ways and, although many of them are dazzled by short-term profitability, the market has also many long-term players ready to take a flexible and more detached view.

A takeover bid or the threat of one usually boosts a share to hitherto undreamed of heights and is a windfall at least to the investor who has no concept of loyalty to a company's management. Such language may not always describe large institutional investors with whom the company's managers may have cultivated a mutually advantageous relationship over the years. The theory is that takeovers are the market's ultimate weapon for punishing inefficiency of management and ensuring the most appropriate distribution of that scarce resource, capital. Offer prices are always well in excess of the prevailing market rate because the assets of the company to be acquired will be put under new management and made to work more effectively as part of a bigger organization.

As a description of the spate of takeovers seen in the UK in recent years and the leveraged buyout craze in the USA, such a description is less than satisfactory if for no other reason than that the companies picked upon have not, on the whole, been conspicuously badly managed by any criterion, and there has been nothing disinterested about the motives of the raiders who have been concerned solely to make a profit or to enlarge their empires. Much use is made of the word 'synergy' in justification of takeover ventures and the dominant interest of the less obviously greedy acquirers has been to build up their own companies through the purchase of assets in related businesses, often in new geographical areas, to achieve a result which would have been much harder if they had had to start from scratch themselves. By some theory unknown to science, it tends to be assumed that if you push together two quite different organizations into a single entity, the sum is going to be bigger and better than the parts.

The just allocation of capital has little to do with the thinking of any of the participants and cost of funds is probably a marginal consideration beside the need to develop the business as a whole in order to compete. A manufacturing company quoted on an exchange always runs the risk of being taken over, no matter how well it is doing, but the larger and more successful it is, the more it will cost to buy and the safer it will be. Size is of particular concern, but even a well-managed and profitable manufacturer is in danger of being swallowed up by a predator who seeks simply to add another arrow to its quiver by incorporating the target company's business into its own. Taking over other companies is also an extremely effective deterrent to anyone contemplating taking you over!

As several companies have discovered recently, synergies look fine on paper but do not always materialize. The price paid or offered for the target company is higher than the market price because, for one thing, one is buying control, and for another, it is necessary to win over a large number of shareholders who had no intention of selling at the normal price or anything like it. It is quite possible for a takeover attempt to trigger an auction as rival companies, reluctant to see a plum prospect go to a competitor, bid against each other. All this is highly profitable for existing shareholders and rather miserable for the company's management who are reduced to spending large sums of their shareholders' money to prevent any takeover from happening.

The actual price at which the takeover is consummated will be as low as the acquirer can get away with and as high as the existing management and the individual shareholders are able to extract. While the battle is going on, the price will rise to a figure approximating to the best offer received, a little higher if rival bids are expected, a little lower if there is some expectation that the takeover may not actually happen, perhaps because of intervention by anti-monopoly authorities. The price/earnings mechanism will be superseded since not even its most enthusiastic supporter will use it to value shareholdings which are about to be turned into cash at a known rate.

Of course, the company resisting acquisition may well appeal to this mechanism to persuade shareholders to hang on. The classical defence to a takeover is to publish a statement to the effect that the company is on the verge of a profits breakthrough and that accordingly even at the price being offered, possibly way above historical trading levels, the shareholders are being asked to give up their shares for a scandalous pittance. Investors, to their credit, normally spot the despair in this type of argument and sell the company to the predator, it being pretty tough for a takeover target to escape if a serious raider is really determined to succeed in the conquest.

If takeovers are a windfall, announcements of losses or liquidations are unhappy events in the extreme. An unexpected loss inevitably gives rise to a drop in share price, but as a loss-making concern has, by definition, no price/earnings ratio the question arises as to what alternative mechanism the market uses. On one level the answer is that the price will fall to the level at which supply and demand are equal, but as that is always true we are not much the wiser.

In actuality, much will depend upon the market's opinion as to the likely outcome: whether the company will be continuously loss making or whether profitability will be restored in the near future. The price is certainly unlikely to fall below the net real asset value backing the shares. Very low prices make takeovers cheaper and loss-making companies are easy targets. The minimum price for a takeover is likely to be around the value at market rates of the assets, since at any lower price an asset stripper could buy the company, liquidate and make a profit. Net asset values effectively underpin share prices for relatively unsuccessful companies.

A good illustration of the psychology of the parties in a takeover comes from an advertisement put out by the newspaper group Fleet Holdings in which they urged their shareholders not to sell out to United Newspapers who were offering to purchase Fleet Holdings' shares with their own. (See Exhibit 29).

What is underpinning United Newspapers' share price?

It can't be earnings per share performance.

In the June 1985 Management Today survey of company earnings per share growth, United ranked only 221st out of 250 (Fleet ranked 8th).

It can't be newspaper circulation.

The August 1985 MMC report showed that the circulation of United's newspapers has plummetted since 1980.

Morning papers down 13%
Evening papers down 13.5%
Paid-for weeklies down 14%.

It can't be asset backing.

Net tangible assets per share have fallen to 25% of their 1982 level.

When you pin down United's share price, where is the substance?

FLEET HOLDINGS P.L.C.

Fleet puts shareholders first.

Exhibit 29

The gist of the argument is that United Newspapers' shares are not really worth the value the stock market places upon them. As any one accepting the offer could immediately sell the shares of United Newspapers for cash, this is not an easy argument to sustain. The advertisement begins by appealing to the earnings per share or price/earnings valuation method to argue that United Newspapers' shares are overvalued. It follows this up with some damning statistics about turnover trends and, lastly, homes in on United Newspapers' falling asset values per share.

Fleet Holdings, which ultimately lost its independence to United Newspapers, is tilting at windmills. No doubt its specific observations may carry some weight, but the advertisement fails to acknowledge that the stock market is using other criteria and evidently believes that United Newspapers is one of the winners in the newspapers game. The share price was high not because it was a balloon waiting to be pricked, but because the City had a healthy respect for the management. There is no reason whatever why a newspaper group should hold balance sheet assets of any size since newspaper printing is a cash business, with low inventories and sometimes old (and hence heavily depreciated) plant and equipment.

How can one use this brief analysis of the stock market to invest in it successfully? Or is all this purely academic? In fact, there are some important lessons here which may not make the reader a fortune but which could prevent some costly mistakes. Equity shares are a risky investment, the principal reason for buying them being expected but by no means certain capital appreciation. Nothing really underpins the price of shares at market rates, and certainly not today's market rates in London, New York and Tokyo, except the willingness of investors to hold them, and the principal component of this value is normally profitability. However, the Random Walk Theory has to be taken seriously if only to the extent that we live in an uncertain world and enormous and unexpected fluctuations do occur regularly in the price of the shares of even the strongest companies. Serious loss of confidence in a share or in a market sector on the stock market will depress the price regardless of underlying asset values, earnings or any other financial ratios. Such losses of confidence are unpredictable and by no means rare.

Some sectors command generally higher price/earnings ratios than others as some types of companies have great growth potential, while others are seen as more solid and stable investments. Perception changes over time and the high-flying high tech stock of yesterday can easily turn into today's albatrosses. Video games and home computers were once going to take the world by storm and the shares of their manufacturers commanded high premiums. A year or two later many of these companies have disappeared as customers have turned to other entertainments. This type of trend can only be predicted by close observation of society, politics and demographic movements.

Risk can be avoided on the stock market by diversification, and business theory teaches that such diversification is assumed in the prices of shares. If you buy shares in only one company, the risk of a disaster is large; buy shares in a hundred companies and inevitably there will be some disasters but these will be matched by some glittering successes and the performance of your portfolio will, in all probability, come close to that of the market as a whole. Small investors can achieve diversification by buying into unit trusts and managed funds rather than purchasing straight equities. Diversification obviously needs to be planned carefully, as do all investment decisions. Just scattering money about may not achieve the desired hedging of the risks, as investments are often tailor designed to appeal to different categories of investor, in different tax situations and even in different countries.

Few people realize that only a tiny handful of investors and investment experts regularly 'beat the market' on their portfolios or recommendations as a whole. To match the market, and to have no other ambition, is not very difficult so long as one has enough capital to invest in a decent spread of leading securities. However, not many investors or investing bodies are content to do that, and the institutional investors employ offices full of analysts and technicians in the hope of squeezing a point or two extra out of the portfolio. Blasphemy it may be to say so, but many of these institutions would do nearly as well with a pin to make random selections!

One way of ensuring that performance does not fall behind the market's is to invest in the shares that make up the indices by which the market's ups and downs are measured. When British Telecom's part paid shares were sold by the UK government at 50p, they opened at 91p and continued rising for days thereafter. The advisers to the government had believed that 130p, the total fully paid price, was as much as the market would bear and the government had taken the added precaution of underwriting these shares at the offer price. Their advisers were completely wrong about the enormous public enthusiasm the issue generated, something admittedly difficult to predict as it was engendered as much by the advertising and publicity as by the quality of the underlying investment.

But one factor that buoyed the price for some time was demand from institutions. They were denied the enormous holdings they applied for because of a political decision to favour the small individual investor in the allocation, and the immediate inclusion of the shares in the Financial Times 30 Share Index (in replacement of Johnson Matthey) made the institutions desperate to acquire a reasonable number. That particular index may not be an especially good indicator of market behaviour, but it is widely followed and reported, and it is used as a benchmark in reviewing the performance of investment managers. They could not afford for British Telecom to be in the index and for their institutions not to hold enough shares. The risk was too great, and with one eye on their jobs and bonuses they were prepared to buy at almost any price.

Short-term equity investment is also highly speculative. The quoted share price is a middle price between dealers' buying and selling rates and to cover the expenses and the margin on small investments requires an appreciation in price of 6–7 per cent, which is substantial for an investor thinking in terms of weeks rather than months or years.

New issues, large and small, appeal directly to the speculative investor. Until a security is established on a trading floor, any valuation is by definition conjectural. To avoid the embarrassment of pitching the price too high and leaving the shares with the underwriters, issuers usually go for a 'competitive' pricing that ensures the market absorbs the whole issue. Investors know this, and it is not unusual for a new issue from a virtually unknown company to be oversubscribed to a ridiculous extent so long as analysts and commentators perceive that it will open in the market as a premium. Wold plc, for example, a new company launched on the London Unlisted Securities Market in mid-1985 with an offer price of 95p, attracted offers of over £150m for the £5m of shares on offer. Being the first attempt at a share issue in London by Citibank, who could not afford a public failure, the issue looked a winner and opened at 105p. When the results of Wold plc started to come in some months later the price dropped dramatically and at the time of writing stands at 45p. This story does not reflect well on the oft-vaunted sophistication of the market makers.

The plain truth is that to beat the market one needs to invest in winning companies and even then it may take luck and patience. A profitable company trading on a price/earnings ratio of, say, 12 will have shares appreciating in line with growth in profits, so long as the price/earnings ratio remains at 12. If its profits are growing at 10 per cent per annum the yield on the investment will be 10 per cent capital growth plus the dividend. Any serious improvement in this performance will render the shares a handsome investment.

Particularly attractive candidates are those companies which, while being essentially sound and well structured, are operating on fine margins and doing only slightly better than breaking even. A modest increase in turnover or margin may well cause an enormous percentage leap in the reported profit and the price/earnings mechanism may well cause a dramatic increase in share price. A company earning £5m p.a. on turnover of £1bn might easily quadruple its profits to £20m on sales little changed.

The danger is that this type of company may easily be pushed the other way into losses and it is as well to avoid highly leveraged companies which are prone to interest rate hikes or which are risky for other reasons. It is unfortunately true that companies meeting all these requirements tend to be sleepy and conservative and may never manage to achieve the breakthrough. However, they do tend to offer a good dividend yield and are prize targets for takeovers as more dynamic companies perceive them as reservoirs of underutilized assets.

There are no easy ways to make a fortune. Trying to outguess the market means pitting your own wits and resources against those of professionals who are much closer to the action and normally better informed. Anyone who imagines he can spot likely takeover candidates and has sufficient staying power should at least know that he may wait for years, while anyone pursuing rapid growth opportunities should realize that these situations are the most risky. In a rising economy and a bull market nearly everyone does well; in a depression and a bear market most get burned.

There is no better tool for investment than a little common sense. In a falling market new investment is generally a mistake unless you are very clever and if a crash is looming it is certainly much better to be out of the market altogether. There were those who made fortunes out of the 1929 Wall Street Crash. They were the investors who saw it coming, sold everything and moved into gold!

11

Industry dynamics—Plotting the future

I never think of the future; it comes soon enough.
Albert Einstein

You can never plan the future by the past.
Edmund Burke

By the time an Annual Report alights on an analyst's desk it will be at least 3 months, possibly as much as 9 or 10 months, out of date. It is old news. The period it describes has gone, vanished, elapsed, and at the company's headquarters the new reporting year is well under way and the executives are drawing up plans and budgets for the next and subsequent years. Analysts are left to pore over dead contracts while real men of business get on with the serious matter of risking and earning money. Other people's money.

Managers do not like to give away much about their ambitions because that information is regarded, not entirely without justification, as confidential. 'Too full a disclosure might be prejudicial to the company's trading interests,' they argue. 'However, the past belongs, more or less, to everyman and we may safely divulge scads of material about past events that hold now virtually no interest at all to us, the company's managers and employees.'

The company, especially if it is a complex and sophisticated one, may supply its managers up-to-the-minute data
on every aspect of the business's performance and condition. Outsiders who merely invest their money in the company have to live with the after-the-event scraps.

Exaggeration or distortion? Hardly. Within a legal
framework, the directors of a company have a virtually
unfettered control over that company's actions and, except
on the matters of raising new equity or selling the company, they do not consult shareholders on even the most
major decisions. Short of calling a meeting to expel a
director from office, an extremely rare occurrence, the
shareholders have no effective control over the activities of
their directors, and usually they seek none. An Annual
Report is, as we have seen, a letter from the directors to the
shareholders giving an account, by and large rosy tinted, of
their activities during the period under review. The style
and backward-looking aspect of the Annual Report are born
of the relationship that exists between directors and shareholders, a relationship not unlike that of the lord and his
trusty factor who renders him an annual account on settlement day, the lord taking no active participation in the
running of his estate in between times.

Shareholders rarely voice their dissatisfaction at being so
kept at arm's length and the divorce between ownership
and effective control is an almost unchallenged feature of
modern big business. It is not a feature of small businesses,
since no proprietor who has built up an enterprise from
scratch will willingly surrender control to a professional
manager without exercising scrupulous supervision of his
activities. But once a company reaches a certain size and
complexity, that degree of personal control ceases to be
practicable and, with the introduction of new wealth and
external shareholders to fund the growing assets, power
and control finds its way into the hands of an oligarchy of
directors and executives.

Investors have only a passive role. That they do not contribute to the development of their company or to its planning may be understandable if the shareholders are a numerous body with perhaps limited business knowledge among them. What is extraordinary is that, being denied control and access to the plans of their company, they are required to make what they can of the historical information and on occasion propaganda contained in an Annual Report and to try to guess on the basis of past performance what their appointees will do in the future. The directors and the managers know, with some precision, what the company will do over the next few months and have a fair idea of likely developments over the coming 5 years. Shareholders can only try to be mindreaders and use what statistical and accounting knowledge they have to extrapolate the trends.

Annual Reports do not make this easy. An Annual Report is management's 'apologia' for what it has done in the past. It is specifically designed to present developments in the best possible light and to justify the management's decisions and stewardship. There is a strong tendency to present a picture of steady, unfaltering progress, and if earnings/profits trends do not contribute to that aim, then the dividend stream may have been managed to present the illusion of ever more magnificent achievements in enhancing the shareholders' wealth.

Not to overstate the case, we can concede that the prevailing order does fulfil many needs, among them the need of the shareholders not to be burdened with management responsibility and the need of the company's directors and managers to enjoy room to manoeuvre and freedom from arbitrary and ignorant intervention. What from the analyst's and investor's point of view is objectionable, is the near total control company managements have assumed over the affairs of the largest companies and their avoidance of true accountability by their restrictions on the data they make available about their activities. Investors want to know about the future. That is why they employ credit and investment analysts. If management were more forthcoming, much investment analysis would become instantly redundant since those closest to a business are likely to be those best informed on where the company is headed. Analysts try to decipher the trends from the past events, and effectively work blindfold. The most effective analysts tend to be those who succeed in lifting the blindfold a little, by drawing on helpful contacts employed by their target companies.

Major companies are aware of their privileged position and as a rule do not abuse it to the detriment of shareholders. There is no huge conspiracy to keep the public in ignorance. Regular management briefings fill the diaries of professional analysts, especially in the USA where freedom of information is a national preoccupation. Unfortunately, management always has an interest to defend and bad news or gloomy prospects will generally be kept from interested parties temporarily if not permanently, where concealment is an option. Rules of confidentiality often preclude parties with important yet sensitive information of this sort from revealing the truth.

Auditors are, to their chagrin, caught in the dilemma. Current proposals from the UK government that auditors should be required to inform the Bank of England of irregularities coming to light in the course of bank audits, have evoked horror-struck responses from banks and accountants alike. Auditors work, in theory, for the shareholders but in practice they negotiate with the directors and managers and consider that latter relationship a professional and privileged one. That relationship would be jeopardized if auditors were required to 'do the dirty' and tell the Bank of England, and auditors do not want that responsibility.

Readers may well be wondering where the public interest is in all this. If a bank is in trouble, it serves nobody except the management, and possibly the auditors, for the full picture to be concealed. To prevent débâcles, the Bank of England has to be informed, and were it not for the panic that would probably ensue from indiscriminate disclosure, there is a strong argument that shareholders and depositors should know too. It cannot be a good thing for the managers and auditors of a bank to haggle over the presentation of its financial statements while both sides are precluded from informing all outsiders when grievous problems come to light, the one by pride and vested interest, the other by strict rules of professional etiquette. That is fiddling while Rome burns. In the USA, material detrimental to banks is regularly published by regulatory bodies and public confidence is maintained by the power and reliability of the Federal Deposit Insurance Corporation. Regrettably, few other countries have similar protection for depositors, so the clouds of unknowing generally go undispelled. The paradox is that only the disinterested will voluntarily tell the truth about a deeply troubled organization, while only insiders know the truth!

So, in forecasting what the future holds, the analyst is deprived of much of that which would be most informative, unless he has access to internal company sources. He has usually no access to the strategic plans, to the budgets or cash flow projections, and will normally have great difficulty in discerning how to break up a conglomerate organization analytically, either into its separate legal entities or into its industrial or economic subdivisions. He is presented with a historical, consolidated record, a commentary heavily biased in the management's favour, notes replete with copious detail of selected aspects of the bookkeeping, and a dearth of worthwhile management accounting information. The whole will suffer somewhat from the traditional reliance on the double entry system. With this unpromising material he earns his living making estimates of next year's earnings!

The banker's or credit analyst's task is in some ways easier, in others harder. It is easier in that a banker needs only to be sure that he will recover his loan plus interest. So long as he is paid, he has no concern for overall performance or profitability and any long-term strategic analysis will be directed solely towards demonstrating long-term solvency. Many multinational companies are much stronger financially than most banks and any time a bank credit analyst spends analysing Exxon or General Electric and writing reports on their creditworthiness is a resource wasted as the likelihood of companies of that size and strength collapsing within the next 5 years with loss to lenders is virtually nil. An investment analyst, however, has to assess the earnings potential of even the mightiest corporation because its future earnings determine the price to be paid for its shares.

The lender's crucial handicap is the absence of data that will help to define the point at which a corporation might become insolvent and fail to pay its debts. Cash flow projections can be run from historical, financial reporting data but they rarely turn out to be very accurate. They have to be derived from projecting a funds flow statement, and the availability of funds for refinancing is always an indeterminate factor. 'Provided the borrower earns a reasonable profit', the unspoken logic goes, 'external funds for debt repayment are unlikely to dry up.'

A banker earns only an interest margin in lending; he does not stand to make an equity profit like the shareholders. He should not be shouldering the bulk of the risk in an enterprise. Although he is protected by the laws of distribution in bankruptcy, he is poorly served by published information that was designed to impress the shareholders and gives little assistance in the determination of expected cash flows. He is entitled to know whether his loan will be repaid from the operations of a business, from asset dis-

posals or from refinancing and he can only know that if he
has cash flow projections that are tolerably accurate and reflect management's own ambitions. In dealing with a small,
weak company, a banker has that control; in dealing with a
major multinational competition has transferred all the
power to the company's financial managers who, beset on
all sides by bankers clamouring to lend them money,
understandably decide that there is little point in souping
up information, at a cost, to make lenders sleep easier at
night. When the obtaining of finance is critical to the
viability of a project, e.g. in a leveraged buyout proposal,
detailed cash flow forecasts are readily forthcoming. Once a
banker is armed with these, little traditional credit analysis
needs to be done. All he needs is an informed judgement—
little enough one might suppose.

Ours is an imperfect world and no one seriously expects
any rapid improvement in the type and quality of company
information available. We have to live with what we have,
and lending and investment decisions continue to be taken
daily on the basis of reliance on the familiar material.
Practical businessmen, not knowing what others will do,
have to hypothesize and commit funds on the basis of their
personal deliberations, and the only practical basis on
which to take sensible investment decisions is to project
the future from the historical statements contained in
Annual Reports. While there exist techniques of some
sophistication for doing precisely that, naturally the future
is always to a degree unpredictable and the past can be
relied upon only to be an uncertain guide. It does not
follow that a brilliant and talented youth will grow up to be
a man of wisdom and discretion, or that the youthful
scoundrel will end his days in penury. Sometimes their
fates are reversed!

If we are looking into the future because we want to
understand risk better, the first step may be to define more

closely in what circumstances certain eventualities are likely to materialize. For example, imagine that we wish to estimate the profit to be earned next year by a company. One approach is to break the problem down thus: profit is difficult to foretell because profit is itself a function of other variables, in particular the absolute levels of revenue and expenses. If, though, we can accept as a hypothesis that there is some arithmetical relationship between profit and sales and we have at our disposal some way of predicting sales, not only can we suggest likely profit figures for a range of possible sales levels, we can also decide which the most likely profit figure will be. This is a useful approach because it both generates a forecast and gives some idea of the sensitivity of that forecast to changes in the key variables, in this case sales.

Unfortunately, there is not in most companies a direct and easily measured relationship between sales and profits. With an exact unitary correlation, one might expect a 20 per cent increase in the one to lead inexorably to a 20 per cent increase in the other. In fact, the percentage increase in profit will tend to be greater because of the phenomenon of leverage and the incidence of fixed and variable costs. These concepts, belonging more to management accounting than to financial reporting, are crucial to any understanding of the dynamics of business and even though they are often difficult, not to say impossible to measure, their effect is ubiquitous and all pervasive.

In essence, there is nothing remotely complicated about the differing nature of fixed and variable costs as they affect an income statement. Fixed costs may be defined as those that do not change but accrue at an unaltered rate in successive periods. Variable costs are costs that are incurred in direct proportion to the monetary value of sales. We assume, for the moment, that all costs in a business are either fixed or variable.

Take now a sample income statement:

	£
Sales	100
Variable costs	(75)
Fixed costs	(15)
Operating profit	10

If sales rise in the next year by 10 per cent to £110, the next year's income statement will read as follows:

	£
Sales	110
Variable costs	(82.5)
Fixed costs	(15)
Operating profit	12.5

A 10 per cent rise in sales, and variable costs, has caused a 25 per cent rise in operating income. One way to express the relationship between sales and operating income is to say that at the end of the first year the company has an 'operating leverage' of 2.5, meaning that for every 1 per cent increase or decrease in sales, there would be a 2.5 per cent increase, or decrease in operating income. The calculation of leverage may be derived from one of two mathematically related formulae:

$$\frac{\text{Sales} - \text{variable costs}}{\text{Sales} - \text{variable costs} - \text{fixed costs}} \rightarrow \frac{100 - 75}{100 - 75 - 15} = 2.5$$

or

$$\frac{\% \text{ change in operating income}}{\% \text{ change in sales}} \rightarrow \frac{25}{10} = 2.5$$

It is important to grasp exactly what is going on here. The operating leverage formulae measure in a simple way the the degree of risk at the end of the first year. By the end of the second year the leverage factor has decreased, as readers may calculate for themselves, to 2.2 as the effect of the fixed costs is proportionately smaller. More important than the trend is the way the calculation allows us to predict operating profit for any projected level of sales. Provided the fixed costs remain fixed and there is no change in the relationship between variable costs and sales, the operating profit is absolutely determined by the sales figure.

As a practical tool of analysis, this method has two, not to be underestimated, drawbacks. The first is that no costs in business are absolutely fixed or completely variable as we have defined them. It is usually said that the costs of raw materials and manufacturing labour are variable and that factory overheads and administration are fixed. That is only half true. Prices of raw materials may vary and the 'margin' earned by the company on its product may contract or expand accordingly. The cost of labour may not respond precisely to changes in the monetary value of sales because workers cannot always be hired and fired to match volumes of production, and there is the age old propensity of workers frequently to demand greater shares of the takings in the form of higher wages. Supposedly fixed costs will inevitably fluctuate over successive periods for innumerable reasons. In reality, no costs are fixed or variable as defined; there is instead a spectrum, some costs being more or less fixed, others being more or less variable.

The other problem is that companies never reveal anything about their cost structure that enables a realistic division between fixed and variable costs to be made. These terms do not appear in Annual Reports where phrases like 'costs of sales' and 'administrative expenses' take their place, the classification being by category rather than by responsiveness to changing sales levels.

One possible way out is to use the second of the two formulae given for leverage and to calculate it from the change in sales and operating profit over two successive years. This would be done by reference to the later year as the basis of the calculation, and in our example the percentage change in sales would be $10/110 \times 100\% = 90.9\%$ and that in operating income $2.5/12.5 \times 100\% = 20\%$ giving again a leverage of 2.2. The danger is that, while this is mathematically correct and the resultant leverage factor can be used to predict likely operating profit for the posited sales figure in the subsequent year, the assumption is again that the company's costs over the two known years can be divided completely between fixed and variable costs as defined in the strictest terms. Since this is almost always unrealistic for a host of reasons—inflation, changing patterns of cost, varying product mix, etc.—the calculation has to be treated with grave suspicion and is in practice rarely worth much. One should note that the technique yields better results as a tool of management accounting, particularly when applied to the numbers for a single product or factory, and with extraneous factors identified and excluded. With the accounts of a multinational company, where many businesses with many different margin products are jumbled together, greater inaccuracy is unavoidable.

We may not be able to measure operating leverage very accurately for a multinational but that does not mean that the effects are not there to be seen. In boom times operating profits clearly rise proportionately much faster than sales, and in years of recession, when sales are falling, once profitable companies can start shedding red ink on quite modest sales reductions.

Two considerations, the proportion of fixed costs to total costs and the closeness to breakeven point, have a major impact on the leverage calculation and on the degree of risk in a company's future earnings stream. A high fixed cost operation is very susceptible to changes in sales level. Take another example:

	£
Sales	100
Variable costs	(5)
Fixed costs	(85)
Operating profit	10

Leverage is 95/10 or 9.5. The corollary of high fixed costs is that the margin after variable costs is closer to unity, and provided the business is profitable at operating level, marginal changes in sales filter almost straight down to the operating profit. If sales were to double in this example next year, operating profit would rise by 950 per cent to 105 as the sales revenue, less the modest variable costs, accrued directly to profit.

Closeness to operating breakeven point renders operating leverage high, as even a small increase or decrease in sales may cause several hundred percent change in operating income, and a company actually at operating breakeven has an infinite operating leverage since any change in sales will cause a profit or loss where none was before and any number divided by zero is infinity. That is only of academic concern, but the fact remains that if a company is making only a small profit or loss, its results are extremely sensitive to changes in sales.

It follows that certain types of company display characteristic earnings behaviour in response to variations in sales. Commodity trading companies, with minimal fixed costs, can continue to earn a profit even in a year when trading volume is severely reduced. One will not necessarily be able to predict how much profit with any certainty unless one has information about margins, but the basic truth holds. Conversely, shipbuilding and heavy equipment manufacturers, especially in countries where labour is predominantly a fixed cost because of employment traditions and legislation, invariably suffer crippling losses if turnover falls to any degree. On a leverage of 10, a 20 per cent drop in sales means a 200 per cent drop in operating profit, that is, operating profit will turn into a corresponding operating loss. Much of British industry is high fixed cost and not always too far from breakeven, and the consequences in a recessionary period are exactly what leverage theory would predict.

We have so far excluded from the discussion two other costs, interest and taxes, that few businesses manage to escape. These too can be factored into leverage calculations. The unreality of the assumption is obvious, but interest is conventionally regarded as a fixed cost and taxes may be regarded as variable, not in respect of sales but by reference to operating earnings after interest. Pursuing our first example another stage:

Operating profit	10
Interest	(5)
Profit before tax	5
Tax @ 40%	(2)
Net profit	3

one can calculate 'financial leverage' from the formulae:

$$\frac{\text{Operating profit}}{\text{Operating profit} - \text{interest}} \rightarrow \frac{10}{10 - 5} = 2$$

or

$$\frac{\text{\% change in net profit}}{\text{\% change in operating profit}}$$

As before, these two formulae are mathematically identical so long as the underlying assumptions, that interest is truly fixed and that the tax rate is constant over successive periods, remain valid. As neither is really true except as a broad generality, the calculation will be distorted.

Taking for a moment the assumptions as given, we can predict that an increase in operating profit of 10 per cent would produce the following result:

	£
	£
Operating profit	11
Interest	(5)
Profit before tax	6
Tax @ 40%	(2.4)
Net profit	3.6

Net profit has jumped by 20 per cent as might have been predicted by the first formula. Operating profit of 10 divided by operating profit minus interest of 5 gives financial leverage of 2 and a 10 per cent operating profit increases net profit by 20 per cent.

Companies do publish interest and tax figures, so there is little call in practice for the second formula. If used, again great care is necessary to be sure of what is actually being measured because variations in interest charge or tax rate will be distorting. The crude use of the two formulae on real companies will always give different answers, not because the company has two different financial leverages, but merely because the two formulae are only identical if the underlying assumptions are true. Since they never are, two different figures, both unreliable, can be expected.

The lesson of financial leverage is the old one that companies with low interest coverage are risky companies in terms of earnings. Tax rates are actually irrelevant to the calculation so long as they do not fluctuate. But an interest charge that consumes the bulk of operating profit, and renders net profit small in relation to operating profit, causes small changes in operating profit to have an extreme effect on the bottom line. Where there is no interest and financial leverage is unity, operating profit and net profit will move up and down in line. High interest charges push financial leverage quickly to high levels, levels in fact approaching infinity as breakeven is neared, and render net profit volatile and speculative. Small increases in operating income may cause many-fold increases in net income, while small decreases may cause profits to turn into losses.

Everyone knows that companies with high debt profiles are risky and the theory of financial leverage clarifies one of the reasons. Interest is not a fixed cost in our definitional sense, as rates fluctuate and amounts borrowed will always vary over time, but interest does have to be paid when due and failure to meet the obligation usually entails the start of bankruptcy or reorganization proceedings. The income statement is actually a poor measure of a company's debt servicing capacity and it should be stressed that the financial leverage test only helps us to evaluate the risk of interest expense pushing the company into losses. It does not say anything about the risk that debt cannot be serviced. It is not income that services debt, but cash in the bank, and as for principal repayments, the income statement is silent. Amounts borrowed are not considered income in the accounting sense, and when the principal is returned to the lender, the income statement is unaffected, both debit and credit going directly to the balance sheet. Crude measures of debt servicing capacity such as 'cash flow coverage', net income plus depreciation divided by interest expense, or 'debt service ratio', the same numerator divided by expected annual principal repayments, are misconceived and in practice are both misleading and dangerous.

To conclude our discussion of operating and financial leverage, we shall look at the concept of 'total leverage', defined as the percentage change in net income to be expected from a 1 per cent change in sales. Mathematically, total leverage is the product of operating leverage and financial leverage as may be seen from the fully worked example we have used:

	£	£
Sales	100	110
Variable costs	(75)	(82.5)
Fixed costs	(15)	(15)
Operating profit	10	12.5
Interest	(5)	(5)
Profit before tax	5	7.5
Tax @ 40%	(2)	(3)
Net profit	3	4.5

A 10 per cent increase in sales will cause next year's income statement to resemble that on the right of the historical statement and we see that net profit has jumped by 50 per cent, indicating total leverage of 50%/10% = 5. The same result could have been calculated by multiplying operating leverage of 2.5 by financial leverage of 2.

Of what value is this information? It wiil be obvious that leverage is a tool primarily of interest to equity investors, who are eager to predict earnings as a step towards estimating likely future share prices. It is a tool that helps the analyst to understand the relationship between net profit and sales. By simplifying the company's cost structure, he can obtain some idea of the dynamics of the income statement and evaluate the risk of major change in net profit. Nothing is said about what earnings will be, only about the potential effect on earnings of sales increases and decreases.

Leverage is a two-edged sword and cuts both ways. In our example, a 10 per cent fall in sales will cause a 50 per cent reduction in net income and larger drops in sales will eliminate profits and start to produce losses. Leverage does not give any indication which way developments will move.

A host of factors have been omitted from the calculation which might in reality spoil the result. Sales might rise by 10 per cent next year and earnings fall by 100 per cent. If this happens, it may be because the relationship between variable costs and sales altered from the previous year, or there was some variation in the fixed costs of operation or the interest charge, or because the tax rate changed, or because there were other items of income or expenditure not taken into consideration, or any combination of these. The point, however, is not that leverage is an inaccurate guide in practice, but that it does give an important insight into potential future profitability. Companies that have high fixed costs, associated either with operations or with financing, are risky companies in that their earnings are likely to be volatile, especially if sales are also volatile. Dramatic improvements in earnings can occur suddenly, particularly if base earnings are low and the company is close to its breakeven point, but alternatively the earnings may just as easily disappear and turn into hefty losses.

The concept of leverage is also of use to a company's managers. Their job is to manage the risk entailed in the business and to ensure that fixed costs do not assume excessive proportions. It is not necessarily wrong to finance a new factory with a bond issue, but such action could easily boost both operating and financial leverage sharply, and total leverage, being the product of the two, will then rise disproportionately.

Finally, the banker can get relatively little comfort from playing with the leverage model. The insights it affords to the investment analyst do not help very much in assessing the risk of getting repaid on time, though bankers are, or should be, aware of the danger in lending to high fixed cost companies with marginal profitability. Bankers are interested in questions of fixed versus floating rate debt and should appreciate that some companies with high fixed operating costs can ill afford the additional risk of floating rate debt and that the raising of fixed rate money, either directly or through a swap, may be an attractive business proposal. What is not a valid test is to plot the calculated levels of operating, financial and total leverage in an attempt to prove that a borrower is becoming more or less risky.

Leverage measurements are tools of prediction, not simple ratios, and the historical trend is virtually certain to be meaningless. A company with total leverage of 5 is not necessarily more risky than another with leverage of 4 and it would not even be fair to say that if leverage had increased in the same company from 4 to 5 over a period that it had become more 'risky' as the term is commonly understood. The change may reflect little more than that the company is operating closer to breakeven point. Leverage is a measure of 'risk' but 'risk' only in the circumscribed sense that a highly leveraged company has an earnings flow proportionately more sensitive to change in the sales figure. That is some way from a banker's idea of a 'risky' borrower.

Before one can use leverage calculations to predict earnings, one must have a projected sales figure. Also, to do any more traditional forecasting the volume of sales must be established. The sales figure is crucial to an understanding of the asset conversion cycle and the amount of money tied up in the cycle. There can be no predicting an income statement without an idea of expected sales, consequently no predicting a balance sheet either since upon sales depend profits and upon profits the amount of liquidity and equity on the balance sheet.

In one sense, an Annual Report gives next to no indication what sales will be next year, in another it gives a pretty fair idea. If we know that over the past 5 years sales have been £1.0m, £1.2m, £1.4m, £1.6m and £1.8m, it does not take much imagination to predict sales of £2.0m for this year. The progression is so obvious that one can see, at a glance, where the company is going. Mathematically, we might say that there is a strong linear correlation between the years and the sales figures and we can illustrate the correlation by means of a graph (Figure 1). The points all fall along a straight line, indicating a perfect correlation, and we can express the line algebraically as $y = 0.1\,x + 1.0$ where y is the sales figure and x is the year. Thus in year 3, the sales figure is $(0.2 \times 3) + 1 = 1.6$. More interestingly, we can obtain values for future years using the same formula, a process analogous to extending the line on the graph and seeing the level of sales indicated for each successive year.

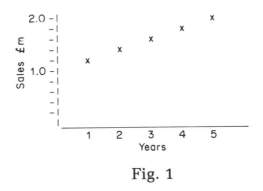

Fig. 1

In real life, the points will not all fall along a straight line though the sales of well-established companies plotted against time may well not be too far away from it, and it will be possible to draw a 'line of best fit' that passes close to the majority of the points. As a general rule, the closer all the points are to the line, the better the correlation and the better the predictive power of the line.

This simple model has presupposed that there does exist a straight line relationship between sales and time, in this case that sales rise £200 000 each year. If this were not so, it might be that a different correlation could be demonstrated, perhaps between sales and gross national product or some other economic variable. Using statistical tables, one could then draw another graph with the economic variables along the x axis (instead of the years) and one would then plot the last 5 years' sales against the value of the variable in each of these years. This would produce another series of points on the graph which might, or might not, fall on a straight line. The beauty of this technique is that official projections are published by governments and economic research bodies and, having established the relationship between the variable and a given company's sales, one can calculate easily the sales levels suggested by the economic forecasts.

Imagine that sales for a company over the last 5 years had been £1.6m, £1.0m, £1.4m, £1.2m and £1.8m. Plotted against time, there is no way to draw a straight line at all close to the points on the graph and we would know immediately that, in effect, time was not the explanation for the changes in the sales figures. If, however, we discovered that gross national product had been £160bn, £100bn, £140bn, £120bn and £180bn over the last 5 years and we drew another graph with gross national product substituted for time, the points again fall in a straight line. If the government is predicting gross national product of £220bn next year, it is reasonable to suppose that sales may not be too far from £2.2m.

This approach to predicting the future is one derived from statistics and the mathematics of regression analysis are fully described in most elementary textbooks on the subject. Our explanation has been rudimentary and we have not even attempted to perform the intricate calculations that can arise. With a basic graph, though, one can see exactly what this technique can do and what its limitations are.

To begin with, it is one thing to draw a line on a graph through a series of points, quite another to suppose that the line has predictive power. In the first instance, of sales plotted against time, although there appears to be a strong relationship between the two, stronger than will ever be demonstrable between two economic variables in real life, it does not necessarily follow that a year later the model will still retain validity. Quite possibly, during the coming year the company will have had an advertising compaign and pushed its sales up more than expected. Alternatively, sales may be much lower for any one of the countless reasons.

The existence of a good correlation, that is a straight line that fits well the points on the graph, does not necessarily establish a causal relationship. In other words, here the passage of time does not cause sales to rise and that fact alone invites suspicion. Where sales, or any other variable, appears closely correlated to time, it is very likely that both are in fact correlated to a third factor, maybe inflation or general economic prosperity, and it is pointless to find correlations that offend against common sense. A close correlation might be found between the percentage of the population owning a refrigerator and that going abroad on holiday. There is obviously no causal relationship and the two variables have in fact nothing to do with one another, except that both reflect the amount and distribution of wealth in society.

It is a weakness of regression analysis that it works best with straight lines. We presumed an increase in sales each year of a discrete amount because that pattern generates a straight line. An increase of, say, 10 per cent each year leads not to a straight line but to a parabola, and other curve patterns are theoretically possible. True straight line relationships rarely exist, just as truly straight lines do not occur in nature. One reason is that our world is unstable and in constant flux, so that it is unlikely that the sales of a company will correlate precisely either to time or to any other variable. It is more probable that some degree of correlation will exist with a number of variables, perhaps exchange rates, interest rates, overseas growth rates or trends in world trade. Mathematically, it is possible to create models to handle such 'multi-linear regressions' but the techniques are extremely advanced and beyond the scope of practical business analysis.

Perhaps the severest limitation on the use of this essentially practical tool is the need to keep drawing graphs, a time-consuming and laborious task. Considerably less wearying is to do the job with numbers rather than pictures and to calculate line of best fit and accuracy factors with a superior pocket calculator or, even better, with a microcomputer. These may be programmed to perform the 'least squares test' on any list of variables and to do in seconds what may take hours by hand. Suitable programs are available commercially, or can be constructed by any statistician with a knowledge of programming. If the calculation can be done in seconds, it is no trouble to try out a whole range of possible variables to find those yielding the best correlations and which may be supposed to have the best predictive power.

Correlation is a statistical technique designed mainly to find relationships that existed in the past. It is a way of exploring history. Extrapolating into the future is of doubtful validity because it is open to question whether past relationships will continue to hold good, and obviously the further into the future one looks, the more uncertain the results become. Beware of the spurious accuracy of the results generated by this technique. The computer may tell you that sales in the year 2000 will be £10 417 324.63 but this is computer language for 'anywhere between £8m and £12m'.

Used sensitively, however, regression analysis can yield quite enlightening results. It is a particularly good way of predicting sales in a company that has a changing product mix. Imagine a company that has shown the following pattern of sales:

Year	0	1	2	3	4
£m					
Steel products	97	84	75	61	50
Engineering	43	27	50	40	18
Electrical components	25	30	34	41	45
Mining	10	12	15	17	20
Total	175	153	174	159	133

What will total sales be in year 5? To do the job properly we could adjust all these numbers for inflation and state them in constant pounds, and then calculate or draw a graph for each product type individually. That would give us a mathematically accurate result but not necessarily one that would turn out to be correct. Probably we can do just as well by observing that steel products are going down by £9–14m per year, electrical components up by £4–7m per year and mining up by £2–3m per year and we will not be wrong projecting values of £38m, £50m and £22m respectively. It is pointless trying to guess engineering turnover because the pattern is so erratic. Having established, perhaps from the company, that engineering is expected to remain static in year 5, we may predict total sales for the year of £38m + 18m + 50m + 22m = 128m, and a continuation of the trend over the last 3 years. Looking at the trend in total sales over the last 5 years, we would have been hard put to make a sensible prediction as the pattern is unclear and the points on a graph would not fall at all close to a straight line.

Regression analysis is nothing more than a method of forecasting that relies on the assumption of past relationships continuing into the future according to an unbroken mathematical pattern. Its great weakness is that the future is ever full of surprises that not even the best statistician could have foreseen, let alone measured with any accuracy. To compound the problem, today's economic milieu is in many ways more uncertain than it has been for decades.

Access to instantaneous channels of communication all over the world has enabled money and commodity markets to operate globally almost uninterrupted, and with the growth in world trade we have become accustomed to a volatility of prices and demand undreamed of by our grand-fathers. Vast sums of speculative money can be moved around the international banking system by people who have only to lift a telephone, and whereas once exchange rates were fixed by governments and moved slowly if at all, the pound can move 3 cents against the dollar within hours to barely a flicker of interest outside the market places.

Competition has never been fiercer and the markets once dominated by entrenched colonial interests are now fought over by established producers and Third World countries alike. Meanwhile, giant corporations struggle to take control of one another, and the rate of technological change quickens. This is not to spread gloom and despondency, but merely to emphasize that our future is a highly uncertain one. In contemporary conditions it makes less sense than ever to chart our way into the future with only a mirror to the past as our compass.

So far in this book we have considered credit and investment analysis in terms of numbers and we have not found much to encourage us. Annual Reports have grave limitations as guides to the past, let alone as prophetic sources about things to come, and remarkably little information is available about specific companies to indicate what may be in store. To be sure, there are press reports, some vague indications from management and, most specifically, reports prepared by professional analysts, but a banker or investor has to have a methodology for making up his own mind in the absence of the company's own budgets and projections.

There is no magic formula. However, one should not underestimate the power of common sense, experience in business and a sprinkling of caution, scepticism and ruthless cynical inquiry. Every time a great corporation suffers a setback, a write-off, a major lost contract, a cut in the dividend, reorganization or bankruptcy, the business community, to judge from the press, declares itself stunned, shocked and horrified. In almost every case, though, danger signs are there to be seen well in advance, at least by those disposed to look for them, and it is not always necessary to have inside information. Businessmen are by constitution optimists, motivated by the refreshing desire to succeed and to make money, but they tend, as a class, to see future profits with greater clarity than they do future losses. In a bull market, there are always plenty of bulls trying to pick the winners. It takes great skill to make money in a bear market and there are many fewer players. Only sophisticates make money out of bad news.

A number of recent examples spring to mind. The collapse of the tin market in London in late 1985 should have been no surprise to anyone. For at least 2 years the International Tin Council, a producers' cartel, had been buying heavily to bolster the price at an unrealistic pitch. One day the moment had to come when finance was exhausted and the price collapsed. It was no secret what was happening, and in financial markets news travels with lightning rapidity. Some of the most conservative and best-managed trading firms had abandoned the tin market months before it closed, wisely refraining to have anything to do with a manipulated market. Some took the sanguine view that it was their livelihood to trade in tin and some never considered that the whole pack of cards really would come tumbling down. These firms are now counting the cost.

No amount of traditional credit analysis of the firms that were caught would have identified them as candidates for the butcher's block. Some were protected by diversification in that that they also traded in other metals, but a specialist tin merchant would, right up until the crash, have produced an upbeat Annual Report giving not the slightest hint of what was to come. One could have calculated every conceivable ratio and done regression analysis and years of projected statements, and they would all have sent out the wrong message. A failure to weigh the risks, and to understand exactly what was going on in economic rather than accounting terms, would have invalidated all traditional analysis.

Tin trading is an obscure world to most of us. Video games are not. When video games first hit the market in 1981 enthusiasm was unbounded. This seemed the perfect product. In the USA, virtually everyone had access to a television and in the gaming parlours and arcades mechanical slot machines, having been around for years, were ripe for obsolescence. A new video game, like Space Invaders or Pac-man, cost little to produce, could be copyrighted and a large proportion of sales revenues filtered straight down to the bottom line. Anyone who could obtain a share of the market seemed set for a golden age of prosperity.

Press comment was, as usual, unrestrained. Nothing could go wrong. This was the new leisure activity to supersede the television, the cinema and the casino! Only a few, unheeded voices pointed out that just as the hula-hoop, the yo-yo and the skateboard had had their day and vanished, video games too would soon pass into oblivion. Perhaps video games are a novelty offering nothing except a repetitive and unedifying distraction from reality, and people will eventually tire of them and go back to more satisfying pastimes. Warner Communications who purchased Atari, the leading video game manufacturer, had to write most of it off within two years.

One is tempted to wonder whether the 'Third World' debt crisis is not another catastrophe in the making, and certainly it is not easy to see its resolution. During the 1930s, default on sovereign debt was far from unknown, a fact ignored by bankers lending money in the late 1970s and early 1980s to many weak nations with histories of unstable government, firm in their belief that 'countries could not go bust'. It was conveniently forgotten that it was much the same countries that had defaulted on their obligations over the previous hundred years that were among the leading borrowers. No one in banking circles likes to suggest that a series of defaults could actually trigger the collapse of the entire international banking system, and as it suits debtors, banks and governments to maintain that posture, the unthinkable possibility generally stays unprovided for.

It would be foolhardy to pretend here to any special insight into the solution of the debtor countries' cash flow difficulties, but the common-sense interpretation, that massive real resources were transferred to the poorer southern nations by the richer northern countries and that there is no way ultimately that the former will ever be physically able or politically willing to repay them, is not easily refuted. Obviously, if interest rates fall and the richer governments assume responsibility for their banking systems to what might be a painful and expensive extent, we may all just escape, but as the prevailing attitude among the banks is that new money lending to the worst affected countries is to be conceded only in response to the most extreme pressure, and there is minimal sign of any governmental willingness to inject more funds, the situation does not look hopeful.

Investors who believe the burgeoning income figures published by North American and other banks with substantial exposure to Latin America, have been warned. These banks have voluntarily released little information about their international lending and investors have had to rely on regulatory agencies to extract even the country by country totals. British banks have generally disclosed such information only because they have securities issued in the USA and are thereby obliged to meet US disclosure requirements. Annual Reports are conspicuously silent on this issue of towering importance to shareholders, apparently because discussion and disclosure of the awful truth would damage the bank by distressing the depositors!

On the international political scene serious question marks hang over the political future of two places with important roles in the world economy, Hong Kong and South Africa. It is very far from certain that Western interests will survive in either place beyond the end of this century, yet investments in neither are considered speculative. Markets and investors seem willing to mark down prices in acknowledgement of an increased risk, yet classically they will maintain their belief in the underlying solidity of their investments until the deluge is seen to be inevitable, when there will be panic. This is not intended as a deprecating observation on the capitalist system, merely as a warning that those who, for example, honestly do not believe that the British style of business in Hong Kong will survive transfer of the colony to the Chinese in 1997, should get out while the going is good and not wait for the market to come to the same conclusion. When everyone is of that opinion, it will be too late.

Clouds on the international horizon, we suspect, do not cause the worry they should because of a mixture of fatalism and optimism prevalent in the investing community. The quality of management is another factor often given less than its fair weight. Every finance student has heard the story of the banker who refused a customer a loan because he did not like the colour of the man's tie. This is not capricious; it is sound business practice! There is no substitute for knowing whom you are dealing with, and this is as true in investing in major international companies as it is in lending to the local widget maker.

Fortune 500 companies are, it is safe to say, normally run by serious people and so are banks, although the demises of Penn Square Bank and Franklin National Bank should serve as salutary reminders to anyone imagining that a bank is necessarily a safe place to put money just because it has the word 'Bank' in its name! However, there are undoubtedly companies run by competent management and others run by bad management and an investor or lender should be separating the sheep from the goats. This is not easy. Directors of companies are routinely listed in an Annual Report, but a list of names does not help much, especially as no reference is made to their abilities or qualifications. British blue chip companies regularly fill out their boards with titled aristocrats who sometimes know next to nothing about business, just for the prestige and the impression it creates. Finding out who actually runs the show can be a vital guide to sound investment.

Much has been written recently about corporate cultures and, with the revolution in financial services currently taking place in the City, the subject could hardly be more apposite. Every established business has its own culture, its traditional pattern of communication, decision taking and action. Companies, as a rule, cope well with the environment they have known for years and which is suited to their particular culture. They have a hard time when the rules are changed.

Banking in London is a prime example. The advent of the American banks into the City in the early 1960s changed the face of banking. Whereas bank managers had previously sat in their offices waiting for customers to come in and beg for money, suddenly there was real competition and success went to those who called vigorously on the customers and sold them services. To the credit of English banks, they survived the transition, but the pain of it has not entirely disappeared to this day, and in becoming more competitive, opening branches abroad and developing new systems they suffered some heavy bruises. The experience in North America of all the English clearing banks was fraught with accidents, not least because they had only limited appreciation of what they were doing.

Past performance is some guide to management capability; any other information is a bonus. Occasionally, one identifies companies totally dominated by, say, engineers while the finance side goes virtually unrepresented at the top level. This type of pattern, indicating an unbalanced management, is a danger sign. It is even more dangerous if the company has a tendency to acquire large operations in unrelated fields, for a style of management suited to one industry may be quite inappropriate in another. Few really large mergers have realized the synergies expected of them, principally because management has failed in the extremely delicate task of moulding disparate and different cultures into a unified whole. The moral is, as always, not to be gullible. Each management vaunts its own competence. All are in fact human with the usual range of human limitations.

Evaluating management cannot be done by numbers. Management skills are intangible and hard to measure. Yet the ability of the management to manage their business lies at the heart of success or failure. A series of poor management decisions can wreck the mightiest corporate colossus, a new management invigorate the veriest weakling. Good management improves confidence and confidence attracts investment. Investment buys time to heal or cauterize festering sores and to reposition. Poor management discourages investment, and money becomes short just when it is most needed.

Much of this book has focused on methods to tease out what is most critical from published material, particularly Annual Reports. We have concentrated on this because traditionally published accounting data have been the starting point for corporate analysis. Our broad conclusion has to be that the nature of the material available, with its bias towards existing management and its focus on past, accrual driven bookkeeping, renders an investigation into the management's ability in the future to generate satisfactory cash flows all but impossible, except in the broadest terms.

The most interesting work being done on corporate analysis has, actually, little to do with accountancy or past or anticipated profits. It is the study, from an economic standpoint, of companies in relation to their industries and it examines a business in terms of its strategy and the relative strengths of the external parties—buyers, sellers and competitors—who interact with a company. The classic statement of this approach is Michael Porter's book, *Competitive Strategy*, in which a methodology and classification system are defined that help an analyst to ask the really pertinent questions about a company, questions that seek to map out the key interrelationships affecting a business, and to discern whether the company is managing them to the optimum. Porter's approach is too wide-ranging to be paraphrased, but a few questions his methodology would suggest might be 'Is the company the lowest cost producer in the industry?', 'How high are the barriers to entry and to exit in this industry?' and 'Can this company produce a product sufficiently differentiated to maintain a price advantage?'

At present, Porter's methodology is just starting to become influential in banking circles. It would be an exaggeration to claim that it has revolutionized thinking among bankers, but interest is growing and the philosophy has obvious benefits for a bank's marketing strategy and for portfolio planning.

Unfortunately, bankers and investors are going to have to construct their own methodologies based on the work already done and adapt its conclusions to their own circumstances. Most students of business are not bankers and have little interest in the banker's perspective. Interest in the academic side of business in the UK lies principally among economists who are interested in analysing and explaining what has happened in the past. In the USA, there is greater interest specifically in individual companies, partly because the study of business is an institution, partly because there is a great desire among people to be educated in investing, managing and, to a lesser extent, lending. Porter's ideas are framed to be of value to managers, managers who need to identify their market position in order to formulate and refine strategy and obtain a winning advantage.

Books about managing and succeeding in business are legion. They describe strategy, tactics and management style, tell the reader how to make product and marketing decisions, and give guidance in making optimum use of resources by motivating staff and handling disputes. Books on accountancy explain the double entry bookkeeping system and the prevailing accounting conventions. Readers learn how to prepare accounts and to some extent what published accounts mean. Books on investing are about the mechanics of the stock markets and the myriad types of investment now available. But books on analysing companies are different. They do not assume a position of strength on the part of the reader. They describe analysis as 'detective work' and there is a heavy emphasis on how to understand Annual Reports with barely a murmur about the inadequacy of those documents. Just as literary criticism is usually perceived as a lower art than original composition, financial analysis is the poor sister of accountancy.

In the fast-changing environment of today, investors and bankers need something better. They cannot expect to go on extrapolating past trends into the future and employing leverage analysis as their fundamental tool for estimating next year's profit. These are crude mechanisms and they have been developed only to help get some value out of published information that is, for the most part, utterly useless to its readers. Too much information is, in fact, available. Much of it is the wrong information and its dullness and detail distract from central issues.

What outsiders need from a company could probably be put on two sides of paper. The figures could be vastly less complicated than those now published, but they should be comprehensive (no off balance sheet items!), include projections and take proper account of inflation. Cash flow should be dealt with clearly and unambiguously. Reliance on historical cost should be minimized, the fair value of assets stated and the emphasis shifted away from presentational requirements to a more flexible management accounting. Provided that it is realistic and objective, the format could be at the management's discretion. In our Utopia, the commentary surrounding the figures would describe not past successes but future sensitivities. The risks would be enumerated and not disguised. More would be said about what the company plans to do, its cost structure, its managers, its strategies and its competitive situation.

Companies belong to their shareholders and others with their money at stake are entitled to a true, fair and up-to-date prospectus. There should be no question of 'detective work'. The present situation has arisen because shareholders have abrogated their power to their appointed directors and managers and failed to force out into the open what they have a right to know. Lenders have virtually given up the struggle to influence what companies publish and only when large businesses are desperate for money do they start to become talkative. It rests with investors and bankers to turn the tide, to start asking the correct questions and to start acting on the answers. The process is too important to be left to regulatory authorities and the accounting profession. Until changes occur, we shall continue to be surprised and shocked every time a big company fails with loss to creditors and shareholders, and individually or collectively we shall continue to pick up the tab.

Paradoxically, there is little reason why companies should object. Share values would rise if no one suspected anything was being hidden. The pressure to spend a fortune on the publication of Annual Reports and to produce constantly rising quarterly earnings would disappear as would the need to go in for window dressing and elaborate off balance sheet financing. Companies failing to disclose what was necessary and desirable would simply lose favour with investors and lenders to their own detriment. Where information was not disclosed for reasons of commercial confidentiality the onus would be on management to say precisely that, and not take shelter behind laws and conventions little understood by outsiders. Auditors might perhaps do more to earn their fee by making some enlightening comments to supplement their little certification that the accounts have been properly prepared.

It is hard to see it happening, but what a brave new world it would be!

12

Conclusion—Arming the risk takers!

Profits are due not to risk, but to superior skill in taking risks.
They are not subtracted from the gains of labour but are earned,
in the same sense in which the wages of skilled labour are
earned.
Frank A. Felice, *The Principles of Economics*

To read most textbooks on corporate finance, accountancy and trade, one would probably conclude that almost every company in the world manufactured one product, in one country, if not in one factory, and that selling that product was little more than a marketing exercise, no problems at all with some splashy advertising and an attractive price sticker. A point we have made earlier bears reiterating: a shortcoming of textbooks on all subjects is that they describe simpler, less convoluted situations than tend to be encountered in the flesh, but we would add that a focus on the simple case may be indistinguishable from a seriously blinkered outlook when it comes to the study and evaluation of multinational companies.

The overwhelming majority of companies that exist worldwide tend to be small and have a very limited product range. Even within a multinational conglomerate, the different activities will tend to be divided among numerous separate legal entities. To that extent, the conventional picture is a true one. However, the organizations that dominate world trade and deal daily in colossal sums of money are organisms complicated almost beyond description. Not only have they numerous different parts, each with separate functions, but the whole in aggregate has a life of its own. Synergy renders it greater than the sum of those parts, at least in theory. St. Paul taught that the Christian church was like a human body in that each member had a specific and distinct role. In the same way, a multinational group may have holding companies, finance operations, leasing, insurance and export oriented subsidiaries, as well as a host of quite varied manufacturing companies. All these have their peculiar characteristics and will respond in non-uniform ways to changing market and economic circumstances.

It is easy to be hypnotized by the concept of 'group'. Investors customarily buy shares in the main holding company whose consolidated accounts form the basis of the Annual Report. Although in some countries separate figures may also be given for the holding company proper, these rarely show anything very useful since the only assets are normally the shares of the next tier of companies in the corporate chain. Investors do not worry about the separate companies in a group; and they are indeed encouraged to view it as a whole.

Older textbooks warn students of banking never to lend against a consolidated balance sheet for the excellent reason that the illusion of these being one company can trick the unwary banker into supposing that all the assets shown are available to settle all the liabilities. In fact, a lender who is owed money by a holding company in liquidation will have no automatic access to the consolidated assets and, at best, will find himself holding the shares of the individual subsidiaries consolidated. Liquidating these companies will bring more trouble and expense, assuming that it proves possible at all. It is a basic tenet of banking that one should lend to operating companies which have readily realizable assets in preference to holding companies which are fundamentally illiquid. Bankers have to know that because the customer will not tell them.

As with so much sound and prudent banking lore, this admirable teaching has been very largely forgotten in recent years as major companies, perceived as first-class credit risks in the market place, have been able to borrow against the strength of the group name. Indeed, lending to operating companies will often be at reduced margins if parent company support in the form of a guarantee or letter of comfort is available to the lender, the idea being that the burden of the obligation becomes a group responsibility.

The perils inherent in this practice are obvious and banks have got away with it, for the most part, only because most multinationals are genuinely strong, are well managed and do generate profit streams which assure them of a ready supply of cash from external sources. A bank lending against a consolidated balance sheet is deluding itself if it supposes that, in extreme circumstances, liquidity will necessarily be moved around within the group to settle 'group liabilities', even supposing that tax and foreign exchange control factors do not absolutely prohibit it. Provided the group as a whole can present a consolidated balance sheet without apparently excessive reliance on debt and an income statement with reasonable profitability, the question of solvency is unlikely to be put to the test.

Each company active in the UK is required by law to deposit a copy of its annual accounts with Companies House, the national registry of companies, even though a great many fail to do so. Abroad, rules tend to vary but are often less strict, and indeed the publication of consolidated figures may absolve management of any responsibility to declare the results of individual subsidiaries. Regardless of the law and the data available, the larger companies of the world do most of their funding at group level either out of the parent company or out of a designated funding subsidiary, the latter sometimes located in a tax shelter area. Subsidiary borrowings tend to be local currency overdrafts, usually with parent company support or transactional trade finance. It is often inefficient for each subsidiary to borrow for itself and a central treasury function serves to reduce overall borrowing and hence interest expense and to maintain financial discipline.

Banks have gone along with and been instrumental in encouraging centralized funding and include 'cash management' products in their package of services. 'Relationship Management' banking is a key concept in many banks' global strategies and a central funding arrangement helps to cement a relationship and make it difficult for rival banks to break in. Unfortunately, the sword cuts both ways and it may not be easy for the bank to leave the scene when it should.

Relationship Management needs sophisticated management accounting systems to back it up, as well as astute marketing officers who know how to use it as a tool without being sucked deeply into unprofitable and perhaps highly dangerous relationships. By no means every major bank that has flirted with the concept has been able to surmount these prerequisites. It sounds catchy and chic, but Relationship Management can easily turn into more expensive bureaucracy and even less control and monitoring of the risks.

This confusion between the separate legal companies and the group hardly affects the shareholder in the parent company; he, after all, is interested in the total wealth under the control of the company in which he shares ownership. Consolidated accounts were invented for financial reporting to shareholders of large groups, to enable the totality of an organization's affairs to be seen in the round, and the compromise is hardly a painful one. The banker's position is quite different, as indeed is the professional manager's, and, given the choice, neither will fulfil his function if reliant upon the group figures.

Managers of a business produce whatever figures they feel they need, using the tools of 'management accounting' to help them manage the part of the organization under their direct control. Published historical data are useless for day to day management and no one actually attempts to use it for this purpose. Bankers, however, do use Annual Reports as their primary source of information about a company, notwithstanding that the material has been prepared for a radically different purpose and reflects an interest in the company that is quite distinct from their own. We have considered at some length the weaknesses of published financial data and here it is necessary only to reaffirm that a banker lending to a parent company on the strength of its consolidated figures is taking a great leap of faith. The danger is that the risk is unperceived and therefore supposed not to exist. That is the way to lose money.

The practice is so ubiquitous in corporate and international banking that it hardly now attracts notice. Few large companies would attempt to take unfair advantage by sheltering behind limited liability and large companies fail with loss to lenders comparatively rarely. What lenders to these companies do not generally realize is how much they are in the power of their borrowers and how little they actually know of what the borrower is doing with the money. An investor may be content to put his money into a company which has shown, in the past, a steady return on equity, trusting that the pattern will not be broken.

It is verging on folly for a banker, who stands to receive only his principal plus a paltry net interest margin, to lend for 'general corporate purposes' relying on that kind of assumption. A shareholder's investment will be valued as a function of the earnings of the group because that is how the market values shares. Profits within the group guarantee that he will not lose his money in the long run. Anyway, he is supposed to be taking a risk! Alas, the banker who assumes that group profitability is sufficient to ensure repayment of a medium- or long-term loan is going one day to get a nasty shock for repayment depends upon the borrower's willingness and ability to disburse funds, not necessarily the same thing!

A banker must know the company he is lending to since that company is the primary source of his repayment and his remuneration. The greatest weakness of modern consolidated accounts is that they conceal, almost totally, the separate businesses and entities that are consolidated together and create the mirage of a single entity. Today, mergers and acquisitions are commonplace. Such a transaction may easily be the most important event in a company's year, yet one will usually look in vain for a detailed financial description of how the deal was accounted for. It is as though new companies acquired are just swallowed up and lose their identity immediately they cease to be independent, hardly a helpful approach when the whole dynamics of the group may have altered as a result of an acquisition.

Occidental Petroleum owns a meat-packing subsidiary, Iowa Beef. This unlikely combination may make economic sense, of a sort, in that it represents a diversification of business activity in Occidental and limits the riskiness in a company otherwise wholly dependent upon oil.

Occidental's Annual Report reveals the total assets tied up in the beef-packing segment but it does not distinguish the assets and liabilities in the consolidated balance sheet or income statement; the information is not considered important and such disclosure is not required by law or accounting practice.

The lender and indeed the investor now have to understand the dynamics of two totally separate and unrelated businesses. Has this diversification really reduced the risk, or has it imported new risks into Occidental? You can only be a little more certain if you are prepared to do a lot more work.

To make a realistic assessment of Occidental that is strictly useful to a banker, one would need to split up the company into its separate components and project the likely future development of each. With time and dedication this type of analysis can be performed, but the lack of anything more than brief segment information robs the exercise of much of its efficiency. Once again, we see how hard it is to analyse a company in any way other than that suggested by the style and direction of the Annual Report.

This book has been about risks. It is usually stated as a dogma that risk and reward are inextricably interlinked and that the market place rewards risk takers in proportion to the risks they assume. That dogma is almost certainly wrong. Risky investments may indeed carry a 'premium' reward but the existence of a precise relationship between the two cannot be demonstrated or verified as there is no objective and generally accepted method of evaluating risk. The measurement of reward is relatively uncomplicated. We know what returns have been generated on historical investments and we can often make a shrewd guess what future returns are likely to be. Bankers build their margins into the structure of their deals and so know precisely how lucrative any particular deal is likely to be. But we cannot measure risk in the same way.

Virtually all the 'tools of analysis' employed by company watchers measure reward or are based upon it. In the context of historical data, as published in an Annual Report, the idea of risk has little meaning and the managers and accountants who write Annual Reports have an interest in not talking about risk. They are motivated by a desire to please shareholders and shareholders take pleasure in the thought that good historical returns on investment may be the forerunners to even better returns in the future. Risk is a dirty word. Just as in a churchyard one might be forgiven for wondering where all the sinners are buried, the uninformed could easily conclude from a study of a pile of Annual Reports that there is no such thing as speculation.

Every decision appears to derive from the most rational of motives. It is unusual for the management of an enterprise to own up to much more than 'a year of mixed results' if the consequences are disastrous.

To discuss risk means to talk about the future and to take a hard-nosed attitude towards what might go wrong. The future is not an entirely closed book. Management makes plans for the years to come, and for anyone needing to understand where a company will be several years down the road, these plans are indispensable raw material. Obviously they will be overtaken by events and soon be out of date. The future may work out totally differently. But we can only start from where we are.

Certain tools of analysis can be used to reveal something about the future. Operating and financial leverage calculations, albeit they are necessarily based on dubious assumptions about fixed and variable costs, help us to perceive what profits may be, if certain eventualities materialize. There is no point in plotting the historical trends of operating and financial leverage to measure riskiness. The figures merely give an indication of how profits may respond to variation in sales levels. To get the full picture we need to know what sales are likely to be.

Projections, sensitivity and regression analysis, the sustainable growth rate test and to some degree coverage ratios can all be used to evaluate risk. But all these are a poor substitute for the company's own honest expectations of likely developments, and as the world economy is now more uncertain than at any time since the War, they are inadequate. Inflation makes a nonsense of much of historical cost accounting. Tax legislation becomes more complicated all the time. Assumptions about the dynamics of large corporations do not hold good over any protracted period and linear relationships which were adequate during the 1950s no longer obtain.

The risks in modern business are significantly greater

now than ever before. Certain huge imponderables weigh
upon the international economic scene and no one knows
what their outcome will be. Of these the most celebrated is
the 'Third World debt crisis', already discussed in Chapter
11. A transfer of resources from 'north' to 'south' has taken
place that has put a near intolerable strain on the
economies of many poor and underdeveloped countries. It
is entirely unclear how these debts can be serviced and
ultimately repaid without banks continuing to roll up
interest payments, a process which cannot continue indefinitely. As it defeats the objectives of both debtors and
creditors to acknowledge the near hopelessness of the situation, complex rescheduling negotiations continue. These
do not produce money or achieve anything of substance;
they merely achieve a form of words adequate to allow the
banks to show these 'assets' as current rather than as the
delinquent debts they are in all but name. Ultimately the
aim is to keep the banks' profits and avoid upsetting the
shareholders back home. The problem is getting worse
rather than better and no one knows how it will end.

Other major uncertainties revolve around the directions
of the US economy. The US government views the raising
of taxes and the cutting of expenditures with near equal
disdain, and the high interest rates which the funding of
the deficit necessitates and the absorption by the USA for
current expenditure of a large proportion of the world's
savings at the expense of other investments are probably
unsustainable in the long term. In the meantime, the weakness of the dollar is a threat to international free trade, yet it
has not stopped the flood of imports from Latin and South
America, the Far East and Europe into the USA. A war of
protectionism could emerge. After several years of falling
interest rates, the trend in 1987 is turning upwards, and
that should throw a few more interesting twists into the
global equation of rates, deficits and trade patterns.

On the corporate scene, the fashion for leveraged buy-

outs, hailed by some observers as a mighty demonstration
of the market's ability to redistribute capital to the most successful entrepreneurs, is replacing stable equity with unstable debt. Advocates of the free market economy, who extol
the efficiency of the market place, do so mainly because
they fear and seek to prevent the imposition of controls,
rather than through any philosophical or scientifically
based belief in total market freedom. The fact is that a
totally free market is a brutal place and, while the efficient
do survive quite justly better than the inefficient, the latter
and their employees face hardship of a type unacceptable
in a democratic society. The Federal Reserve has at last
recognized that the issue of junk bonds in quantities
limited only by the market place's appetite is not in the
national interest and is taking steps to control the leverage
buyout merchants who float them.

No one should be surprised when chronically weak,
debt-ridden companies finally bite the dust and go into
liquidation. That they are not kept going indefinitely is one
of the positive characteristics of healthy capitalism and
something that distinguishes efficient economies in the
West from the sluggish, centralized regimes of Eastern
Europe. It may not help to so observe in retrospect, but those
banks that lost money in the AEG reconstruction in West
Germany in 1982 had years of warning that the situation
was deteriorating. Perhaps their desire not to be left out
from doing business with a leading West German manufacturer overcame any reservations they may have had about
the credit risk. Many of the same bankers had lost money to
the department store chain Neckermann, money they had
lent happily at the sight of the name on every high street in
West Germany. Twice bitten, not shy at all!

Sudden collapses are something different. A single unexpected incident may bring serious setback or even catastrophe to the very largest companies and it is probably fair
to say that few organizations or investments are as risk-free

as they appear. Johnson & Johnson survived the maniac in Chicago who laced a few packets of their Tylenol aspirins with cyanide in 1982, but at a cost running into tens of millions of dollars. The company changed the packaging to try to prevent a recurrence, but were hit by another maniac early in 1986. There seems to be no managing this risk.

Disasters such as that at the Union Carbide plant at Bophal will continue to happen from time to time and cannot be predicted. It pays to remember though that the unpredictable does occur. That an oil giant like Texaco is in Chapter 11 bankruptcy proceedings after a lawsuit would be incredible were it not a fact, and if Texaco is not safe against the current craze for litigation and sky-high judgements in the USA, one can with justice wonder who is.

Legal liabilities have broken several power utilities in the USA, companies until recently considered prime investments for 'widows and orphans', as regulatory bodies have denied them the right to recover the costs of failed nuclear facilities from their customers. Such is the fear of incurring astronomical damages that insurance cover is becoming hard to obtain at the necessary levels.

While the future is a great unknown, it does not follow that all attempts to evaluate and predict likely future events are futile. No one can expect total accuracy, but skill and imagination can put the thoughtful and experienced analyst ahead of the pack. Everything depends upon asking the right questions, probing and with luck penetrating to the essential determinants of prosperity and failure. We have tried to give some hints as to how to do these things and how some elementary concepts like the asset conversion cycle and cash flow can be brought into service.

Unfortunately, much of the established literature points in the wrong direction. The bias, frequent in the USA, but less so elsewhere, towards the stock market as the supreme arbiter of corporate wisdom is to a degree ideologically motivated and fundamentally unhelpful. Nor are complex statistics and formulae the answer. What matters is risk. Business is about people as much as it is about money. That tends to make business, like the course of history, unpredictable.

The uncertainties will never be eliminated entirely, but we believe that very soon something is going to have to be done about the type of material companies publish about themselves. Annual Reports are not adequate for people making long-term investing and lending decisions. What goes into an Annual Report is determined too much by accountants and management and too little by the users of accounts. The quite shameless lobbying that now precedes any change in accounting standards or financial accounting law is little more than a power struggle. The system has already fallen into disrepute with the proliferation of 'off balance sheet lending and borrowing' and sophisticated deals structured explicitly to avoid disclosure in the accounts, especially in the main financial statements. In years gone by, this kind of business activity would have elicited some very impolite designations.

The changes that are needed are fundamental and revolutionary. It is simply not right that producers of financial information should have the loudest voice and that they should use it to prevent adequate disclosure. It is also questionable whether the accounting bodies around the world have much hope to offer. Their basically unproductive dialogue on how to account for inflation has produced virtually nothing of any permanence and the profession has been unable really to accept that, in inflationary times, historical cost accounting fails as a method of representing a business accurately to outsiders. Historical cost accounting is a poor mechanism for the presentation of complex modern companies and dangerous in that its weaknesses are not visible on the surface.

Few industries illustrate this so well as banking. The final risk in a bank is that an event triggers the depositors to want to withdraw their money all at once. The more money is withdrawn, the weaker the bank becomes, and naturally the bank collapses. Although often the result of years of mismanagement, the final episode is sudden and comes without warning. Depositors rarely lose money in a bank failure, as governments or deposit insurance agencies usually come to the rescue rather promptly, but they may suffer the inconvenience of having their funds tied up for a while until the chaos is resolved. Even in the USA, where government intervention is politically unpopular, so substantial a bank as Continental Illinois cannot be allowed to fail completely, for fear of a general collapse of confidence in the local and national banking industry. Depositors are specifically protected by the Federal Deposit Insurance Corporation.

These key elements in the risk assessment of a bank are nowhere to be found in a bank's Annual Report. These documents simply do not talk about what happens either to the depositors or to the shareholders if the bank gets into trouble. Nothing is said either about the quality of the bank's assets, whom it has lent to and what the problems are in getting repaid. An Annual Report is of limited value if it does not tell the reader the proportion of lending assets in South America! One of the few banks whose published reports are moving in the right direction is First Chicago where a glimpse into the businesses of the bank has been made public.

However, what readers of a bank's financial statement expect to see is an income statement and a balance sheet that conforms to common notions of what a bank's financial statements should look like. The Bank of England, having taken over the collapsed Johnson Matthey Bankers, declined to publish a report until 15 months rather than a year had elapsed, reportedly because the restructuring had not yet taken place after 12 months. It was felt that there would be unease in the international community at dealing with a bank showing negative net worth, notwithstanding that it was wholly owned by the Bank of England! It is common practice in the industry to set up interbank lending limits by reference to the size of a bank's equity. Never a sensible policy, it would obviously fail altogether in the case of Johnson Matthey Bankers. So much for the market's much vaunted sophistication in evaluating risk! More sensible evaluators of bank risk take a great number of factors into account, often in a highly interactive mode, to render a judgement on a bank's risk profile and 'capacity to borrow'.

It is too early to see what developments in accounting and presentation may be expected. Recent improvements in funds flow statements are encouraging but there is still a long way to go. Promising, too, are some of the bankers' packages being assembled for special financing with their emphasis on cash flow. Undoubtedly, it will take some more spectacular, unexpected yet quite predictable disasters, with goodly sums lost by innocent individuals, to persuade governments and business that those who entrust their money to hired managers are entitled to know precisely what is being done with it and that the balance of power needs to be shifted back to those in whose hands it rightfully belongs, those taking the risks.

Index

Haig J. Boyadjian is an American banker who was based in London for a number of years. He had served in senior management positions with US European and British banks and had over twenty years of strategic and tactical experience in a wide range of international finance activities, joint venture negotiations, marketing, corporate finance, financial controls and long range planning as well as management training.

This book was largely based on his extensive lecturing notes on the Financial Analysis Seminars he set up for a major British bank where he was Controller of Lending and Assistant General Manager. He was assisted in this effort by James F. Warren. These seminars were also successfully marketed internationally.

Mr Boyadjian received his BA from Swarthmore College and his Master's degree in International Economics from the Fletcher School of Law and Diplomacy. Due to illness, Mr Boyadjian retired from his position of Senior Vice President in corporate banking in 1988 and has been working on another book related to management issues.

James F. Warren was an English banker who was associated with Mr Boyadjian in structuring and lecturing on these seminars. He worked in England and the USA. In 1987, he resigned from his banking position to enter the Harvard Law School. He graduated magna cum laude in 1990 and now practices corporate law with a major law firm in North Carolina where he lives with his American wife and two daughters.

Mr Warren took a double first in Classics and Oriental languages at Cambridge University.

FINANCIAL ANALYSIS SOFTWARE PACKAGE
Designed by Haig J. Boyadjian
in conjunction with the publication of

RISKS
Reading Corporate Signals
by Haig J. Boyadjian and James F. Warren

An easy to use yet unique and innovative personal computer software package has been designed as an invaluable tool in the analysis of corporate financial statements. The Program, designated HB/FSP™, generates historic and projected balance sheet, profit and loss and cash flow statements based on the penetrating analytical approach rendered in the book, structured around the twin and related concepts of the asset conversion cycle and cash flow.

The program also calculates a wide range of structural and performance ratios shown in modular profiles as well as graphic representations of the financial statements, sensitivity analysis, regression analysis, and a net present value module. The HB/FSP™ is available at $795.00 and includes a floppy disk (Lotus 1-2-3™ compatible) formatted for financial analysis, printed spread sheets for spreading of published account data ready for input and comes with an instruction manual.

To order, please complete and return the slip below.

Return to HB/FSP™, Haig J. Boyadjian, 31 Walnut West, Mahwah, New Jersey, 07430, USA.

Please send me .... copy(ies) of HB/FSP™. I enclose a certified check/ payment order for $795.00 (tax included) payable to HB/FSP™.

Name ....

Address ....

....

Signature .... Date ....